By Al Young

Fiction
SNAKES*
WHO IS ANGELINA?
SITTING PRETTY*
ASK ME NOW
SEDUCTION BY LIGHT

Poetry
DANCING
THE SONG TURNING BACK INTO ITSELF
GEOGRAPHY OF THE NEAR PAST
THE BLUES DON'T CHANGE
HEAVEN: Collected Poems 1958–1988*

Non-Fiction
BODIES & SOUL*
KINDS OF BLUE*
THINGS AIN'T WHAT THEY USED TO BE*

Editor
CALIFÍA: *The California Poetry* (with Ishmael Reed, *et al*)
YARDBIRD LIVES! (with Ishmael Reed)

*Books published by Creative Arts Book Company

THINGS AIN'T WHAT THEY USED TO BE

Musical Memoirs

by

Al Young

A Donald S. Ellis Book
CREATIVE ARTS BOOK COMPANY • BERKELEY
1987

Several of these selections, in slightly different form, have previously appeared in *Air Cal Magazine, Berkeley Monthly, Black Warrior Review, Image, Quilt, TriQuarterly,* and *West.*

"Ac-cen-tchu-ate the Positive" appeared under the title "Unripened Light" in A World Unsuspected: Portraits of Southern Childhood, edited by Alex Harris (University of North Carolina Press, 1987); "A Nightingale Sang in Berkeley Square" originated as liner notes commissioned by Carl Jefferson for the Concord Jazz album: *Stephanova* (with Stephane Grappelli and Marc Fosset).

The author wishes to thank Reginald Gibbons, editor of TriQuarterly (an international journal of writing, art and cultural inquiry published by Northwestern University) for permission to reprint "Jazz and Letters: A Colloquy," which appeared in its Winter 1987 issue. The author also thanks editors Jim and Amy O'Neal and the University of Mississippi Press for permission to quote from their John Lee Hooker interviews, which were published in the journal *Living Blues.*

For information contact:
    Creative Arts Book Company
    833 Bancroft Way
    Berkeley, California 94710

Typography: QuadraType, San Francisco
The cover painting, "Jazz Singer," is from one of a series of jazz paintings by Stephen Henriques, a San Francisco artist, ©1987.

ISBN 0 – 88739 – 024 – 2
Library of Congress No. 87 – 71146

Printed in the United States of America.

"There is music that makes one feel like jumping and dancing; there is music that makes one feel like laughing and smiling; and then there is music that makes one feel like shedding tears. If one were to ask a thoughtful person which he preferred, no doubt he would say, 'The last; the music that brings tears.' Why does the soul want sad music? Because that is the only time when the soul is touched. The music that reaches no further than the surface of one's being remains only on the surface. It is the music that reaches to the depths of one's being that touches the soul. The deeper the music reaches, the more contented is the soul."

—Hazrat Inayat Khan
The Music of Life

To the memory of my brother
Richard Young;
born in July of 1945
at Ocean Springs, Mississippi;
gone by July of 1984;
Hollywood, California

TABLE OF CONTENTS

THINGS AIN'T WHAT THEY USED TO BE

Musical Memoirs

Prelude

Since beginning this series, it has taken some time for me to realize how flexible and unpredictable a so-called musical memoir can be. There's no defining it, just as there is no way to define poetry or the blues, which are, by nature of the indomitable life-spirit that feeds them, unruly and wild. The minute the academy thinks it has poetry or the blues theoretically mapped out, wrapped up or coldly codified, along comes some ignorant or unassuming genius—someone who either does or doesn't know any better—to make a poem do something it's never done before, or make a blues line uncoil and snake its way into places where other blues haven't gone.

For readers new to this eccentric series of books, it's important to remember as you read along that they're all about music as a way of remembering. All the experience covered in this and previous volumes—*Bodies & Soul* and *Kinds of Blue*—are, in one way or another, linked to song. Sometimes the remembering takes the form of story or personal myth. At other times the interaction between author and song or body of music gives birth to a related narrative or account, formal or informal, or a reverie, a fantasy or an inspired soliloquy.

As a pre-school kid, I used to like to sit in front of the family's coal-burning heater in winter with even younger brothers and listen to our father's 78 rpm records. The little heater had an opaque screen on its door that allowed us to glimpse patterns the flames made as they raged and smoldered. While we listened and stared into that fire-screen, the Ravens jazzed "Ol' Man River," Louis Jordan and His Tympani Five asked "Is You Is or

Is You Ain't My Baby?," the Mills Brothers cut up on "Paper Doll" and the Nat Cole Trio took it on out with "It's Only a Paper Moon." Johnny Mercer advised us to "Ac-cen-tchu-ate the Positive" (we thought the song was called "Don't Mess with Mr. In-Between," just as Duke Ellington's "Don't Get Around Much Anymore" to us was "Mr. Saturday Night"), Xavier Cugat samba'd us with "Brazil," Artie Shaw's Grammercy Five drove us home to "Summit Ridge Drive," wherever that was, and numbers like pianist Eddie Heywood's "Begin the Beguine" transported us to some happy inner spot we could feel, even if we couldn't always talk about it.

While we were seated or standing in front of that active heater, it was no big deal to picture in the screen-framed flames anything musical our innocent ears picked up from the phonograph or radio. And this was especially so of *wordless* song, popular or classical. We'd project our pictures of *Scheherezade* or Benny Goodman's "Song of India" right out there—the way we always do our thoughts, our feelings, when there's a fireplace or an ocean in front of us—and, if necessary, we could step right up to the screen and point out or trace the shapes of our mind-pictures, for there they danced, illumined in firelight and shadow, before our very eyes. And these images never played the same way twice.

"Thinking and singing the world into existence," anthropologist Gary Witherspoon wrote in *Language and Art in the Navajo Universe,* "attributes a definite kind of power to thought and song to which most Westerners are not accustomed." For the late bassist and composer Charles Mingus the blues weren't a color, but a feeling. And now physicists say we appear to be co-creating the universe at the same time that we're participating in it. But that's the beauty of music and every other art and science that springs from the human imagination by way of intuitive intelligence; the truths they express are so simple as to seem child-like to the windowless grownup mind.

The law of entropy tells us the same thing we get from reading just the title of the Nigerian storyteller Chinua Achebe's most famous novel: *Things Fall Apart.* This law of thermodynamics states that, unless fresh energy in the way of careful maintenance is introduced, records will scratch, pianos get out of tune, machines come unglued, houses get messy, roofs start leaking, weeds take over, topsoil erodes, farms bottom out, cities get crowded, economies and international relations grow shaky, and galaxies explode.

"This city is going to the dogs," a Manhattan taxi driver told me as we cut through Central Park on the way to the Upper West Side. It was February, late in the morning; glacial but honeyed with sunlight. "I mean, they take a whole five- or six-block area and give it one damn address, then I'm supposed to know exactly where to drop my passengers off. Who'd you say you were going to see? I know it's got to be somebody famous."

"Mercer Ellington," I told him.

Glancing over his shoulder he said, "Duke Ellington's boy?"

"Well, yes, sort of—Mercer's quite mature now."

The driver laughed. "Well, you tell Mercer when you see him that he and his father, they've given us a lot of good music and there's a lot of us out here that love them madly. But you tell him that the next time he gives somebody directions to his place, he's gonna have to do better than this. I been driving a cab in New York for 27 years now, and I *know* this town; used to know it anyway. But now they slap these big condo complexes up overnight, put some address on it like 50 Vanderbilt Place, and got 5,000 ways to get in there, and I'm the one comes out looking like a fool."

"Well," I couldn't help reminding him, "Mercer Ellington said it in that song of his."

"Which one is that?"

"'Things Ain't What They Used to Be.'"

"You can say that again. And you know what else?"

"What?"

"They never were, and they never will be."

Because they're still in the process of finding out what they themselves are supposed to be, even these musical memoirs keep changing on me. And why shouldn't they? I'm not exactly gathering moss, and neither is the music scene. It has been my pleasure, this time around, to have some guest commentators sharing these pages with me. One of them is Larry Kart, the man who wrote the text for *That Old Ball Game,* a photographic history of baseball's early days. He also translated Eugenio Montale's *Mottetti,* and writes regularly about jazz, poetry and other arts for the Chicago *Tribune.* Michael S. Harper, world renowned poet and professor of English at Brown University, is at work on a book about South African photojournalist Ralph Ndawo whose recent death in that country has raised many questions and eyebrows. Harper's most famous book is arguably *Dear John, Dear Coltrane.* The three of us, under the auspices of the Associated Writing Programs, got together at that organization's annual meeting in Chicago in April of 1986 and spoke extemporaneously—how else?—about jazz and letters. The excitement created during that morning session was such that I've been moved to include it here. Rarely is the subject discussed in either musical or literary circles, and even rarer is the opportunity it provides general readers to look at how music affects the thinking and feeling and hearing and seeing of artists who happen to be working in language.

My man O.O. Gabugah has been around, it seems, for as long as black pepper. Our association is heavily sprinkled across the years, and there are those who have commented that Brother Gabugah sometimes seems to be pepper to my salt and, as it were, mean cop to my nice cop. Many old-timers will remember him as the author of "What You Seize Is What You Git," from his revolutionary days when he was writing books like *Off the Pig and Git Yo'self Some Chitlins* and *Love Is a White Man's Snot Rag.* But, like other firebrands from the Sixties and Seventies, like Archie Shepp and Bob Dylan and the People's Republic of China, O.O. Gabugah has mellowed. His comments and memories as they relate to some of the heartier, meatier Motown classics and to trumpeter/singer Hugh Masekela will be sure to hold your attention.

As always, my only reason for pulling this book together has been to have a little fun and to share it. I want to thank Mercer Ellington for taking the time, during a visit to this country from his home in Denmark, to explain how he happened to write "Things Ain't What They Used to Be," and for allowing me to preserve it in print. And I'd like to thank James Brown for penning what could be viewed as the corollary to that truism.

"Money won't change you," Brown once sang, "but time will move you on."

May the rhythm of life and how it works as sounded time move through you invitingly while you think and sing back into danceable existence what has merely been notated here.

—AL YOUNG
Belgrade, Yugoslavia–
San Francisco, 1984–1987

I'll Remember April

Gene DePaul, composer;
Don Raye and Pat Johnston, lyrics

Everyone thinks drivers are wary of hitchhikers, but it works the other way around too. When the driver backed up almost a full block that morning in Berkeley to pick me up, I didn't know what to think. He was driving a beat-up car and, climbing into the backseat, the first thing I noticed were the books on raw foods and other esoterica. As for the driver, he was balding, white-haired, had big bushy white eyebrows, seemed to be in his fifties, but the most salient characteristic was the glow he exuded.

He and his teenage son sat up front and as he chugged uphill, away from McGee and Dwight Way, where they'd backed up to get me, I had a feeling deep in the center of my solar plexus that something was up, but of course I didn't know what.

"What do you do?" the driver asked.

"I go to school," I lied.

"Up here at Cal?"

"Yes."

In the rear-view mirror I watched his eyes squint curiously at me while I wondered why I was telling him this. It wasn't his business, I rationalized, and besides, in a sense I *was* going to Cal. I was working for a Ph.D candidate in psychology, a man who was setting up experiments in conformity around town in various public schools. And I was, after all, a student of life.

"And what is it you study up there?"

"Anthropology," I said without missing a beat.

"What's that?"

"It's the study of man."

"The study of man, eh? Well, that's interesting. I never got beyond the fifth grade myself, but I've been studying hard to make up for it. I read a lot—histories and dictionaries especially. I've got five kids and I gotta leave 'em something, something they can use.

"So you study anthropology?"

"Yes," I said, beginning to feel uneasy.

"I don't know anything about that, but I have had some of these U.C. students babysit for me and, from what I can tell, they don't know much of anything."

I laughed at this and so did the driver's son. We were approaching Dwight Way and Telegraph, where he would be dropping the youngster off at the vocational high school that used to be there.

"From what I can tell, all they seem to be teaching those kids is more stuff to keep 'em ignorant." He glanced back over his shoulder at me. "There's a reason you got this ride, you know."

"There is?" I had picked up the ancient volume on raw foods and had nervously begun to flip through its well-thumbed pages. It looked and felt like the kind of item you'd find in the cheapie sidewalk bins in front of a good used bookstore.

"Yes. You notice how I backed all the way up like that? I almost missed you. We saw you out there with your thumb stuck out, and I told my boy: 'We have to go back and get that guy.'

"Listen," he said suddenly, "you've read a lot and studied a lot, haven't you?"

"Yes, I have," I told him, feeling more tentative than I ever had before.

"That's what I thought." He took one hand off the wheel, his right hand, and thrust it back toward me with his palm open. "So," he asked, "can you give me 'A'?"

"I beg your pardon? . . ."

The driver wiggled his fingers at me. "You heard what I said: Can you give me 'A.' Just give me 'A.'"

At this, the driver's son, a tall, handsome lad, turned to face me fully. I've never forgotten the wry smile on his face and the way his eyes twinkled at me as if to say: "You don't know what you're in for, do you? This father of mine is something else." What he really said, however, as his father slowed and pulled to the curb for him to gather his own schoolbooks and notebooks, was: "Pleased to meet you."

While his son was getting out, the driver motioned for me to move up. "C'mon, up front," he said.

"No, thanks," I told him, "I'm comfortable back here."

In no time at all, we were back in traffic.

"Where you headed?" asked the driver.

"LeConte Elementary School," I said.

"Oh, is that where you work?"

"For today yes. We move around to different schools."

"What do you do in these schools?"

"I help conduct a psychology experiment."

In a low, gentle voice, the driver put another question to me. "And what are you doing with those kids?"

"We're working with them."

"But are you teaching them anything helpful or useful? Or just playing around with 'em, helping keep 'em ignorant?"

At once the way I really felt rose up into my throat in one big awkward rush of confusion and guilt. What *was* I doing? When I thought about it, it seemed to go something like this: At each scheduled school, we would arrive early, set up our electronic circuit boards and little booths, our screen and projector, tape player and P.A. system. The kids—who had either volunteered themselves or were urged to volunteer for the project by their teachers—would come into the room, then sit and listen while I gave a little talk about how this little experiment was going to run.

"Don't worry about a thing," I'd tell them. "When you sit in these little booths next to your pals and classmates, you'll have a little board in front of you with lights that light up to tell you how your cronies are reacting to whatever we flash up there on the screen or play over the loudspeaker. All we ask is that you don't push any buttons until it's *your* turn, and the board will tell you when it's your turn to answer. You got that? OK, so now just relax and have fun."

And that's what we'd do: get them all rounded up and seated in these tiny stalls—seven or eight kids at a time—into little slots with a partition between each one and a light-dotted board in front of them. The stalls were just high enough for the screen to be seen. So, say my boss Ron or his other assistant Sherwin snapped on the slide projector and flashed onto the screen a line marked Line A that extended perhaps two feet along the length of the screen, then, in rapid succession, flashed Line B, which

was obviously a full foot shorter than Line A. What I would ge-
nially ask the kids to do was indicate, by pushing a button,
which was the longer line. And that was exactly what they'd do
but, precisely because it was a psychology experiment, I needn't
tell you that there was something funny about the whole setup.

This was how the thing really worked: Each student, going by
fraudulent information dished out by their circuit board, was being led to believe that everyone else had answered before them
and that he or she was the last one to be registering a response.
When we got down toward the end, down to the music part of
the so-called test, where Ron would give Sherwin the cue to play
28 measures of Beethoven's *Fifth Symphony*, then 3 measures of
Sousa's "Stars and Stripes Forever," then ask the kids which
piece had lasted longer, the air in the room would usually be
crackling with emotion. Working through a host of factors and
cross-factors, my boss Ron's objective was to find out which
kinds of students surrendered fastest to majority opinion and
which ones held out in favor of their own perceptual judgments.
What I found curious was that the more middle-class and white
the community's school, the less apt students were to cause
trouble or make waves. In the marginal or lower-class or
black neighborhoods settings, you could count on someone acting up in the middle of the experiment. They would either bust
out of their stall and look over at their neighbors' circuit boards,
or yell something like: "Hey, what the fuck is goin' on?
Y'all deaf or blind or somethin'?" And, I must confess, I liked
those kids.

This is what whooshed through my mind while the driver, the
quintessence of the mysterious stranger, sat waiting for my answer. What could I tell him? Obviously what we were up to
wasn't helping those youngsters in the least. Not knowing how
to reply, I allowed my own uncomfortable silence to do the talking for me.

"Like I said," the driver went on. I've got all these kids and I
need to leave 'em with something they can use. They need to
know the truth. How much truth do you know? If you had to,
could you explain God to an eight-year-old?"

By then we had reached the very corner where I was to get
out. The driver parked in front of the school and, there in the
dewiness and sunniness of a warmed-up April morning, he

turned to me and said, "You still don't know why you got this ride, do you?"

I shook my head.

"You're looking for something," he said again, "and I'm gonna try and give it to you—if you'll let me." He clicked off the engine and turned to look directly at me. "Don't you know why you suffer?"

"Well," I began, but that was as far as I got.

"You suffer because of your desires," he said, looking into my eyes with such feeling and depth that something inside me fell away altogether.

Then, recalling the language of the many books and texts I had been devouring of late on Eastern mysticism: yoga, Vedanta, Buddhism and Taoism—books like Alan Watts' *The Joyous Cosmology,* W.Y. Evans-Wentz' translation of *The Tibetan Book of the Dead,* and Paramahansa Yogananda's *Autobiography of a Yogi*—I managed to utter a single word. "Karma," I said, reluctantly of course, because it seemed to be inappropriate given the person I was saying it to and his plain-spokenness.

He smiled and said, "All right, well, karma, yes—if you wanna put it that way. But it's like this: There really isn't any such thing as hell, and certainly not the way you've been thinking about it. You know where that comes from? Comes from those days back there when they used to drag all those dead bodies off to the edge of town and set 'em afire and burn 'em— that's where. Don't you remember?"

Honestly, I was scrunched into that backseat, as scared as I could be.

"They'd have a slow, steady fire of those bodies going all the time," he continued, "and that's where the concept of hell comes from. You're going through hell right now, though."

And it was true; I'd inwardly reached one of those blind alleys where—or so I thought at the ripe age of 24—that I'd looked down every street and backroad there was to examine and, no matter how closely I scrutinized their mapped-out paths, they all led to nothing, and nothing added up to zero. A few days before this hitchhiking interlude, one of the grand events of my youth, I had been feeling lonely and hungry for something unnameable. During a lunch break, I had excused myself from Sherwin's and Ron's company to go and have my sandwich on the Berkeley

Pier. And, standing there at the railing, in the tepid sunlight and the fibrous, mind-stretching offshore winds of high spring, I remember looking out across the choppy, troubled blue-green-muddy bay waves and the way the gleaming noonday light was speckling and coating and riding them. Aha, I had thought, so that's how Jesus walked the waters! Something was happening inside me; some soulful craving was beginning to unravel and unfold. I hadn't understood it. I had gone home and drunk copious quantities of a friend's home brew to try to drown it out, but that soul-hunger I felt kept right on on expanding; it wouldn't go away. Later, in a poem, I would refer to it as the craving for infinity. Yes, I had begun to look for something, and with an intensity I must've been broadcasting obsessively.

"And so," the driver said. "What you must do is study and think. Study and think, that's what you must do. This situation is awful; it's a mess. You've got eyes; you can see. We've got a lot of my kind messed up in this thing, and a lot of your kind."

If I said anything after this remark of his, I can't recall it. Mostly I remember wanting to get the hell out of that old beat-up car and on in the school to start setting up the first morning experiment, even though I now knew I wasn't going to be sticking with that job for very long.

"You know," the driver said, peering, I swear, down into every nook and cranny of my secret self. "You've been to a lotta schools and read a lotta books, right?"

"Yes," I told him, baffled about what he was driving at.

"Nobody's ever been able to tell you *nothin'*," he said. "You were always ahead of 'em. And now here I am, the first one to come along and kick your ass."

I had no idea then what he had meant, except in a broad, generalized, you might say college outline kind of way. It was true that I had usually been rated and placed in the accelerated classes along with all the so-called smart and high I.Q. kids. But all along I had known that the kind of intelligence that fed me wasn't the kind that produced mathematicians and physicists and paleontologists and political strategists and literary structuralists and demographers and business tycoons. I always worked out my answers to problems and questions in a round-about fashion, slipping up on truth through the side door, as it were.

Acknowledging my discomfort, the driver beamed at me and said, "Poor guy. You've been through a lot and you've still got a lot to go through. But you know what? One of these days you're gonna slip right out of that cloud you've been buried in and find out for yourself what's really going on. In the meantime I want you to study and think. When you can explain God to an eight-year-old, then you'll know something.

"Oh, just look at you," he said. "You're so frightened of what I've been telling you about yourself that you've just about had it—right here." He touched his throat. "Had it right up to the gills. But don't worry."

He pulled the front passenger seat forward to enable me to climb out of the car. After I'd gotten up, he stepped out too and stood beside me next to the cyclone fence and, beyond it, the playground.

"I know I said all that stuff about kicking your ass," he said with the oddest of smiles, "but in a moment I'm going to shake your hand, then you'll realize I didn't really mean that. You'll know what I really meant."

At this, he placed his warm hand around mine, which might've been trembling, and shook it with a sureness I had never before felt.

"Good luck to you," he said, "and think about what I've been telling you."

No sooner had his thick, hairy fingers slipped from mine than I felt myself becoming light and balloon-like, but not in the head. It was my body that felt as if some enormous bone-crushing weight was being lifted from it. I waved to the old man—being 24, I thought he seemed rather advanced in age—and watched him motor away. In fact, I stood there in a daze and kept waving, knowing how Ron was going to give me, heh heh, hell when I stepped into that classroom, 20 minutes late at least. But the giggly high that was puffing up past my throat and into every cell of my self just then said: Man, aren't you sick and tired of going around worried and anxious about stuff that couldn't be helped anyway? Frankly, I didn't care if Ron fired me on the spot; I'd get by. Something would turn up, the same way the sky was opening up for me and those treetops and birds and the sunlight itself seemed intimately aware of what I was feeling.

The beautiful fact is that I wandered about for days in this blissful condition. But it was that night, going for a walk, standing on the sidewalk and looking at the full moon, that I realized—*realized,* that is, *knew* and could *feel* as distinct from understood—that there was no distance whatever between that lighted orb hanging out there above Sacramento Street, above the Bay, above Berkeley, Oakland, San Francisco, California, the West Coast, North America, this whirling ball of mud and stone and greenery we called the Earth, and myself. The moonlit blood my heart continued to pump throughout and around my bodily constellations was winking to me that there was only one distance anywhere.

Did I go looking for that bushy-eyebrowed, gray and balding gentleman again? But of course. I stood on that same corner morning after morning, two blocks from the cottage my wife and I shared, and never laid eyes on either him or his son again. Every time I'd walk by that vocational school when classes let out in the afternoon, I'd look for his son in vain. For years I kept an eye peeled for them. Gradually, though, I came to realize how useless it was to keep scouting out the messenger when the message had been all I'd needed.

Every time a band or a singer strikes up "I'll Remember April," or when I rudely pick it out on piano myself, and for more Aprils now than I care to remember, I've been meaning to tell this little story. Except to a closed handful of sympathetic friends, I've figured it might be best to keep my mouth shut about it. But now that an entire horizon of clouds is beginning to break, when at least I can feel the warmth and nearness of that cloud-melting sun, I'm ready to sing it to the world.

"This lovely day will lengthen into evening" is the opening line Don Raye and Pat Johnston came up with back in 1942, describing, without meaning to, an unforgettable life in the day of a poet who, 22 years later, would remember Edna St. Vincent Millay's "Second April" and poet Bob Kaufman's "Second April" and the wistful melody of Gene DePaul's timeless "I'll Remember April" (from the motion picture, *Ride 'Em Cowboy*) and all the people who've played it and played with it and played to it and danced and hugged or kissed and made love to it to the thunder and lightning, in their souls or outside. And, facing the music, how could this poet forget the people who've gone to war re-

membering that song, who whistled and hummed it absent-mindedly in the trenches of duty or ignorance or tipsy or dead drunk at the edges of some soft, breezy, terrifying daybreak or black hole of night or while stitching up a stomach or sitting in the cockpit of a high-flying bomber, pressing a button to unleash enough computerized missiles to wipe out an entire village that will neither see nor hear its coming and going as it whizzes over-head in the rural sky of some Buddhist countryside while the pi-lot listens in the comfort of his cabin, his luxurious stall, to Miles Davis or Lee Konitz or Charlie Spivak's Band or Ella Fitzgerald or Linda Ronstadt doing "I'll Remember April."?

And that poet, no longer able to masquerade as an innocent bystander, the victim of circumstance, a helpless but worldly hitchhiker, will have to swallow hard and face the music, then put his own words to what he has seen and heard and felt and done and learned and lived before he can know what to go back and tell that eager, wide-open, moon-pulled part of himself that never grew older than eight.

I'll Play the Blues for You

Albert King, 1977

There's something unalterable, unutterable and yet perfectly if not totally expressive about feeling-states the blues instill. I mean this from the ground-zero center of my heart—arteries, blood-run and blood count.

Having reached the turning point in my life—that thin bend in time where you turn the corner and twist inexplicably down some other street, an altogether unmapped street as unfamiliar to you as tomorrow, except you can sometimes see exactly where and how it's been blooming from seeds you've been sowing all along—having reached that intersection of Earthly Street and Heavenly Avenue, such ripened beauty as Albert King sings about comes to my ears as the blues. And the blues are about as soothing an expression of the basic human condition as ever there will be.

It's true that there are nights when you're so lonesome, so lonely, that it just wouldn't do for anyone to show up to befriend you or to try and startle you out of your solitude. On the same wavelength, there are times when you're so horny, so randy for the world that even the most intimate and prolonged contact with it—say you get close enough to the woman of your dreams to be able to verify from candid observation that it's got to be jelly 'cause jam don't shake like that—well, such closeness could only leave you feeling unfulfilled.

So what's all this got to do with Albert King? When Albert King in his gruff, tender way promises, "I'll play the blues for you," you go for it headlong, the way a simple mackerel snaps at fishing pole bait. And when, in his easy cocktail lounge intermission manner, he makes good his promise, plays the blues so plangently and directly—gathering momentum chorus after chorus while he rolls down the hillside of your sorrow, rounding off the edges of your sadness—you know that by the time this Saturday night dissolves you'll be 50 bucks in the hole, but all those green wigs of moss that love to make their home on stone will have rocked down to sea level. And by the time that's happened you'll be as cooled out as the sand and grit and gravel at the bottom of King's hilly voice.

Go right on, Albert, with your multidirectional self! Play the blues for me. And you can pour it on because I'm already up to my ears with major blues. But I'm so tickled with the sound of your minor blues, I'm thankful I was born with ears.

Last Tango in Paris

Gato Barbieri, 1973

Forget about Marlon Brando and Maria Schneider and the buttered-up sex and mooning. Forget the title shot and also the sadly erotic tawdriness of tit and ass pavilions. What you really want to concentrate upon is how it must feel to be rushing around the streets of St. Germaine des Pres with a fluttering at the back of your skull that's opting for joyful, frontline hits.

Add all this up and hear how Gato Barbieri scored. Listen to the lush but simple accordion statements of melody he's penciled into the arrangement. People are driving around America with bumper stickers that read: PLAY AN ACCORDION, GO TO JAIL, THAT'S THE LAW, but they don't know how beautifully particular players can squeeze those boxes. This accordion is from those gritty streets of Gato's childhood, where time was tapped to shoe measure.

Remember, if you can, those warm-throated pre-Peronista nights, an evening barely begun. Violet light is flooding the eye's heart. Overcome with desire, that light is neither sure nor understands why it is being set daffy with longing.

So where does this tango lead? Where do all tangos lead? No place but up to Gato's place, that space just in back of his heart, yellowed with taxis. And if an August rain's begun to fall in April or in May, this could make it an even juicier visit. This could send the tango wandering into some smoky shadow of a corner, to find its partner, to do what it takes two to do.

Ah, the tangles and entanglements of love let loose like light let in, whisking and snatching you gently and crazily every broken-legged way but loose!

Imagine all of this for background while you listen to *Last Tango in Paris*. Put yourself in the picture. Expand to the *duende* of this intoxicant, the movement of the music itself. At long last you've got your damp palms wrapped around each other's waists; the feet are working, doing whatever they should; the mustachioed musicians are all but winking at the both of you from between the wheezy cracks in the squeeze and shudder of keys and buttons, the sounded breeze the accordion makes. The wind is so slow moving in the flowered room that you can take your time breathing in the smells of smoke and drink, perfume and sweaty euphoria. You make that little ethnic pass around the floor. What's that they call it? Tango's as good a name for it as any.

The crowd, such as it is of a week night, looks on. The light even glistens in the elongated sliver of scalp your partner's parted hair reveals. For sure, it's a perfect match for her now-lowered, now-undulating cleavage, all dew and shine in the heave of her smart yet simple blouse. These are not champagne and chauffeur people; these are the descendents of cowboys, gauchos, laboring people and scufflers. Both your busy foreheads are lathered in salt. The moon is nowhere to be seen, but the tide of the tablecloths you keep brushing from your laps and the glide of the tango are the only things spilling from this ardent moment now, like fruits and vegetables from an old-time horn of plenty.

The tango is everything, all this moment is made of. It's almost as if there's never been anything else in any season of your sweet and bitter passages. Along the giddy edges of your stomach and the nape of your neck, you sense this moment isn't going to be your last. But you aren't certain about how you mean that. Last as in "last night"? Last as in "there ain't no more"?

The sting of demon time is poisoning your blood. What will become of this casual passion about to wane and recede like practically everything you've ever tried to clutch or make last?

Saxophonist, songwriter, epic builder Gato Barbieri—perhaps with Pharoah Sanders and John Coltrane at the back of his inner ear—has picked up all the pieces and saved them for you, that's what. Barbieri saw his shot when director Bernardo Bertolucci sent for him. Yes, of course, that's got to be it. It could only take an Argentine out of Buenos Aires to coax the last ounce of romance from Parisian myth musically for all the rest of us.

Forgive me, Gato. And listen, reader. Nobody knows about any of this except you and me, and I swear I won't say any more about it if you don't.

Flyin' Home

Lionel Hampton, 1942

Somehow are we not forever flying home somewhere? Speeding there in our automobiles, tooting our own horns the way we do cocaine, or smacking our way home on a spoon of heroin, coming or arriving soon? Decisions, decisions. To be or not to be.

To be a kid and listen to the sound of Lionel Hampton's "Flyin' Home" was to be grounded firmly in the 20th Century of arrivals and departures by way of rhythm and being. And rhythm was a matter of being with 'em, if you'll excuse my Afro-boa-constricting loa, this spirit that rides and rides its lordly horse.

Tell my horse about the time when you were growing up in Detroit, Michigan and Lionel Hampton would come to Detroit. I'd be riding that crowd so hard when Hamp's band struck up "Flyin' Home" that even after he'd walked down off the stage and led them all out into the streets and around the block for a musical walk in under the stars they'd still be so charged and ready it was all I could do to try and restrain them so they wouldn't tear up the theaters the way managers reported they did after Hamp's band had trouble getting booked back in at the Fox and the Greystone and the Paradise Club and those other theaters the following year.

What was it about "Flyin' Home"? What was it that made them want to boogie in the aisles and all out on top of parked cars at the curbs and in the parking lots and all on top of each other so hard they forgot it was only a tune—highly charged, admittedly—and took it perhaps to somehow mean more than Hamp had meant it to mean?

Wasn't it because of the yea-saying, life-affirming ring of

Hamp's vibes and Illinois Jacquet's and Arnett Cobb's church-like voices reaching toward some kind of heaven? We even memorized and would sing Jacquet's solo, note per note, and as recently as 1980, when Jimmy Carter invited Hampton to play at the White House Jazz Festival, Zoot Sims got up and swung that classic solo of Jacquet's.

Even if it was smoky and boozy and jazzy and coarse; even if it did hover above the band's brass and saxophone choirs and all those palpitations out there in the pulpit, this heaven at hand that Hampton evoked was rapidly reachable. To get there, you didn't have to crawl, limp, walk, swim or row. You didn't have to hitch up no wagon to no mule, or sit up all night on some train with a boxed chicken lunch, or doze while you drove there on some bumpy highway where, when you got hungry, you had to go around to the back of some God forsaken greasy spoon to get a bite to eat. And don't talk about the times the only thing that kept you driving into that night were the dark spots along the road where you could hide behind a tree to pee and let well enough be.

No, you didn't have to go through all that to get to heaven with Lionel Hampton's band. You plunked down for your ticket, you got yourself either an aisle or a window seat, and, depending on your needs, you either clicked your seat belt into place or took your own sweet chances, but, doggone it, you took the trip direct, the same way you posted your letters Air Mail Special. You closed your eyes and patted your feet and let the music pilot your body to heaven and, before you knew it, you were flying home.

Keep On Truckin', Mama

R. Crumb and His Cheap Suit Serenaders, 1970

The topic of Angelfood McSpade had popped up somehow on that steamy afternoon at the Café Mediterranean as I sat with with pal Leslie Perry over coffee and Italian sodas. I was telling him about something mildly unbelievable I'd been reading in the latest issue of *Zap Comix*. It turned out Leslie had never read or even heard of cartoonist R. Crumb.

Crazier Than Thou was the name of the game everyone was playing, it seemed, in Berkeley by 1970. There was so much grotesquerie to behold and acknowledge that it was easy to get anyone's attention, but practically impossible to hold it.

As I told Les about Crumb's inky black amazon Angelfood, he began to get restless. Finally he leaned across the wobbly little round table and said, "Where'd you say you saw this funnybook?"

"At Moe's," I said, "right across the street."

Les smacked his cup down, dragged the paper napkin across his beard and jumped up. "C'mon," he said, "let's go!"

"Go where?"

"I can't believe what you're telling me. I gotta see it for myself."

I could see he was steamed up, but it wasn't always easy to tell with Les because he tended to be dramatic. After all, he was an actor. He had also just written a play about Frederick Douglass that he would later star in and become something of a Bay Area celebrity.

I followed while Les jaywalked across Telegraph Avenue and straight into Moe's Book Shop.

"Where?" he asked.

I pointed to the underground comic book section. Les' eyes
got big and then narrowed as he surveyed the racks that bulged
with all those gaudy and often racily illustrated covers of *Slow
Death Funnies, Young Lust, The Furry Freak Brothers, Fritz the Cat,
Yellow Dog* and other scuzzy favorites.

"What'd you say this thing was called?"

"*Zap Comix,*" I said, reaching and handing him a crisp new
copy of the very issue I'd been describing over refreshments at
the Med.

With flaring nostrils, Les leafed through it, and I could see he
wasn't taking lightly the outrageous and unsavory shenanigans
of Angelfood McSpade and all her dwarfish and doofus-looking
sexual partners, to say say nothing of the reprehensible and
sometimes swinish antics of Crumb's other characters. Here was
Angelgood engaging in coitus with some wimpy white loser. And
here was Mr. Natural with his snowy, long beard, jumping nasty
with some sweet young thing. And how about this drawing of
one of Crumb's big-legged young hippie females in a miniskirt
as she crouched to pay lip service, right there on the sidewalk, to
some pop-eyed black pimp flashing regulation gold teeth and
sporting gassed, patent-leather-looking hair?

Les didn't crack so much as a smile at any of it. Not even at
the spectacle of the zaftig Lenore Goldberg, her copious blue-
jeaned behind spread all over the seat of the roaring Harley between her legs, on her way to terrorize a cowering roomful of
effete East Bay intellectuals with the cutting salutation: "Hi ya,
smarties!"

"Hey," Les said, comic book in hand, "I'm calling 'em on
this shit!" And turning on his heels at once, he stomped over to
the ponytailed clerk at the cash register.

The clerk said, "You gonna buy that?"

"Hell no," yelled Les. "I wanna file a protest!"

The clerk, who had probably witnessed by then every manner
of madness go down in Moe's, looked more irritated than surprised. "A protest about what, man?"

Les whacked the *Zap* flat down on the counter. "This so-called
funnybook your store is selling."

"What's wrong with *Zap Comix,* man?"

"First of all," Les told him, "quit calling me *man!* You got
that?"

"Shit, are you ever uptight!"

Les' intensity was even taking me by surprise, for I had no idea he would ever carry the thing this far. But there was nothing to do now except stand back and watch.

"You're goddamn right I'm uptight! Just look at this! Look at the filthy and obscene ways black people are being depicted in this racist publication! I don't find this shit funny worth a damn!"

The clerk's ponytail swung as he looked on and turned the pages of the comic. To me he looked absolutely lost and dumbfounded.

Leslie Perry opened up the *Zap* and started pointing out specific drawings he found offensive. "Look at this," he raged. "And look at that. Don't come telling *me* this isn't racist."

The clerk patiently noted each illustration as Les' finger fell upon it, yet he still seemed not so much alarmed as puzzled. "Yeah," he said. "So?"

"So we want this kinda garbage outta your store. It's racist and it's disgusting, and that's *all* it is!"

"Hey," said the clerk, "I can't do that, man, uhhh, I mean . . ."

"What!" Les hollered. "What the hell you mean, you can't do it? Then lemme talk to the boss. Get Moe over here!"

"Moe's gone home for the day."

"Well, *some*body's gonna have to do *some*thing!"

Trembling, the clerk snatched the comic out of Les' hands, then spread it flat on the counter again. "Look," he said, obviously trying to be as calm and as reasonable as he could, given the circumstance. "I'll agree with you that this publication might be sleazy and it might even be sick, but there's no way you can say it's racist."

"How's that?" I asked, curious to hear what the clerk would say, even though I didn't believe in censorship.

He nervously brushed at the *Zap* page on display with one hand and said: "How can I say that? See for yourself. Everybody in this magazine is sick—and that's the fucking point! They're all sick, Robert Crumb is probably sick, you're sick. Fuck, it's a sick fucking society! And you," he raged on, turning to Les, "you're coming in here telling me we oughtta stop selling it. Shit, that's sick too!"

Suddenly Les, who's fair-skinned, turned a deep incendiary shade of red. His gray-green eyes were smoldering. He did another about-face and pushed past me. While the clerk was still holding forth and turning *Zap* pages, Les raced back over to the underground comics section and pushed and flung and kicked every item on display to the floor.

Heads turned.

I took a deep breath.

The ponytailed clerk's voice was quivering as he shouted: "Don't you ever come back in here again, you sick sonofabitch!"

"Keep stocking those racist funnybooks," Les yelled over his shoulder, "and see what happens!"

And with that, Leslie Perry, his handsome face aflame, stepped unhurried out the front door.

When I caught up with him outside, Les patted my shoulder and, smiling, said, "Hope I didn't embarrass you too much, man. But somebody's gotta show these peckerwoods we know what's going down. . . . I'm glad you told me about that stuff."

The Avenue, as they call it in Berkeley, was jammed with people, and as I took a quick look up and down the street, absolutely everybody my eyes fell on looked as if they'd just stepped straight out of a *Zap Comix,* including the fragile professor clutching a copy of *China Reconstructs,* who was emerging at that very moment from the Café Med, which old-timers still called the Piccolo.

And somehow I sensed that if Les and I stood out there chatting long enough, Lenore Goldberg or Mr. Natural or even Angelfood McSpade would be certain to turn up too.

Moody's Mood
for Love

King Pleasure, 1952

What we liked to do at Hutchins Intermediate School in Detroit was get together—a whole gang of us, say, half a dozen to ten kids—and either walk through the halls or hang out by the grocery store over there off Woodrow Wilson, or step through streets singing "Moody's Mood for Love" in loud unison with a vengeance calculated to blow grown people and other squares clean away; keep them right there where we wanted them—at a distance and out of our business.

In the motion picture soundtrack of your mind, you can easily envision and hear us all silly and feisty; arrogant as city mice out to pull the rug out from under our slower, country cousins; that is, anybody who didn't know the words to this tricky vocalese version of an alto saxophone solo James Moody had cut on Prestige Records. From beginning to end, Moody never stated the melody line of the tune whose chordal layout he was bouncing from—Jimmy McHugh's "I'm in the Mood for Love." One wonders why he didn't bother claiming composer credit, for this was how the beboppers had learned to fatten their royalty checks—when they were lucky enough to even get royalties—from record companies and from BMI (Broadcast Music, Inc.), or ASCAP (the American Society of Composers and Publishers). The copyright office said you couldn't copyright a chord progression, only a specific melody. So Moody, living in Europe, had borrowed an alto saxophone from Swedish bopster Lars Gullin and made this three-minute cut, which might have gone the way of many a fine but forgotten jazz solo if it hadn't reached the ears of a mystic and singer named Clarence Beek out in East St. Louis. Clarence Beek changed his name to King Pleasure.

"There I go/There I go/There I go/Therrrrre I go . . ." is what Pleasure had heard Moody whispering as he began to poeticize the
urgency of his emotions in a solo that gathered candor the way
an object approaching the speed of light accumulates mass,
grows tinier and tinier until time stands still. That's all Einstein
had been talking about, and there Moody was—like any other
outstanding jazz artist—telling such a story in musical notes and
tones that Pleasure broke down into language that was far from
sounding like the airy sweet nothings we'd been brought up to
expect from popular songs: "A. You're adorable,/B. You're so
beautiful,/C. You're a cutie full of charm," sung by Perry Como
or Doris Day—and, don't get me wrong, Doris Day could
sing—but there was something about this invisible collaboration
between James Moody and King Pleasure that was irresistible to
us as adolescents.

There are rumors that the lyrics were really Eddie Jefferson's.
But whoever wrote them, these were love lyrics that cut across
neat little bar lines and formulas; that were lofty yet earthy —
"Pretty baby,/You are the one who/Snaps my control." There
was something awfully close to real about them and, because
they followed the heated build-up of Moody's soar-and-cruise,
the way stories in jazz are traditionally laid out, these were also
words that we could taste in our mouths as we sang and said
them. By the time we each felt the first climax approaching, the
whole gang of us would stop in our tracks and flail our arms toward the sky. All we could do was peep around at one another in
anticipatory glee an instant before the beat told us it was time to
belt it right out: *"Ohhh, baby,/You make me feel so gooood!/Lemme take
you by the hand. . . ."*

Singer and lyricist Jon Hendricks, whose first record was a
vocalese duet rendition of Stan Getz' instrumental, "Don't Get
Scared," has told me how shocked he was to go into the studio
with Pleasure to find out that Pleasure hadn't written words for
Hendricks to sing. On that recording, Pleasure sings Getz' tenor
solo and Hendricks sings baritone saxophonist Lars Gullin's.
But when Hendricks had asked Pleasure where were the lyrics
he'd have to sing, Pleasure had to remind him that this was still
jazz and that Hendricks was going to have to write his own.

I don't know whether Blossom Dearie had to do the same
thing for the passionate but cool response to Pleasure's wolfish

plea on "Moody's Mood for Love," and we didn't even think
about anything like that back at Hutchins. All 6 or 10 of us
would simply shift from baritone or tenor into falsetto register
and gurgle out the girls' part too. And who can ever forget how
she opens? Perhaps Dearie's coyness suggests what we were all
probably too macho or unconscious to accept or understand:
namely, that the seducer and the seduced are always in cahoots,
and usually there isn't much question as to which has the upper
hand, not in "Moody's Mood" anyway. Dearie, taking Swedish
pianist Thore Swanrud's piano part, sings: *What is all this talk/
About loving me,/My sweet? . . ."*

And, on that sly note, just when they're off to find "a place
where we can use a loving state of mind," Pleasure, like all good
Victorian storytellers, draws the curtain on the ensuing scene,
leaving to the imagination what didn't need to be said anyway.
Then, telling James Moody that he can come on in there, man,
and he can blow now, "we're through," the song ends as breath-
lessly as it began.

Most of us didn't really know who James Moody was, but
there was a kid at school named James Moody, a rather prominent gang leader himself; he was the neighborhood head of the
Shakers, a hardball pack of youths, ranging in age from 13 to
30, that terrorized Detroit in the early Fifties. The story of how
I, who belonged to no youth gang, managed to coexist on turf
that both the Shakers and their rivals the Ooloos warred over
regularly, and yet steer clear of both gangs diplomatically, would
make a novella in itself. James Moody happened to like the
song, though. He basked so completely in the reflected glory of
this musical salute that he actually grew to believe that he'd
composed it, or something.

The truth is that we were all composing it, over and over,
everytime we sang it. Even now when I listen to Aretha's version, still regarded as offbeat and too jazzy to be commercial, I
remember how it was played over the rhythm and blues station,
WJLB, on "Rockin' With Leroy"—a show upward-looking Negro parents didn't want their kids listening to, even though an
awful lot of grown-ups' auto radios were glued to that 1400 spot
on the dial. Leroy Holmes, the deejay, spun out a powerful line
of jive, and when he put on "Sixty Minute Man" by Billy Ward
and the Dominoes or "Baby, Don't Do It" by the Five Royals or

Hank Ballard and the Midnighters doing "Work with Me, Annie" or their outrageous sequel, "Annie Had a Baby (Can't Work No More)," my folks would voice concern about what the world was coming to, but they were fascinated all the same. Only the most daring of white kids at school knew anything at all about it.

"Are you guys making that up?" one kid asked us in the locker room one morning while we were doing a round of "Moody's Mood for Love."

"No," some wisecracker told him, "James Moody wrote it."

"Oh," the curious kid, onlooker and listener, said, pulling up his sweat socks, "I didn't know he did anything but fight."

It was all about territory, I suppose; physical and mental, cultural and emotional; what was pure versus the adulterated and the adult, you might say. But, above all, it was still about square versus hip. Mainly, our feeling about what we sang and how we sang it and where it came from was this: It wasn't nobody else's business.

Just the Way You Are

Billy Joel, 1977

1 / MARCIE

"Love you just the way you/love you just the way you/love you just the way you . . ."

That wasn't like Stan at all, I kept thinking. There's any number of negative, even mean things I could bring up about him, but sloppiness wasn't one of them. Stan was smooth, especially when he was on the air. And melodious. He had one of the most melodious radio voices to ever ooze through me. It's hard to believe I hardly listened to his shows the five years we were married.

That's what you get, Marcie, I told my skinny new self in the mirror after I got up out of bed and walked to the bathroom for a glass of water. It's hard to lie still and listen to a stuck record playing the same nick over and over. By the time I slid back under the covers, I figured, he'll have nudged the needle over, or something. What a pity. That's my favorite Billy Joel record too. In fact, that's the *only* Billy Joel record I can say I really like. I just knew Stan would come back on the air and say something hilarious that would make it sound like he'd been planning this all along.

I got back into bed expecting to finally hear Joel sing, "I love you just the way you are," followed by that bright, lush sax, but no! It was still stuck. I felt like I needed to do something—phone the station or pound my radio; it was making me jittery.

But, like I said, that's what I get listening to my ex late at night while my boyfriend was out of town. Why I was doing it's hard to say. Maybe it was because I hadn't heard from Stan at

Christmas. I mean, he usually gets in touch on my birthday, at Christmas and on Valentine's Day, which also just happens to be the day before his birthday. But the holidays had come and gone—and nothing. It wasn't the biggest worry in my life just then; the little ad agency was taking priority over everything else. And I wondered if that didn't bother Stan?

Justin, the guy I'd just started to see, who happens to be a good lawyer, kept saying Stan and I were in cahoots with one another. He figured two years was long enough for divorced people to stop getting all mushy on birthdays and holidays. I don't know if I agree, but I'd gotten pretty tired of being Stan's ex-wife. We were luckier than most; we didn't have kids, there wasn't any big property settlement, and there hadn't really been any big, crushing or devastating circumstances that had caused us to split. It just didn't work out the way we thought could if we worked at it hard enough. But Stan wore me out, and I figured life was too short to be spending it making somebody else miserable by trying to make them happy.

Even after we'd decided to bust up, he was slow getting the message; he wouldn't go away. Finally I went out, found him a place to stay, borrowed a pickup truck, helped Stan pack and move, and the poor bastard still didn't quite get it. Was it because I was three years older? Was it because I couldn't help mothering him the way I used to play mother to my kid brother and Dad after Mom took ill and became an invalid? Therapy had helped a lot, but it still hadn't totally melted that tight, little burr at the center of my heart that was guilt and nothing *but*.

While I was sitting on the bed, getting spaced out into my own train of thoughts, the phone rang. You know how scary it is when you're up past midnight and not expecting anyone to call and you hear the phone. Well, that's how I felt: real wobbly yet ready for anything as I picked it up. I knew it wasn't Justin because he'd gone home and turned in right after dinner because he had to be in court bright and early.

2 / STAN

How dumb can you get? At first I can't believe what's happened, then a voice at the back of my head says, "Believe it!"

Walked clean out of the studio, let the door click shut behind me, and then there I am in the KJOY parking lot with this expanding knot in my stomach that says, "You are just about to get washed all the way down the drain, Stan Logan."

First I lose my talk show down in Monterey, just when the network affiliate in San Francisco is about to bring me up there for a shot at the big time—or so they were hinting at anyway. Then, like a fool, I hook up with Abner Heath—and Abner's track record in this business, you gotta admit, is nothing short of formidable—and Abner offers me a piece of the action on this new station of his. What would you do?

I like working at KJOY because it's a little like being back at college. You get to cue your own records, pull and play your own stuff. And there's nothing computerized about it, not yet. Abner's out there raking in the advertisers, and people like us because we're an underdog station, the way KFAT used to be when I worked over there in Gilroy playing country western, so we're moving up in the book, our ratings are climbing, and here I have to step outside on a Thursday night for a hit of fresh air and lock myself out of the studio.

I wanna cry, then I remember I've got an extra KJOY key in the car. So I groan a little and hightail it across the lot, stepping around all those puddles to reach the Honda. I get there, take a peek inside and realize I am indeed losing it all—and fast. It sinks in while I'm hunched over, peering inside, that the Honda keys are in my raincoat pocket. And where's the coat? Why, locked up in the studio, of course. The last time this happened was on a camping trip with Lorna. We ended up having to smash the side vent to get inside to hot-wire the car—Lorna did. Her dad's an auto mechanic; she knows that stuff. That set me back some, yes indeed!

I know the phones are gonna start lighting up. I also know Abner's got nothing better to do than monitor the station at odd hours of the day and night. He'll have a fit! It's moment of truth time, for real!

That's when it hits me about the extra set of keys. When I first bought the Honda three years ago, when our thing was on the skids, I left an extra set of keys with her. Just for safekeeping. I'm more than notorious for being absentminded. I'd be a professor if I could, but professor of what?

Believe me, Marcie's the last person in the world I wanna be calling at a time like this. I'm starting to stand on my own two feet; even if they are two left feet, they're mine. I don't need to hear her tell me what a klutz I am, what a fool I am, or that all-around rejoinder of hers: "Grow up!" I didn't even call or drop her a card at Christmas—which took all the guts I could muster, and a little applause from Lorna who kept saying, "Well, just see if she calls *you* for a change!"

But now I *have* to call her. If I let this gig get away from me, it's gonna be bleak. I don't need bleak. If I keep my nose clean and walk the straight and narrow this time, I'll get over. I can feel it. I can hear Stan Logan coming out of every radio in the Bay Area, with my own show and taping spots for everybody else all up and down the dial. Just like Tom Campbell or Emperor Gene Nelson or Russ "The Moose" Syracuse or, hey, I'm talking maximum saturation: way up beyond and above top of the hill, Daly City.

3 / MARCIE AND STAN

"Hello? . . ."

"Marcie?"

"Yes . . . I don't believe this!"

"It's me."

"I know. What's going on?"

"Marcie, I'm in a jam. I need your help."

"Where are you?"

"At a pay phone, downtown San Jose."

"Stan, what's going on over there?"

"What do you mean?"

"The record's stuck. The same skip's been coming out over the air for five or six minutes now."

"You mean, you're actually listening to the show?"

"How else would I know?"

"Marcie, that's terrific."

"Stan, why aren't you at the turntables? Are you OK? You aren't stoned, are you?"

"I locked myself out."

"Huh? That sounds serious."

"I know it's awful to be waking you up like this, but I need those keys."

"What keys?"

"Keys to the Honda. Remember? I gave you that other set in case I ever did anything crazy like this? Marcie, can you hear me?"

"Sure . . . I hear you."

"So? You know where you put the keys?"

"I keep 'em on the same ring as my keys. But I don't get it. What good are car keys when you're locked out of the station?"

"Never mind, you don't wanna know. If I give you directions, is there any chance you might drive over here with the keys, honey?"

"Please don't call me honey. I still don't understand."

"Pleeeeeze! This is heavy stuff! It should only take you a couple minutes to get here; we're not far from State campus."

"Uh . . . Give me a few minutes to get dressed, all right?"

"A few minutes might be too late. Can't you just throw something over your nightgown and get in the car and—"

"Oh, for crying out loud! I'll be right there."

4 / MARCIE

I don't remember anything about that drive except the rain. It seemed right. Stan and I met in the rain, it was raining the day the divorce was final, and now there I was hurrying through the rain at some dreary hour to save his ass again. I do remember trying to sort out whether I was being too hard on the man, in retrospect.

What was it about us? If I were a songwriter, which is what Marc, my kid brother, still thinks he wants to be, then maybe I could tell it all in a few verses with some kind of clever chorus. There wasn't much to it: Girl meets boy at San Jose State after she's finally saved up enough money to quit work in an insurance office and go back to school. She studies art, commercial art, and he's fooling around with journalism and broadcasting. He's funny, ha-ha funny, and they both like to laugh a lot. Even when she's so incensed with him she can hardly talk, he still has the power to make her laugh. He's good looking too, in an awkward sort of way. She likes drawing him sometimes.

But here's the flip side: I stopped being a girl; never was really, certainly not after Mom got Parkinson's. That was when I was starting middle school in Stockton. How I managed to make it from there to the Bay Area without looking back much is something I'll have to take time to figure out one day. I was crazy about Stan; I loved him. Even now, even at 35, he's still got this helpless glint in his eye that makes me want to smother him in my arms and make everything OK. Am I the last fool of a woman around that's like that, or what?

When I pulled up in front of the station and rolled down the window to hand him his damn keys, Stan stuck his head in and looked at me up close. He was tan, he looked great and I could feel that old, pure, raw, blind energy of his bouncing off on me again, but all I said was, "Good luck."

"You're coming inside for awhile, aren't you?"

"No."

"So that's what it sounds like," he went on anyway, bending closer to hear the voice of Billy Joel hiccuping on my car radio. It was almost like a mantra now: *"Love you just the way you/love you just the way you/love you just the way you . . ."*

"Think you'll survive this one, Stan?"

"I don't know. All I do know is that one of the lines that'll be flashing when I get inside will be Abner Heath himself, and Abner might have a good radio personality but in real life he's about as good-humored as the flu."

"What are you going to do?"

"I don't know. Remember that time I was interviewing that ecologist and hadn't read a word of her book and had to fake it the whole hour?"

"No, when was that?"

"When I was doing the talk show in Monterey."

"I only heard you a couple of times then. It just didn't feel like a healthy thing to do."

"Oh?"

I pointed to the car radio. "Don't you think you'd better? . . ."

"Yes, ma'am, I sure do."

I watched him make a dash through the rain for the Honda. I suppose I should've offered to drive him the few rows of cars to his, but I didn't think of it until it was too late.

Driving home, I kept my ear glued to the station to hear how Stan was going to handle this.

5 / STAN

Sometimes you do a show that's special, and you know it's special while it's happening. That's the secret. You don't try to do the show; the show does you. You sort of serve as the instrument, the channel—if you'll excuse the wordplay—for all that takes place. That's what happens after I get back in the studio. Like I figured, every line is lit up, including Abner's. I don't answer a one! No, I clamp my earphones on, fade old Billy Joel down, and come riding in real soft and low on top of the music, right up next to the mike.

"That's one for Marcie," I say, "somewhere out there in Greater San Jose. . . . As for Billy Joel, I suspect the man has been trying to give us a message, wouldn't you agree? There's nothing quite as anticlimactic as climax itself."

And then it comes flashing down all around me like invisible lightning. I don't even know I'm 'bout to say it until it comes pouring out with a buttery chuckle, and I hear my voice melting on top of the song: "Tell you what. . . . The fifth caller to get through on the KJOY Joyline who can tell me how many times Billy Joel repeated that phrase in the tune we're hearing will receive a pair of complimentary tickets to see and hear Tom Petty and the Heartbreakers next weekend at San Jose Civic Auditorium. . . . That's the fifth caller only, pleeeeze! . . . And now a word about the most dramatic sale on personal computers and software in the history of mankind! . . ."

That show had light all around it. Sometimes I think the title "disk jockey" is too mundane and lame a description of what I do, I'm more like that character Jack Nicholson plays in *The King of Marvin Gardens* who's sort of a radio poet, an artist who's turned broadcasting and studio shots into an art form, you know?

But there you got it. Time to wrap it up, play the theme and sign off for now. Your whole heart's gone into some show and then all of a sudden it's all over, it's all bubbles in the air.

When Joan comes in to take over the six a.m. slot, we do our usual joking around, but just Joan's presence—the way it always seems to do after you've been up all night talking to yourself and working up a genuine, deep-down sort of lonesomeness—makes me start thinking about Marcie. If Joan didn't happen to be Abner's girlfriend, and if she wasn't pregnant, I think we could've hit it off. She's nothing like Marcie. Marcie's almost as tall as I am, a little over six feet, and Joan's petite. But this morning, coming down and not wanting to come down from the high of doing the show, I remember how sweet it used to be to get back to the apartment early in the morning after I'd been doing graveyard shift and slip into bed beside Marcie and get all heated and snuggly before she seguéd into dayshift consciousness.

How can you be married to somebody as long as I was to Marcie and still not understand them? I never wanted the divorce; that was all her doing. She says I'm not supportive. Maybe she's right there. I liked it when she was drawing ads for department stores and furniture stores and clothing stores. But she wanted to have her own agency. She stopped drawing and started scheming and getting into business. That would be like me not jockeying, and being like Abner instead—a station owner and manager.

I know the station's gonna get some mail behind that stuck record routine. Maybe I'll leak the story to Herb Caen or somebody, just for the fun of it.

6 / STAN AND MARCIE

"Stan, it's 6:45 in the morning. I didn't get any sleep last night to speak of, and I have to be at the office early. We're meeting with a new client."

"I know; I don't mean to bug you. But I had to stop by to bring the keys back."

"No, those are *your* keys. I don't want 'em."

"Marcie, aren't you gonna invite me in for a cup of tea or something?"

"I don't think that's a good idea."

"Not even for a hug, for old time's sake?"

"I don't think it's a good idea."

"I can tell you got a new guy."

"How can you tell that, Stanley?"

"Hey, I gotcha! You never call me Stanley unless you're *real* ticked."

"Stan, isn't Lorna somewhere waiting for you to come home?"

"We broke up."

"When?"

"Around Thanksgiving."

"Oh, is that why I didn't hear from you this Christmas?"

"No, well, not exactly."

"Stan, just go away. Let's finally get this thing right. Go away, please, and stay away until . . ."

"Until what?"

"Until everything's gotten mellow."

"And when will that be? I mean, aren't we even allowed to be civil to one another?"

"There's a difference between being civil and dropping by someone's place at a quarter to seven in the morning. I've got isometrics to do. I've got things to read over. I still have to call Justin."

"Justin? You still seeing that yuppie?"

"He's hardly a yuppie; Justin's older than I am. Just because he's a lawyer doesn't mean he's a—"

"OK, so he's a muppie: a middle-aged urban professional."

"I don't buy any of this, Stan. You're being rude and I'm asking you to leave."

"All right, you don't have to talk like that. I'll go."

"Now, don't go trying to look hurt. You know I think the world of you, but I don't want any intimacy with you again. It just doesn't work."

"Thanks for bailing me out last night, Marcie."

"I'm glad I could do that."

7 / MARCIE

I hated having to be so cold, but finally I could see that there was no other way. I waved and watched Stan turn away, looking sort of professionally vulnerable. Something told me that if I could bring this one encounter off, then both of us might be free. I wondered if I was just making that up.

When I caught myself crying in the shower—with the water so hot and steamy all around me—it felt right; it felt *all* right. I sang to myself and tensed muscle after muscle, and quietly let go of the years.

I figured if I heard from him the day before his birthday, then I would find out for sure which one of us was hopeless.

Bohemia After Dark

Oscar Pettiford, composer

The story, as I got it, was that Oscar Pettiford, a magnificent bassist and cellist, used to get a kick out of getting people to try to play the bridge of this song of his, popularized by renditions Cannonball Adderley, George Wallington and other jazz colleagues recorded across the years. O.P., as intimates called him, was part Cherokee and the bridge to "Bohemia After Dark" has an Amerindian tribal tom-tom trickiness about it that floored most players the first time they tried to read the actual notes he'd scored, and this is said to have given Pettiford considerable pleasure. But it isn't so much this story that floors me as it is the mere notion of Pettiford's having titled a piece of music "Bohemia After Dark," which always makes me think about bohemia.

In *Who Killed King Kong?*, an unpublished collection of essays that won him a Hopwood Award at the University of Michigan in the Fifties, the poet X.J. Kennedy—known to intimates as Joe—included a memorable essay about bohemia and its origins. Joe had tracked it back to the European Middle Ages, to the days of the Goliards and other wayward students and scholars: drunken boisterous types, defrocked priests among them, who would gamble away everything they owned, including their books, and whose overriding characteristic was the din, the racket, the noise they kept up. All traditional bohemias, according to Kennedy, were noisy.

The bohemia I fell into in my teens certainly grew loud at times. Music—and jazz especially—was very much a part of it. For the most part, bohemia for me meant running with an older crowd, people five to fifteen years older than myself, who knew about art and literature and Marxism and Freud and Zen

Buddhism and African primitivism and Leadbelly and Scots-Irish balladry and Hindemith and Thelonious Monk and the fact that prizefighter Jack Johnson ran around for a spell with other American expatriates in France and wrote a little poetry himself. As a matter of fact, boxers have always been a part of America's black bohemian scene. Sugar Ray Robinson and bop singer Babs Gonzales rubbed shoulders in the clubs, and one of the things that attracted amateur boxer Miles Davis (who had recorded "Ezz-thetics," composer George Russell's musical tribute to Ezzard Charles) to pianist Red Garland was the fact that Garland had fought professionally.

There was no more professional musician than Oscar Pettiford. He played hard, drank hard, lived hard, wrote hard-to-play tunes and, even though I was a very young man when he died, I still miss him. Sometimes in the bohemian night when I'm humming his most famous song or listening to some bass player tackle his composition, "Trickotism," I think of handsome, balding brown-skinned trickster figure Oscar Pettiford, who probably knew all about Coyote, fighting his way through the music jungle, dragging his bass into Greenwich Village's Cafe Bohemia for a three-night stand.

Heroic in the midst of all that noise and smoke, for unlike their classical brethren who do their performing in genteel settings, jazz musicians are expected to create beauty and ply their wondrous necromancy in taverns and saloons, I can picture images of the Indian reservation in Oklahoma playing through Pettiford's head, and early days when he tap-danced with his father's territory band, and what it must have been like for him to study tailoring on the side just in case showbiz became too threadbare and raggedy. And, thanks to all the lovely music he left to warm and tickle us, Oscar Pettiford's artistic, intellectual and athletic bohemia grows lighter and brighter as the years get shorter and my ears get bigger.

Marta

(Rambling Rose of the Wildwood)
Arthur Tracy, 1931
Tony Martin, 1952

Marta? I'll tell you about Marta, no rambling rose of the wildwood like in that Cuban Moises Simon's song with words by L.
Wolfe Gilbert that used to be Arthur Tracy's theme, but a real
woman with a way of blowing fragrance and musk and sweetness and thorns into your life that's almost soothing to an old
beatnik like myself, pushing 65 now on this multi-laned freeway
of life and still hearing myself as nothing more than Radio's
Street Singer of Bop Prosody. When the clock goes beep and it's
time to hit it, I roll out the sack, hungover and glooped, a
reacher for Marta, the solid fleshiness of her, hee hee, marta-
dom, even when she isn't there, even when she's across town or
not in town at all. When she's across the Bay, say, in the very
east of San Francisco-ness, stiff to her pantyhose from wayward
Hayward lovemaking, even then, I'm right there, fast by my
Hermes, swift and clean of herpes, delicately, writerishly, hunt-
ing and pecking my gallant way thru the grand Kerouackian
confusion of America cum laude—past master of all her con and
fusion. America, suddenly grown older into elderly like a sinful
sunflower in the wishful kitchen of her desolation—a dark dish
browning and buttered, much like myself: the literary toast of
this town, though unmarmaladed. But marmaduked like Bird,
like Charlie Parker, like Charlie Yardbird O'Rooney relaxed
into the savoir-faire Savoy Ballroom of the soul. Oh, the spade
in me flows Negro in such splendid indigo!

Color. Marta might've been the one I caught myself trapezing
over in a freefall circus act back in my dreary, psychoactive
twenties. But I was into benzedrine then when all my benny
buddies never knew how high the moon or when to stop and

neither did I, Bud Powell be my witness!—even though the Buddha in me was steady busy buzzing, dig?

But who was Marta then? Nothing, believe me, but the seam of a gleam in her sad daddy's eye of Mexico, which is the elixir, the gentle twister that puts all the lemon and peel of this glad and woeful cocktail of a confession into full and tasteable form, starting afresh in Oaxaca and Salinacruz and salted beercan top places of the Teotihuacán heartbeat all foamed over with dark and luscious Tecate where my lips go crazy with explaining. Don't worry about forms or comprehending any of this for now since all writing is the river home of alluvial sands washed up on the shore grain by grain in a yoyo-ing of consciousness.

It's all so easy to describe, so simple and linear and seemingly complete while all the while singing, zinging winds whip around me in both tropical and arctic regions of whatever remains of me when I think about Marta in the Sears store, the one in downtown Oaxaca the summery morning in the equinox of June when I walked in looking for the right-sized stopper to plug my decorticated sink (I was collapsing at the Hotel El Águila on Calle 16 de Septiembre)—and there in the dusty light of women's wear just as I chanced to be huffing and puffing past, for I smoked the worst and strongest of Mexican cigarettes in those days—Faros, which people later told me were manufactured from butts the pulque heads and winos picked up off the streets and collected to turn in, like bag ladies and Howard and Sixth Street winos do aluminum cans now in San Francisco, so the already smoked filaments of remaining tobacco can be removed and "new" skinny cigarettes produced—but *ouch!* Just the sight of Marta in that aisle bent over a pile of bikini swimsuits all crissed and crossed and tangled up in snarls of green pink lavender orange red black brown blue and geometric long-gone creative fashion design confusion made me want to hurry over and ask her something in Spanish or in English or in Zapotec or Aztec just to hear the sound of what I knew would have to be a voice nothing short of melodious and commodious because the curl of her mouth and the light around her savage and ennobling nostrils were right there and then enough to drive even the raciest of racing drivers mad mad mad with confusion as the subtlest of collusions began to form between the two of us at once along the rangier borders of love in the Mexico of suddenly connecting.

Did she actually look at me then? It's hard to know and even harder to remember because of the stopper I was determined to come up with or forever let the dirty water that was life for me just then gurgle down the drain. That was all my mind of scantly royal emotion could handle at that moment. To have passed Marta by in that trivial mind-state would've put me in the dungeon of you-had-your-chance-and-you-blew-it, so I knew feeling alone was all I had to go by and that I'd either have to go straight for it or forever bob and weave through the glittery, spidery threadbareness of what I'd let get away.

Marta ignored me at first, then she rattled off something in a Spanish so local and hopeless—to my shaky comprehension anyway—I actually pretended I was just another dumb gringo strayed into the wrong part of the store, which was the truth, except out of sheer and willful ignorance and contempt for this laid-back culture of the Aztec moon and sun gods and goddesses against a calendar that crowds out every saintly calendar date but one. And this just might be the day! Sensing this, that this just might be *el día de los difuntos* (The Day of the Dead) and that I might even be able to do some picnicking in the cemetery that happened to be what I thought my life was at that time of not exactly effortless Mexican exile, I sensed too I might be able to wend my way *poco a poco* and little by little into the precious confines of her generous-hearted presence, lingering warmly under a thin golden dress of fragrant post-girlishness there where with an exclamatory yum I could focus so easily on the swirling of classic hair beneath her arms as she raised them to direct me in gentle feminine irritation to pause and take a good look at what could only have been her gardenia'd conception of a sticky-fingered me, all thumbs, pondering other choices, other ruins.

"Or ewe oil rrrrright?" she asked of me in a fragmented English so fragile, so sweetly intoned that I grasped right off she meant to have me hear "Are you OK?" instead of what flowed from her in breath as rushed and tasty as the last winds of October turning into November at the foot of the stateliest hill surrounding such ancient sites as Mitla or Monte Alban.

But it was the look that went with it that signaled to me the already completed meaning of our not-even-yet-dreamed-of longtime liaison that would lead into another October, this one far away in the San Francisco of my spiritual longing when we'd be

tight as tight as tight can get without snapping, and the only way
to tell it all is not from the beginning, but sideways and crabwise
and kitty-cornered all crazy-legged and feverish-armed in a
clamp-to-clamp embrace of warm-bellied togetherness.

And when finally that second October arrived in the mind
and all the warming trends cooled the way weather does right
when leaves are blowing every which way in irreversible shades
of earth light, I sat down in literate sadness to begin this unfore-
seen narrative or navigation. Trees in the breeze can put your
mind at ease, but I was flying into the face of all I ever thought
was true about myself, so in love with Marta my San Francisco
geisha I hardly knew up from down anymore—and certainly
there was a thin tune bambooing out of all that lushlife hush of
the soul I'd been living from the first moment Marta and I had
kissed somehow in her pitiful shack of a house outside Oaxaca
on her ex-busdriver of a boyfriend's stop-and-let-the-tourist-
passengers-wait route.

I didn't know what time it was. I didn't know what our days
and nights meant by the time we set down in San Francisco once
it'd hit me in my gringo gut just how mean the ticks and tocks
of love can stab you as they swing back and forth in the heart—
little thorns of darkness and recall, give and take, soothe and
ache—with its age-old wrap-the-rosebud-tight-around-me bloom
of love. And this, I warn you, careless reader you probably are
and always were my star, that this is my hour-by-hour report of
the crazed flower of Marta's and my growing.

There ain't no time, strictly speaking. You know. I was only
conscious, that's all, and none of this ever happened, except it
did in theory, which in ancient Greek got all mixed up with the
same root—*theōros* (spectator), *theasthai* (to observe) and *thea* (a
viewing). It's all theater of the mind, any way you look at it. So
this is all about how I—the horny and brassy and fiddling and
saxophonic player of such a tale would sound the drum if you
asked me, either *pianissimo* or *fortissimo,* to write a book.

And what better book to start than this—scrawled haphazard
on leaves of leftovers? I walk into this hello apartment, say goodbye to Marta and suddenly two hearts the color of bananas
slowly go crazy—

Duke Ellington's "Ring Dem Bells" is tolling all around me in the lavender California dawn creeping through a window-shade become more crease and crack than cover— And the room is not roomy at all, but pigeon-colored, the color of loneliness which is all I've ever been in this mendicant world, this Novembered slice of life barely remembered—

And Marta is gone, the moon is gaunt, the gone of the stomp of time stampeding past, the goneness of being here—all a clouded ocean with winds to churn the tide—

There was a time (and the very now of it keeps threatening to crush me in its spell) when I could've got up and walked away from any cheap hotel and gone out into the papered streets, prose rising inside the rosiness of my headfulness like spinning newspaper headlines in old time-chronicled Thirties movies, but those days and nights are fades and blackouts now, the unlasting—

October 29, 1930: "I Got Rhythm" again with Eddie Lang on guitar in New York City— Where's Joe Venuti?— Where's Dino? Where's Jerry? My favorite Marxists: Groucho, Harpo, Chico, Zeppo?— It's a pity the Depression was on and none of this got righteously writ, and so I'll have to smithy the subconsciousness of my Gallic race from the day I got born, airborne—

Look, Ma, the dig and shovel of earthy old time is burying me back in that prickly rose wildwood where from on my grave and solemn site the soul ups and does a trapeze flip back out over the free-fall circus act of my dreary twenties, but I was numbed and dumb with benzedrine then, and all my benny buddies didn't know how high the moon any more than I did, even the Buddha was budding forth from me with loving intensity, dig?

I Left My Heart
in San Francisco

Tony Bennett, 1962

There are two of me in love with San Francisco. The one is
smart, knowing, discerning, debonair and likes to think of himself as urbane and polished; the other is childlike, playful, easygoing, spontaneous and open to adventure. Often, as might be
expected, these far from identical twin halves of mine find themselves quite at odds with one another. Let's call the restrained
one Mr. Young, and the looser one Al.

Mr. Young hadn't quite blossomed fully when Al arrived at
San Francisco in 1960, fresh out of college at Ann Arbor and,
like so many immigrants from the Midwest and the East and
the South who have settled in the Bay Area, anxious to start life
afresh, to do something different. A writer was what Al wanted
to be. At that time the highly publicized Beat Generation and
its literary notables—Jack Kerouac, Allen Ginsberg, Kenneth
Rexroth and Gary Snyder, among others—were instrumental
in bringing attention, through their unpredictably wayward
but exhilarating writings and antics, to the "San Francisco
Renaissance," as it was called. Poetry and jazz, Zen Buddhism, the intellectual and socially aware comedy of Mort Sahl
and Lenny Bruce, Enrico Banducci's hungry i nightclub with
its off-beat entertainers, Beat poet Lawrence Ferlinghetti's City
Lights Bookstore, the Coexistence Bagel Shop on Grant Avenue, the eternally experimental community of Berkeley across
the Bay—all of it was heady stuff that had a mighty pull on me
when Al was making the transformation from late adolescence
to young manhood.

In the span of that two and half decades, I've lived and
worked all around the San Francisco Bay Area, most pertinently

as a disk jockey for the jazz FM station KJAZ, a folksinger at the Coffee Gallery in North Beach, a yardclerk for the Southern Pacific Railroad at the old Third and Townsend station (yes, where novelist Kerouac once worked), a shipping clerk at the Bethlehem Steel parts warehouse near the Naval Yard and, of course, as a writer and sometimes teacher.

Having had the opportunity of looking at this radiant dream of a city from numberless angles, I would pick Golden Gate Park as my all-time favorite place to be in it. I love nothing better than to turn up there early of an afternoon and roam leisurely through the California Academy of Sciences, Steinhart Aquarium, Morrison Planetarium, the Conservatory and the DeYoung Museum. Whether I'm there alone or with others, Golden Gate Park, in its lush expansiveness and inhalable beauty, is always calming to the mind and freeing to the spirit. When my son was small, my wife and I made regular weekend outings to the park, and the fact that it's the first place I like to take guests and visitors from out of town must, in itself, be telling.

But this is what usually happens when the two sides of me arrive at this heart-bracing setting, which, viewed from within, seems perfectly endless, although it's actually only a mile wide and three miles long. Mr. Young, the driver, will be poking along John F. Kennedy Drive, the main park thoroughfare, admiring the statuary and thinking how pleasurable it's going to be to spend a few heady, contemplative hours strolling through the Conservatory, taking in—with eyes and breath—all the exotic tropical and semitropical plants especially. With a bit of imaginative abandon, it isn't hard for me to feel and smell something of the jungle while I'm experiencing the Conservatory.

"Hey!" Al's voice will rudely cry out. "Let's not go to the Conservatory first!"

This will annoy the Mr. Young in me, but because I have learned—through meditation and patience—to live at peace with the Al in me, my response will be polite. "Well, where would you like to start instead?"

"How about the Academy of Sciences? We can see the dinosaurs, and look at all the stuffed elk and caribou and sea elephants and birds and stuff in the North American Hall. Then we can go check out all those rocks and gems and crystals in the mineral room."

"But that's an entire afternoon right there!" Mr. Young explains.

"So? What's a day off good for if you can't have a little fun?"

As sometimes happens, neither self wins out. Because Golden Gate Park is so vast and many-sided—with its Arboretum, its Japanese Tea Garden, the Music Concourse, Stow Lake where it's a joy to rent a rowboat, the Center of Asian Art and Culture, for scheduled delights alone—I frequently end up resisting the usual year-round exhibits and simply walk around the grounds instead. Walking is my favorite form of exercise in a universe gone delirious with joggers. And there's no better walking to be done than around Golden Gate Park. As the light shifts from the gold of midday to the tangerine of sunset and fades into violet, I love to walk with my thoughts as I behold the countless bicyclists, kids and grown-ups whizzing by on rented roller skates, the proud-looking police officers on horseback, the working-class and middle-class and no-class passersby from the neighborhoods. Families and couples, loners and organized clusters of tourists from all over the world—I notice them all. The eyes of foreigners, I've noted, inevitably grow wide as they move through this wondrous setting we locals take for granted. However, it hasn't ceased to astonish me that Golden Gate Park, which borders on the Pacific, was once all sand dunes. And that reflective side, the Mr. Young side, that has always been attracted to mild nature, as the English call it, and occasional gardening, still has trouble believing that all this quiescent greenery surrounding him has been planted and cultivated by hand.

Hardly ever, though, do I miss a chance, once I've set foot inside the Academy of Sciences, to queue up for one of the astronomy or Laserium shows at Morrison Planetarium. Mr. Young, you see, is deeply touched by these first-rate, well-researched presentations and—like all the ancients of his species—has a congenital fascination with the heavens. But it takes someone like good old Al to remind Mr. Young why he probably enjoys the planetarium shows so thoroughly and repeatedly.

"You just like to come in here," Al says, "to get away from wandering around and sightseeing for a spell. Here under that big domed sky, you know it'll be like nightfall once they hit that button and the stars come out. And you can take off your shoes, recline way back in your cozy seat and drift off into the peace and quiet of Never-Never Land."

Mr. Young and Al are in complete agreement on that.

It is, after all, the Never-Never Land aspect of San Francisco that perennially delights me and keeps drawing me back again and again. If this city strikes those viewing it from afar as a place where dreamers, eccentrics, pilgrims and seekers choose to settle or "do time"—as the late and colorful writer William Saroyan has termed it—that's perfectly understandable. The enchantment persists as much today as it did over half a century ago when he was a penniless scribe about to become world famous with such masterpieces of the page and stage as *The Daring Young Man on the Flying Trapeze*, and *The Time of Your Life*.

From how many other American cities can I set out by auto and, in less than an hour, be in the mountains, or all by myself by the roaring sea, or winding through farmland so poignantly picturesque it could pass for the Midwest in which I grew up. In fact, many of the farmers in the Sacramento–San Joaquin Valley are either the descendants of immigrants from Michigan, Ohio, Nebraska or Iowa, or themselves first-generation transplants, "Let a hundred flowers bloom," is an ancient Chinese maxim that expresses the notion of tolerance and diversity. I would cheerfully add that, when it comes to this region known as San Francisco, not only do hundreds and hundreds and hundreds of flowers bloom, but they moreover enjoy their own respective microclimates to bloom in.

When I used to visit a poet friend who lived up on Rhode Island Street on Potrero Hill—where each street is named after one of the states—the moment would inevitably arrive when we'd be standing at his living-room window, looking across the the way at Twin Peaks. My friend would always sigh and say, "Man, I sure feel sorry for all those people over there. I know they must be freezing!" It didn't matter if it were warm or chilly there on Potrero; we knew people were wrapped up in sweaters or overcoats over there on Twin Peaks. "I know," he'd say, "because I used to live there, and I couldn't get any of my avocado plants to even sprout, much less thrive the way they do over here."

Climatically, the months that hold me rapt in San Francisco

are September and October. That's when things start warming
up and cooling down at the same time. It's customary for me to
pack a sweater, coat, T-shirt, long-sleeved shirt, sandals, regular
shoes, a scarf and umbrella in the trunk of the car when I'm nav-
igating my way around town in early autumn.

Sometimes when the almost munchable fog is rolling in at five
o'clock from across the Golden Gate Bridge, and I'm either
walking around Fisherman's Wharf to see how the tourist trade
is doing, or wending my way through the crowds around the
Cannery or Ghirardelli Square close by, time stands still. That's
when I catch myself pausing and thinking: "Don't you ever get
enough of this fish and seafood cocktail aroma mixed with sour-
dough French bread and popcorn and chocolate and the
ocean?" The answer is obvious, and I've even experienced in
such instances, deep and luminous flashes of having walked
these very winding, climbing streets of this city before in some
other life. The Al in me, of course, is quick to remind me that
what is agreeably familiar has a way of seeming like it's always
existed.

While I'm in that part of town, I know that somewhere—
usually at the foot of the steps on Beach Street that lead up to the
complex of Ghirardelli Square shops and restaurants—I'll stop
and listen to one of my favorite street characters. It's a black
street musician, ageless in his tortured felt hat and turtleneck
sweat, who never reveals his name or age, but who has been
playing for a bit of eternity in this same location. Mr. Young
would guess his age as 65 or possibly a youthful 70, but Al would
say: "I'd put him at 15 going on 100!"

There doesn't seem to be a song or ditty this gent doesn't
know, or can't fake if you'll hum a few bars of it. And he can
surprise you when he seriously gets to picking that battered guitar and singing in his sunny, clipped Caribbean lilt. The man's a
comedian and knows languages, too, smatterings of them anyway. Spanish, Japanese, Chinese, French, German, Dutch, Ta-
galog, Russian, Italian, Greek, Swahili, Swedish, Bengali—he's
got a sharp ear for them all, much to the delight of the tourists.
Watching him grow younger on those very steps as the years
ripen, I've also listened to his voice grow hoarser and coarser.
And I know he has to keep his singing at a level that surpasses
the traffic, the crowds, the boat whistles, the cable cars' melodic

clang and the cries of barkers, seagulls and other nearby street artists.

Not far away from this venerable sidewalk entertainer stands the sultry, wistful-eyed Gypsy woman who sells flowers. I've watched her blossom from girlhood into full womanhood in this bustling part of San Francisco. Although neither of us knows the other by name, we nevertheless always register what I perceive to be a palpable twinkle of friendly, mutual recognition whenever our paths cross. Or perhaps I should say when my path crosses hers.

For all its latter-day hubba-hubba hucksterism and ultra-touristic sensationalism, North Beach—with its Old World European and Asian populations—is still quite special to both halves of me. Al and Mr. Young both regard it as the heart of San Francisco. If you start with the idea of California being an exceptional state, and move on to the notion that San Francisco is an exceptional city in an exceptional state, then, as far as I'm concerned, North Beach would have to seen as an exception within an exception within an exception. To circulate in a zone where, traditionally anyway, Chinese or, more properly, Cantonese culture and Italian culture and a seasoned bohemian culture are at least on nodding terms with one another—well, that isn't exactly an everyday American experience. Except, that is, where North Beach and Chinatown intersect. Of course, this doesn't mean that invisible territorial lines of demarcation haven't been drawn.

I love to move in and out the various restaurants there: the Basque family-style places, the Italian, French, Vietnamese, Laotian, Greek, Indian, Arab and Korean restaurants. Two of Mr. Young's favorite places to eat, in a glorious city for eating, just happen to be in North Beach. One is Yenching, which has recently switched from Szechuan to Thai cuisine, but its old-fashioned booths, which can be curtained off by request, remain. I used to love that whole steamed fish they prepared there and served with a scrumptious, peppery sauce that was literally breathtaking, Now I'll be going right next door to Hunan Home's on Jackson Street for the same dish.

Thankfully I've grown deaf to the truculent yip of sidewalk barkers along Broadway, whose paid job it is to hook passersby into the gaudy, bumptious topless joints—"C'mon, sneak a free peek!"—because my other favorite, Vanessi's, is along that noisy, glittery strip. When Mr. Young is out with family or friends or professional associates, he likes to sit at one of the tables or booths out back and enjoy his *calamari* or pasta or salmon. But when I'm out by myself with lunch in mind and haven't bothered making the requisite reservation, then Al doesn't mind at all sitting up front at the counter where he can watch the chefs, many of them Asian, in their floppy white hats busy at the grills, sprinkling prawns and squid and other toothsome delicacies and goodies with white wine from bottles with perforated caps attached for just that purpose. Ah, and the appetizing aroma of the blasts of hot steam rising as the wine hits the grill and sizzles! The Al in me loves that!

But Al's *special* dining experience in San Francisco is still the annual visit he makes to John Lehr's Greenhouse Restaurant on Sutter Street, an adjunct to the Canterbury Hotel. It's the Sunday buffet that side of me has never gotten over, and this has been going on for a good 15 years. Picture, with your eyes closed, the most diverse assortment of people you can imagine, then open your eyes and see us all lined up to plunk down $15 apiece for tickets to get inside the sumptuous dining room, which really is a greenhouse.

There, among hanging and potted floor plants—many of them evocative of the Conservatory at Golden Gate Park—in the soporific, filtered light, a waiter or waitress will bring you a fresh plate as soon as you finish whatever it is you've been snacking on or eating in earnest. The buffet usually includes egg dishes, crepes, breads, pastries, bagels, lox, vegetable delights, fresh fruits, fruit cocktails, endless salads, yogurt, cottage cheese, whole baked salmon and other fish dishes, warm and chilled desserts, lamb, beef, bacon, ham, caviar, chicken, liver pate, and on and on. Naturally, while Al is shamelessly sampling everything savory, Mr. Young will sit with a dish of scrambled eggs, say, and watch the staggering quantities of food other less inhibited diners put away.

Mr. Young will always have his pet San Franciscos just as Al will always flaunt his. And, of course, whether I'm driving or walking or clinging to the side of a Powell Street cable car—

which has been accurately described as the most exciting urban transit ride in all of North America—I never forget that the main reason I love San Francisco is precisely because there are so many San Franciscos to love.

Squirrels scampering up and down the leafy trees along the Panhandle or Russian Hill or Telegraph Hill must have San Franciscos. Sleepy women working away in sweatshops tucked away in rooms above the rainbow glitter and neon glow of Chinatown at night have their San Franciscos, just as the newly arrived Cambodians and sad bag ladies and eccentric winos who work against all odds and at all hours prospecting for recyclable aluminum have their San Franciscos. And those doleful-eyed Slavs out there on Geary Street, who've been here since the Bolshevik Revolution and still speak more Russian than English. And black kids in the Fillmore and Western Addition and Chicanos and Nicaraguans and Salvadoreans in the turbulent Mission and Samoans and Tahitians on Potrero Hill—they all have their San Franciscos.

It's one thing to fall under the spell of a place while you're experiencing and absorbing it for the first time. But it's quite another to find the magic still dazzling you a quarter of a century later. I must love it; I keep coming back to San Francisco. And whether it be as Mr. Young or Al, the more I get to know this town, the more there is to be discovered.

Motown Review

*Who would have thought all those clackity old Motown singles from the
Sixties and Seventies would end up being the musical measure—the pop
measure, for sure—of an era? It never seems to start out that way. Like
any sensible record company, Motown started out to make money. Its
president, Berry Gordy, Jr., sent out memos and directives to his staff to
make certain the inspirational element didn't get left out of the company's product: whatever Mary Wells, Smokey Robinson and the Mir-
acles, the Supremes, Martha and the Vandellas, Stevie Wonder, Tammy
Terrell, the Jackson Five or Marvin Gaye were doing. And the
songwriting team of Holland-Dozier-Holland were certainly more interested in getting hits than they were in preserving the cultural concerns
and mores of an epoch. Yet here we are, decades later, warmly and
fondly clutching a legacy; holding on and shopping around and hearing
it through the grapevine with our my-guys and my-girls uptight and virtually clean out of sight.*

*Even though we've learned again and again that beauty's only skin
deep, that in matrimonial transactions you'd better shop around, that it
might be wise to wipe away the tears of a clown, that two can easily
do—especially on Cloud 9—what's so hard to be done by one, even if
you happen to be a superwoman and understand that ain't no mountain
high enough, we keep on hanging on.*

*There must've been more in those Motown grooves than first met the
ear because people are still dancing to them and aging with them and the
20th Century is about to run out. The so-called Motown Sound—and I
still can't forget that purple banner with gold lettering that used to flutter
in the carbon monoxide breeze up over Motown's offices and studios in
downtown Detroit. All it said was:* HITSVILLE U.S.A. *My worthy*

constituent Brother O.O. Gabugah has penned these little reruns, which are like prose-poems, some of them, and he joins me in urging you to come and get these memories.

—A.Y.

Reach Out,
I'll Be There

The Four Tops, 1966

I don't know what it was like where you were, but around New York it was startin' to get real crazy back around 1966. It was nowhere near as crazy as it was gonna get, but you could tell it wasn't about to slow down yet. I'd managed to stay outta Vietnam, but all my old block buddies—the ones that survived—were turnin' back up and actin' all strange. The ones that weren't strung out on skag or speed were goin' around so depressed you couldn't hardly relate to 'em anymore.

You take Tony Bolger. Now, me and Tony go all the way back to the Fifties together; we were real tight; ran track together in high school, worked at the car wash, took out girlfriends to the same dances sometimes and talked about what we were gonna do. But after Tony got back from Saigon, man, you just couldn't tell what he was subject to do. Look like he resented me 'cause I stayed in school and squeaked by gradewise just enough to keep the draft board off my back.

Tony always did kinda think he was slick, but after Nam he was ruthless. You could go to Tony and get anything . . . for a price. Didn't matter what it was: pot, skag, stereo, color TVs, cars, clothes, watches, white college girls, anything. He even started takin' classes himself at Hunter College in business and accounting, I guess so he could do a better job of managin' his own operation. He ran that scam like a corporation too. I missed our old friendship though, and I missed not bein' able to talk with him. Even though he didn't personally seem to be on dope, he had turned into some kinda money addict or power addict.

Finally I was able to pull him off to one side and ask him if he knew what he was doin', and wouldn't he like to get together and maybe go hear Stokeley Carmichael speak. Tony looked at me like I was tryna serve him with a summons or somethin'.

He looked me up and down, stretched his hand all up in my face, then, from outta nowhere, he went: "O.O., you know I'm wearin' more money on my wrist and little finger than you probably gonna earn if you keep workin' till you turn 65."

I looked at the diamonds and gold and silver he was sportin', and I said, "Yeah, brother. And you tellin' the truth too, cause right now I'm wearin' these J.C. Penney and Sears suits—too tight in the butt and too loose in the waist."

Tony could get down and talk about the white man and the system along with the best of us, but he said, "Vietnam gave me all the political education I need, O.O. Had us over there killin' and gettin' blown up so General Motors and General Foods and General Electric and Exxon can expand their business operations and pay their stockholders a dividend. That white boy Bob Dylan is right: We ain't nothin' more than somethin' they *invest* in. So I'm takin' care of my own business now. I'm lookin' out for numero uno, and then maybe when I get big enough and powerful enough I'll be able to send some people off to do my fightin' for me."

"Tony," I said, "Tony, what's happened to you, man? Don't you ever have any fun anymore? Don't you ever dream?"

Tony got quiet, then he said, "Yeah, I have dreams. But the shit I'm dreamin', I swear, O.O., it would scare you to death."

I kept away from Tony Bolger after that, but that wasn't all that long because somebody got to him and blew him away. It happened right there in his place. Somebody walked in and shot him all in the head and chest. They found him in his kitchen, and the *Daily News* had a picture of the body on the front page with the bullet holes and the blood tricklin' out all over this fancy carpet where he fell. You know how tasteless the *Daily News* can be. I mean they're the ones that when Jimmy Carter wouldn't give federal funding to the city of New York to save it from bankruptcy, they ran that headline that said: FEDS TO CITY: 'DROP DEAD!'

I cut out the picture of Tony's corpse and was sittin' down to paste it in this scrapbook I keep when the Four Tops came on the radio singin' about how all you had to do was "reach out for me" and "I'll comfort you." And it made me think about all my dead buddies and I thought about my mother and how nice she was to go with me to Tony's funeral.

"I still think he was a nice boy," Moms told me, drivin' home. "This country's gonna have to pay for the way it keeps messin' up its youth and its elderly and its poor and black people. If it wasn't for Negro soldiers they couldn't raise no Army to fight no Viet Cong."

I had never heard Moms say anything like that before. "What do you suppose went wrong with Tony, Moms?"

"It's just the times, O.O., that's all. People done got so far from doin' what's right, they got the whole thing upside-down."

I knew she was warmin' up to that Jesus stuff and she knew I didn't wanna hear it. I mean, even if there was such a thing as God, then why would he let all this evil stuff go on with people sufferin' and dyin' and offin' one another? That's the one question I never could find nobody could answer it. Not even Moms.

But while I was fixin' to paste Tony's picture in my scrapbook, the Four Tops came on the radio talkin' about how it is when your best just ain't good enough and, "I'll be there" with all that old soulful feelin', and my nose and throat went to stuffin' up, and I felt like they were singin' directly to me.

Heat Wave

Martha and the Vandellas, 1963

It probably helped that "Heat Wave" came out when it was hot, a July or August night—that's how I remember it anyway. Isn't it funny how it all gets blurred in the smeared mascara of time? Now, that's the way Al Young might open up on somethin' like "Heat Wave." Me, I got another perspective on it. And people'll know where I'm comin' from if they ever used to get into those crazy block parties where the city would come out and open up the fire hydrants in black neighborhoods and let the water skeet all out in the streets. I mean it was scaldin', the weather was and the only way to cool down was to get into somethin' drastic, and openin' up the fire hydrants was about as drastic as you could get. I liked visitin' my cousins in Detroit.

Martha and the Vandellas—and I'm still tryna figure out what a damn Vandella is, though I suspect she got that idea from lookin' at old Archie Andrews comic books or somethin'—now, they were a trip. Martha Reeves and them they got over on nothin' but rhythm, but I was one of the millions of people out there doin' the rhythm with 'em. I'd be out there all musty and sweaty and slippin' and slidin' around in the water with that lit- tle woman I used to be so crazy about—Jola was her name—and my little cousin Truman, he'd be up there in his Detroit Tiger T-shirt—and wasn't too many people on the East Side all that crazy about the Tigers 'cause they were about the last major league team to even think about getting some colored in their farm leagues. We'd drive all the way to Cleveland to root for the Indians before we would even drive by Briggs Stadium, that's how strong we felt. And Truman'd be up there jumpin' around to "Heat Wave" like today gonna be the last day and I'd be thinkin', well, so it's hot, but that don't mean you gotta be singin' about it. I mean, it's like bein' on the freeway all jammed up and somebody on your car radio is talkin' about how it's all jammed up. Say what?

Sorry, I know the song's supposed to be about love and all like that, but this was the way I heard it when the temperature was makin' me funky and dizzy.

Where Did Our Love Go?

The Supremes, 1964

Since my man, Al, or Mr. Young, or whichever, invited me to
write a few of these things for this book, I'm gonna tell you
straight off the top that I been knowin' him goin' further back
than he wanna admit. Tell you the truth, I think it makes him
nervous sometimes how much I know about him and his history,
which is maybe why he lets me get my two cents in sometimes
when he be writin'.

"O.O.," he said, "I want you to do some of these rhythm and
blues and soul and disco numbers. You seem to have a flare for
that sort of thing."

"Do I can a credit?" I asked him.

"O.O. Gabugah," he said, "have I ever denied you a credit?
You're actually better known than I am as an author in many
circles."

"Hey," I said, "let's not get into that competition stuff. Just
tell me which selections you want me to do and I'll do 'em,
OK?"

So all I'm doin' is runnin' straight down the list Al Young
handed me. But lemme warn you: I don't believe in mincin'
words and if sometime I come right out and say how I feel about
a piece of music or the artist performin' it or whatsoever, don't
get mad. Eloquence ain't everybody's style, you know.

Now, I'm gonna tell this just the way it happened because I
was there on the scene, runnin' side by side with Al when he
heard "Where Did Our Love Go?" by the Supremes the first
time. And guess where it was? No, it wasn't in Detroit and it
wasn't in Chicago or New York or even Oakland, California.

No, Al Young heard that thing in Asilomar, California of all places. Say what? That's right, Asilomar, California, which is this fancy resort setting right on the ocean outside Monterey and Carmel and Pacific Grove.

It was at a writers' conference; the Negro Writers' Conference is what they called it, even though there were plenty white people there, like that poet Kenneth Rexroth and Harvey Swados who wrote a lot about working-class people and Nat Hentoff the jazz critic and his wife Margot was there, and all types of unknowns.

Al was one of the unknowns; he'd just started gettin' stuff out in little teenie magazines out there on the Coast, but I know for a fact that he had to crash this event. Didn't have no enrollment card no ticket no reservation nothin'—just walked on in and acted like he belonged. He woulda done all right too if he hadna gone messin' around in the dinin' room; actually had the nerve to go waitin' in the lunch line with some of the big-time writers, then when the woman on duty, standin' up there with a ticket punch in her hand, asked to see his meal ticket, whoa! My man had to get back because he'd been fakin' it every step of the way.

He got into everything he wanted to though and even met some of his heroes at that time. Probably the one that fascinated Al the most was this little dude that went by the name of LeRoi Jones. I'd been kinda halfway followin' the joker myself for awhile because he was on that so-called Beat scene and was doin' a magazine called *Yugen,* had put on an anthology called *The Moderns,* in which he said wasn't nobody doin' anything much that was all that fresh except him and Jack Kerouac and a handfulla his beatnik buddies. All right, I didn't much agree with that. I was still knocked out by what James Weldon Johnson and Countee Cullen and Langston Hughes and Ann Petry and them had accomplished. And there was this brother over in Europe, Chester Himes, who'd been puttin' out these not-to-be-believed thrillers with these two Harlem detectives named Coffin Ed and Gravedigger I thought were pretty fresh and tough. But, you know, the Civil Rights was happenin' and we were all tryna integrate and hang together and kinda half-ass love one another. The so-called Movement was makin' itself up as we went along.

Al really kinda idolized the dude, you know, like he'd read all his stuff, his book of poetry, *Twenty Volume Preface to a Suicide Note* and some of that bodacious novel of his, *The System of Dante's Hell.* And Jones even had a play openin' in New York right after the conference. *Dutchman* was the name of it. See, Al kept up with all that kinda stuff. I mean, he was livin' in Berkeley but he could just about tell you what was goin' on all across the country when it came to things he was interested in, and literature and art and jazz and poetry and philosophy and stuff like that he kept track of the way a seagull keeps track of every ice cream cone and potato chip somebody done dropped on the Coney Island beach.

They were puttin' everybody up in these sort of cabins on the beach there at Asilomar, so one night Al decides to get up the nerve to go and knock on Roi's door. Me, I kinda hung back in the shadows of the hallway that evenin' to see how it was gonna go.

When Roi opened the door, Al Young said, "Uh, Mr. Jones?"

Roi looked at him like he was nuts and said, "You wanna come to my party?"

"Yes," Al told him.

"Then why are you standing in the doorway talking all this 'Mr. Jones' crap? Just come on in."

Well, the minute Al got his foot in the door I just slipped right on in there behind him and didn't nobody say anything.

It was a festive bunch, now that I think about it, and what was interestin' to me was all the records LeRoi Jones had dragged from the East Coast with him. He had 'em all boxed up in crates. Musta been two to three hundred LPs and 45s that man was travelin' with. I thought right away about this piece I'd read in *Ebony* about Sammy Davis, Jr., and how he used to travel with two and three *thousand,* and all I could figure was the same thing me and Al talked about later on when we went for a walk on the beach. We both got this take on how addicted soul people were to music, but it was only after you'd reached a certain stature that you could actually afford to pack your jams up and fly around on airplanes with 'em. I think that impressed Al that night more than anything LeRoi Jones did or said.

But, like I say, it was quite a night. What tickled me too was that Roi was pullin' albums out those crates and playin' 'em in fronta Nat Hentoff, and doin' a kinda wrap-up or summary of what the music was supposed to be about. Like, he'd pull out some things I hadn't heard before—some Albert Ayler and some Bill Dixon and some Cecil Taylor, those old E.S.P. disks with all that disturbed, mental-soundin' music on it—and Roi would put it on the turntable and start commentin' about how it's important to know about this horn player or this drummer or that piano player or composer and all like that. And the whole time Roi would be runnin' this shit down, Nat Hentoff would be sittin' there right across from him—and I know because I was sittin' just behind Hentoff—writin' down everything Roi was sayin'. I remember the way Hentoff lit his little pipe, then got his notebook out and then took out his fountain pen and, while Roi was playin' a jam called *My Name Is Albert Ayler*, Hentoff was writin' on the top of one of the notebook pages: Post-Coltrane Tenors.

Al and I both peeped this at the same time so we kinda gave each other one of them easy on the sly glances, I call 'em, that meant: Hey, are you seein' the same thing I'm seein'?

Well, it was startin' to get pretty wild with all those way-out sides they were spinnin', and that little apartment of Roi's was startin' to fill up with people that didn't seem to be in no mood to be talkin' all intellectual about avant-garde anything. So then Roi did somethin' Al and I will never forget.

Reachin' in the crate that had all the 45s he'd brought, he yanked out this little thing on the Motown label and put it on the turntable and cranked the volume up.

Next thing I know, we're hearin' *STOMP STOMP STOMP STOMP/ STOMP STOMP STOMP STOMP* and then these little sisters, sound like they couldna been more than 18 or 19, started in with that *"Baby/Baby/Baby, don't leave me/Pleeeeze don't leave me/ All by mysel-el. . . ."* And that changed the whole mood right then and there. People quit lookin' all tragic and sad and Reichian and contemporary and existentialist and Dadaist and Marxist and Kwame Nkrumah this and James Baldwin that and Ralph Ellison this and started havin' a little fun.

Roi was wearin' this little seersucker suit and had a straw hat he'd picked up in some junk shop on the Lower East Side; called it his Van Gogh hat. He took it off and showed it to Al and said, "Paid 50 cents for this. Now ain't that a baa-aaddd lid?" and then they'd slapped hands. That was when this young actress named Mary Berry, who was after Roi that night, came over and asked him to dance. But Roi was slick; he was Br'er Rabbit, man. He wasn't gonna commit himself to any of the women there—and there were a gang of 'em, black and white, eager to get next to him.

Kenneth Rexroth earlier that afternoon had told me and Young: "LeRoi Jones is the W.E.B. Du Bois of the Nineties, but he doesn't have to call me a Nazi simply because I disagree with some of his political philosophy."

Roi kept pullin' out one 45 after another and spinnin' 'em on that portable record player of his, but he would always come back to "Where Did Our Love Go?" which musta kinda meant somethin' special to him at the time. I wondered what.

Pretty soon—you know how literary people are—everybody was knockin' back liquor and partyin' to the hilt. I mean, you'd go outside where the cars were parked and see *old* heads, as we called 'em back then—people gray-haired and old enough to know better—and they'd be done slipped off from the party and coupled up out there in the dark, takin' turns pullin' off a half pinta whiskey or gin while they sized and felt one another up. Some things don't never change, right?

Well, the partyin' got to be so good that pretty soon you can guess what happened. *WHOMP WHOMP WHOMP!!!* There was this big, awful-soundin' knock like some kinda demon tryna break the door down the way they did in that movie *The Haunting.* Then everybody got quiet while Roi went to see who it was. You know the story; it was the police.

"Sorry to bother you," the officer said, "but I'm afraid you're going to have to tone it down a little. There's been a complaint."

At that moment, I couldn't believe what I was hearin'. This little colored poet, this LeRoi Jones, startin' talkin' back to them peckerwood cops in German. That's right, in German, man! I don't know what he was sayin' 'cause the only European languages I ever paid much mind have been French, so I can get around the Continent, around Africa, especially the Ivory Coast, and a little bit of Spanish, just enough to make my way around places like New York and L.A. and Chicago and Houston, you know.

So the whole time the cops were tellin' him to knock it off, Roi was rattlin' off stuff in the German language. Later Al told me the brother had an M.A. in German philosophy from either the

New School or Columbia University, where he'd done some kinda thesis on Heidegger.

"That's funny," Al told me, "because Charlie Parker, Bird, used to read the German philospher Heidegger, and you know what Bird concluded?"

"What'd he conclude, man?"

"Bird said that what Heidegger boils down to is this: That the more you get to know about a thing, the more its appearance changes. So you ain't gon never get the goods on anything *no* how."

Al laughed after he explained all this. Now, where he was gettin' his information is beyond me, but I believe it was from some kinda autobiographical essay in *Esquire* he'd come across. See, that's the way my man works, always puttin' things together and synthesizin', you'd say nowdays. I never had time to be strainin' my brain with all that information. I liked action. Even after I got into the black revolutionary thing—and I was what the French would call a real *bête noir!*—I didn't like sifting through all that shit the way people like Al used to do. I liked to listen at what they had to say and then pick up on all the hip sayings and licks and drop 'em in my speeches and poems and start blowin' and spreadin' the word.

The police, they looked at LeRoi Jones kinda funny, so there was a white dude in a suit and tie, I forget who it was, musta figured this didn't look right with this Negro talkin' German like that, so he ran to the door and started actin' like a go-between, like some kinda ambassador or somethin'.

"May I ask who lodged the complaint, officer?" this fellow asked.

The policeman said, "I'd rather not."

"Not so much as a hint?" the paddy dude said.

"Well," the big athlete-lookin' cop said, lookin' at the other one. "It was whoever lives directly above this apartment."

Once they were gone, Al asked Roi why he wouldn't talk to the officers in anything but German.

"Hey," Roi said to a quieted-down room. "you ever sit up late and look at those all-night movies where that SS officer be knocking at your door in the middle of the night?"

Later Al explained to me about Roi's marriage to a Jewish woman named Hettie Cohen, so I figured he must've identified with some of what his old lady's people done been through. I'm sayin' this, but I don't know what this German kick he was on was all about, do you? You know me, I'm quick to just call whatever goes down the way I see it, and the way I saw it was the brother was just bein' consistently himself; that is, as weird and as unpredictable as *any* of them Negroes on the East Coast that listen to a lotta bebop and run in them beat and off-beat circles and shit.

The next day—while me and Al were checkin' out panel discussions on the state of Negro Literature and Richard Wright and all such, with people like Horace Cayton (who co-wrote *Chicago: Black Metropolis* with a sociologist name of St. Clair Drake way back in the Thirties) and the distinguished writer and scholar from Fisk University named Arna Bontemps and other heavy brothers and sisters—LeRoi Jones figured out that Arna Bontemps had been the one called the law on him. And he was so got off with after he found that out, he didn't know what to do.

But Al Young will tell you, there wasn't much time to stay in any one mood at that conference because everything was pilin' up fast. Ossie Davis, the actor, who was about to bust out with his wife Ruby Dee in a picture he'd written called *Purlie Victorious,* which he read aloud to us from manuscript, came up to Al and said: "You know, you sort of favor me, the way I used to look before my hair turned gray." If you don't believe me, go ask Conyus Calhoun, the poet; he was there too.

Oh, that made Al's day! And even though he was disappointed that Ralph Ellison never showed up to give a scheduled talk, he enjoyed listenin' to Adam David Miller deliver the text of Ellison's speech. But it was LeRoi Jones who'd been the highlight of that four or five days when he'd heard "Where Did Our Love Go?" And you know how Al is; he likes to get all deep and mysterious with his stuff, like those old jazz players he's so crazy about. You know what he told me years later? He said, "Maybe that Supremes number we heard that night was prophetic."

"How you mean, prophetic?" I asked.

"Well, look what happened. Everything moved rather quickly after that from integration and passive resistance and civil disobedience and trying to turn the other cheek and put the Judeo-Christian ethic of loving thy neighbor into practice—it went from all that into hatred and rage and separatism and disenchantment in almost no time. Like, you know, where *did* our love go?"

"Aw, man." I told him. "It was a happenin', that's all. You always read more into things than you need to. But that sure keeps you crammed up with stuff to write about, right?"

Al went and got out his copy of the Supremes' *Greatest Hits* and played it with a twinkle in his eye.

The Way You Do
the Things You Do

The Temptations, 1964

I never was good in poetry at school. The best I ever pulled was
a C plus once in Mr. Riley's class at P.S. 147. I don't know what
they had the white kids downtown readin', but up there in
Harlem they had us readin' stuff like: *"The curfew tolls the knell of
parting day,/The loving herd winds slowly o'er the lea,/The ploughman
homeward plods his weary way/And leaves the world to darkness and to
me."* Now, who said that? Don't worry, I ain't about to hit you
with no quiz or anything, but that's the kinda poetry Mr. Riley
had us memorize. Sir Thomas Gray's "Elegy Written in a
Country Churchyard," and Robert Frost and Edna St. Vincent
Millay and Robert Browning and Wordsworth. I kinda liked old
Wordsworth a little bit 'cause whatever else you say about him,
the sucker wasn't dull. He was always comin' up with some jive
you wasn't expectin', like: *"Water, water everywhere/And not a drop
to drink."* Now, that's got a little grit and zip to it. I could always
relate to that, and that's the way it still is too, at least 'round here
in New York with all this pollution. You go out and look at the
East River and, I guarantee, you sure wouldn't wanna be
caught drinkin' none of that old nasty-lookin' water.

So what's all this got to do with the Temptations and "The
Way You Do the Things You Do"? Just this: The first time I
heard them goin', *"Good looks by the minute/You know you coulda been
an hour,"* I just about fell out! Here at last, I thought to myself,
was some poetry I could get right into and stay there. It was on
time, it rhymed, and you knew the woman whose lover was
layin' down sweet-talkin' lines like that wasn't gonna hesitate
when it came down to takin' care of business in the love and
physical affection department. I mean to say, that's one pretty

song, Jim! It's really too bad me and Jola had busted up by the time this one came out. Her daddy had got this white man he was workin' for mad at him and the man had called up Immigration, so the whole family, except for her, got shipped back to Barbados. By Jola bein' a U.S. citizen, her family wanted her to finish out school here, so they sent her to live with her aunt up in Queens. I was real sorry we'd broken up because that girl really did have a smile so bright, you just knew she coulda been a candle.

That's the jam started me to writin' poetry myself.

Hitch Hike

Marvin Gaye, 1963

"I'm goin' to Chicago/but my next stop/just might be L.A. (L.A.)/Now, what I say? (L.A.) . . ."

The calls and responses of Marvin Gaye didn't end when he stopped leaving space for listeners to chorus in their own rhythmic fillers. Right after he was killed, I happened to be in L.A., out on West Adams where a cornerful of black people'd gotten together with tapes and records right out there on the street to commemorate Gaye's passing. If there ever was a singer who spoke directly to most of the people all of the time, it was Marvin Gaye. Those lines of his echoed on into the hungover dawns and sparkling pharmaceutical afternoons of whatever that poignant appetite is that Gaye's sonic energy conjures up in us.

When he sang "Hitch Hike," his first Motown smash, you not only danced to it; you could smell the grease along all those exit ramps just off the freeway of love—which is all Gaye ever sang about—and not just those "hot dogs and french fries" the Coasters croon about in Carole King's "Under the Boardwalk" —but the bacon and smoky links and the flame-broiled Whoppers and the donuts and the Church's chicken and the fried okra and the hot sauce on the tacos and the chuchifritos, and all those Colonels still to visit.

And when, down in the mouth and pitiful, he sang "I Heard It Through the Grapevine," you could practically reach out and pluck the grapes, bite down past their thick, bitter skins and end up in a juice-squirting sweetness so delicate and musky you could spit the seeds out right there in the middle of the dance floor—unless you happened to be outdoors.

What got me about that neighborhood commemorative

gathering in L.A. was the spontaneous look and feel of it. While Marvin whined and moaned and purred from the speakers of ghetto blasters set up in store doorways and at curbside, young and middle-aged men and women danced along with boys and girls right there on the sidewalk. Try imagining the sound of two hundred people all singing the words to "What's Going On" or "Inner City Blues (Make Me Wanna Holler)" or "Pride and Joy" at the same time.

One recent night outside Detroit at a party of journalists and writers that had finally reached the dancing stage, somebody put on that cut of Gaye's from that album he cut in studios all across Europe, where, through multiple tracking and synthesizers, he sang and played almost all the instruments you hear—*Midnight Love*. To the rhythm of the hook on "Sexual Healing," L.A. Times reporter Itabari Njeri closed her eyes and moved out onto the floor with a satisfied smile. As she began to move as if she were snug and encapsulated in a magnetic field, or in a state of suspended animation, I said to her: "Marvin Gaye's lyrics don't leave much to the imagination, do they?"

"No, no," she answered from some place deep down inside her entrancement. "He didn't have but one thing on his mind. All the time. And that's what he sang about."

Listening to that sensual voice, you know it couldn't have come from any place other than from church, and you know too that the pain that Marvin Gaye was capable of singing about in a way that almost made the hurt feel good, you know that this pain must've been genuine.

What we hear in Marvin Gaye goes deeper than the words to "Can I Get a Witness?" or "How Sweet It Is to be Loved by You" or "Ain't That Peculiar?" or "Mercy, Mercy Me (The Ecology)." It's that same primal cry you hear in tribal religious music all over the earth, and although it might sound like a cry it's really at the source of all joyfulness. It all seems to depend on whether you want to listen to it in the shadows or out in open sunlight. But it's that very thing Coca-Cola, for all its extravagant advertising and geopolitical leverage, can never be: the real thing.

(You've Got to)
Ac-cen-tchu-ate the
Positive

Johnny Mercer, with the Pied Pipers, 1944

"Papa," I told my grandfather that morning on our way to that distant part of his farm we called the low field. "I wanna tote me a watermelon back to the house, too."

Papa gave me one of his stern, knowing looks and said, "Skippy, you b'lieve you can handle one of them big old melons?"

"OK," I said. I was four and, for some reason, the slang term OK was beginning to fascinate me.

My cousins Jesse Earl and Inez were walking with us, and they were far wiser to the ways of farm life than I was because they lived full-time with Papa and Mama there in Pachuta. Situated in Clarke County in the southeastern corner of Mississippi, Pachuta was a comfortable driving distance from Ocean Springs on the coast where I felt at home with my brothers Franchot, Billy and Richard. It was rare for me to be away from them, visiting my grandparents on the farm.

"Wha'cha know, Skippy?" Inez asked.

"OK," I drawled back.

The four of us were taking our own good time stepping through the weeds and clay along the path to the low field. There were several ways of getting there, but the route we chose took us through the chicken yard, around the smokehouse, under my favorite pecan tree, past the rows and rows of corn that led to one of the cow pastures. After that you walked for a long time through clusters of pine and other nut and fruit trees until you came to a clearing.

My maternal grandfather, Jordan Campbell, was doing all right for himself back in 1944, and he'd been doing well from the earliest years of the century. He was raising cotton, corn, sugarcane, potatoes, peanuts, hogs, cows, poultry and timber. Papa owned the vast acreage and the house that stood on it, a poor-Black, country-style wooden structure built up on stilts. As a kid, I figured the space up under the house had been provided for me and Jesse Earl and others our age to crawl around and spit on long pieces of haystraw to stick down dirt holes and catch doodlebugs.

Sweet Inez's mother, as my own family would do later, had taken that train known as the Chickenbone Special up to Detroit to seek out new opportunities. My Aunt Mae, Jesse Earl's mother, was working at the army base down in Biloxi on the Gulf, right near Ocean Springs but, like Aunt Ethel who had blazed the trail, she, too, would wend her way up north. But for then, during the warring Forties and the upcoming Cold War Fifties, everybody was wandering back and forth, and grandchildren were forever being farmed out for long and short spells to the old folks.

"Look out when you step 'round here." Cousin Inez was saying. "Look like it might be rattlesnakes crawlin' 'round. Y'all remember Mama tellin' us 'bout Uncle John gettin' bit by one some place 'long in here?"

Inez was a big girl, in my eyes anyway, and I loved her long legs, long hair, luscious brown skin and big, dark, soulful eyes. She must've been twelve to my four, but age didn't matter; it was the gentle, girlish motherliness of her awkard kindness and innocence that would endear her to me for the rest of my life.

"Hmmph!" said Jesse Earl, who was only a couple of years older than me. "Naw, I don't reckon we oughten take no chances."

Jesse Earl, even then, even at six, was what they used to call a good little man. Among the grandchildren, he was papa's favorite and, to this day, I believe the old man loved him every bit as much as he did any of his own kids. But what keeps coming back every time I think about Papa is the wrinkly-browed cheerlessness that seemed to hover around him the way gnats and moths buzzed around our kerosene lamps at night.

"Oooo," I said, "I don't wanna get bit by no rattlesnake!"

"Then just look where you goin'," said papa. "It's plenty

other stuff besides rattlesnakes can mess you up while you walkin' these weeds, you ain't careful."

That was Papa to a "T": blunt and curt, although well-meaning and wise in his sullen way.

By the time we reached the low field, which took forever, my little legs were tired. I wanted to sit down some place and catch back all the breath I'd lost trying to keep up with the others. It was Jesse Earl's tough country savvy that I aspired to; that's how I wanted to be. I was a little boy craving to be looked upon as a big boy capable of holding my own and doing my share.

When Papa saw me panting and looking for someplace to plop, he bent down and, looking me right in the eye, said, "Wha'cha know, Skip?"

"OK," I told him.

"Well," he said, "this here's the low field, and them's the watermelons over yonder. What say we go look at 'em?"

We walked down the rows of melons, we barefoot kids and grand old workbooted Papa. To me the watermelons looked like magic itself as they sparkled on their bellies in the dirt, still connected to their source by vines. I didn't yet know about umbilical cords and childbirth, and yet I distinctly recall the whole feel of that warm morning vibrant with sunlight. Toeing and stepping around what looked like millions of melons—baby ones, mother ones, daddy ones, and great big grandpa and grandma ones—I began to get it. It was the first time I'd ever begun to become aware in an adult kind of way of how connected up everything was to everything else.

There we stopped and fooled around for a moment, looking at ants crawl totally unfelt across our happy, callused feet. Inez and Jesse Earl stalled and stooped around for the longest while before they got Papa to cut off a melon they could carry.

When it came my turn to pick one, I fell to my knees over a round, compact green-backed, yellow-bellied baby of a melon. Right away I saw it was the only one I could possibly carry all the way back to the house. But I pointed instead at a bigger, long-headed melon I thought looked more like the size and kind the big people were choosing.

Papa snapped open his pocketknife and said, "Why don't you try it out first before I snip it?"

Jesse Earl and Inez looked at each other and laughed.

"Dog, Skippy," Jesse Earl groaned. "How you gon tote some'n that big?"

I got up and lifted the watermelon. Deep down I knew good and well it was more than I could comfortably carry, but when I saw Papa take off his straw hat to fan his face, keeping his eyes on me all the while I was trying to prove my secret point, I decided then and there that, come what may, I was going to heft that thing from the low field and tote it the whole quarter-mile— a *good* quarter-mile—home.

Already I could picture myself arriving at the back door, the back steps where chickens roamed and cats and kittens hung out, where Mama was going to come rushing out of the kitchen, wiping her hands on her apron, to say, "I declare, Skippy! You mean you toted that melon all the way from down there all by yourself?"

"Yes'm," I'd say.

And Papa would tell her: "Ain't he some'n this little boy of Mary's?"

While Inez and Jesse Earl held their melons to their chests, Papa squatted and sliced mine free from its vine, then stepped back to see what would happen.

"You gon be all right, Skippy?"

"I'm OK," I grunted, wobbling a little on my legs and arching my back to make sure the melon was balanced smack up against my belly for the long march.

Papa grabbed a huge watermelon for himself and carried it under one arm, which tickled me. "We better get on back," he said. "Mama'll be waitin' with dinner, and we can slice one of these for dessert."

Whatever we talked about walking back to the house swept clean past me. I was straining and struggling to keep up with everybody else. Maybe nothing was said at all. Papa wasn't the most talkative of men, even when he was feeling good. The truth, though, is that all three of us kids were concentrating with all our might on keeping those watermelons aloft.

Papa was the main one whose OK I wanted. That's because I'd been hearing so much about him from the rest of the family that to me he seemed like a monarch of some kind, a patriarch certainly. I was too young, of course, to know what a successful man he was, with all those lovely daughters and handsome sons, all of them loquacious, to say nothing of his respected standing in the community. All I remember about the walk back is how hard I had to work to keep my simple feet moving and the sun out of my eyes.

We'd got as far as inside the front gate, the place where I could feel relieved because the back porch was only a few more steps past the well, around the big black iron clothes-washing pot and the honeysuckle bushes that looked out from the side of the house onto the vast and seemingly borderless cottonfield.

OK, OK, OK, OK, OK, OK, OK kept bumping through my hard little head, spurring me along, grunt upon grunt.

And then—with Papa, Inez and Jesse Earl staring right at me, as if at some galaxy through an oversized telescope—the weight of it all finally caught up and overwhelmed me.

"Uh-uhhh, look out!" I myself hollered. And in the same breath I came back with: "OK, OK, OK!!!" The meaning of *OK* by then had shattered, and each dinky shard and broken piece of it seemed to mean something different. I didn't understand any of them. All I knew was it sounded OK to say OK right when I was about to fumble everything, just when the watermelon could no longer stand the tortured care and attention I'd been giving it, just when it must've been feeling its loneliest for the vine and all the other brother/sister melons it'd just been severed from back there in the low field.

The thing, I swear, just slipped and squirmed and worked its way free from my hands and, *zoop!*, went splattering to the ground. The moment it happened I could smell its cool sweetness begin to spread through the sunny air and blend with the sugary fragrance of honeysuckle. And right away the bees began buzzing around the seeded red flesh and green and white rind of it as watermelon fragments whizzed every which way.

"Uh-uhhhhh!"

Whether it was Inez or Jesse Earl who groaned that final uh-uhhh I still can't say at this bend in time, but I've never forgotten what Papa said; it was something that was going to affect me deeply for a long time to come.

"Mmmm-mmmm," he hummed deep down in his throat, surveying the wreckage with one hand in his overalls pocket and the other fastened around his own totable melon. I wanted to vanish

on the spot and slip off to that part of the barn where they stacked hay and where it was possible, or so I thought then, to turn into pure straw simply by wishing.

Papa set his watermelon down and jammed both hands into the pockets of his faded blue hitch-em-ups.

I gazed up at the permanent, wet half-moon circles of dark sweat in his workshirt armpits and made a connection I wouldn't be able to take apart and understand, not even halfway, until forty more years had passed.

"You see," Papa said to the sky that morning, but in reality declaring himself to everyone and everything that lay within reach of his vibrant voice. "This boy of Mary's will never amount to the salt in his bread."

I did the only thing a four-year-old could do under the circumstances: I burst into tears.

In later years I would continue to do everything I could think of to win Papa's approval, but eventually I had to accept his being the habitual grump he was. Consider the photograph of him and Mama and my Uncle Noah, still a baby, taken by the side of the old house in Pachuta in 1909, some thirty years before I would come back to Earth, and a good thirty-five years before I dropped the watermelon not far from that same shuttered window in back of them. I love this picture, which had always been around my grandmother's rooms. Later I would learn from Mama the story that frames it so perfectly.

"That's your grandfather and me with your Uncle Noah, our firstborn," she explained.

"Mama, you're beautiful!" I told her.

"Why, thank you, son."

Well into her nineties now, Lillian Campbell lives in one of the modest apartments that her church provides its elderly members. Arthritic, Mama is confined to a wheelchair and dependent on my Aunt Lil, her youngest daughter, Aunt Mae, Uncle Noah, Uncle James and others for the special care and attention she needs. But her mind is as clear as the mineral water springs running through the backwoods of the old Pachuta homestead.

"This was taken around the side of the house off the dining room," she said. "You remember the dining room, don't you?"

"Mama, you might not believe this, but to this very day I can

tell you everything about that dining room you'd ever wanna
know."

"Like what?"

"Well, like all the jars of fig and peach and apple and pear
preserves and jellies and jams you had stored on that shelf
against the wall across from the table. And those sheets of newspaper spread out up on the wall behind all the mason jars, I can
even tell you some of the articles printed there."

"Is that a fact?"

"Sure, like the Letters to the Editor column where the colored
citizens of Laurel are writing to thank the white folks for letting
them have the town park to hold their annual picnic."

"You remember all that?"

"Yep."

"That don't surprise me. From the beginnin' you was kinda
like a little old man. You used to like to get a hot cup of tea and
get off by yourself in the kitchen corner over there where the radio was and read and listen at Arthur Godfrey."

This made me laugh; it was absolutely true.

"You got a good memory yourself, Mama. What else can you
tell me about this picture?"

I watched her smile and get that wistful look—part pleasure,
part pain—she used to get late in the day sometimes when I was
staying with her. And, thinking back on those days of hers, it's a
wonder she can still smile about any of it. My maternal grandmother, who hummed spirituals from morning to night, got up
at five o'clock mornings, prayed, chopped wood, carried water,
cooked, gardened, sewed, washed clothes from soap she'd made
herself, ironed, cleaned, looked after kids and grandkids and
chickens and cows and pigs and mules, and there's no telling
what else.

"I'm seventeen years old here," she said, staring back at the
photograph, piercing its surface and peering deep down into it
as though it were only some soft cipher laid out in shadow lit
cryptography that she alone knew how to unscramble. "And
your Uncle Noah isn't even a year yet."

"How old is Papa?"

"Mmm, let's see . . . That would have to make him forty-one
or forty-two, cause I wasn't *but* sixteen when we got married—
and he was forty."

"That's a pretty gown you wearing."

"Thank you, thank you. I'd just finished sewin' that dress a few minutes before the photographer got there. Unh-hunh, I'd just got through hemmin' it, and the second I got the last stitch done, looked up and there the man was ready to set his camera up. You know, in them days gettin' a picture of any kind taken was a *real* big thing. You didn't just jump up and snap no picture the way people do nowadays, and ain't even got the patience now to wait for these instant pictures to jell."

"Mama," I said, "Papa doesn't look too happy about any of this."

She laughed. "That's 'cause he wasn't. I had to call him from out the field to come and get dressed up and pose for the picture. And I know you know enough about your granpa to know how much he hated for anything or anybody to take up his time while he was busy workin'. Facta business, far as he was concerned, this was all foolishness that could wait till he got through plowin'. Papa couldn't wait for the man to come out from under that black cloth and start packin' up so the picture-takin' could be over with and he could hitch Jack and Jenny back up and go back to plowin'. That's just the way he was."

"I'm glad the picture did get taken."

"I am, too, son. But, you know . . . If I had it to do all over again, ain't no way I'da married that man and put up with all that hard work and mistreatment. Papa didn't know how to relax or go easy on *nobody.* He was hard on all of us."

I told her about the watermelon episode.

"See," she explained, "your granpa would say somethin' like that on accounta he and your mother didn't get along all that good. She'd done run away from home while she was still a child and married A.J. over there in Laurel and had you. She was just as hard-headed as her daddy, and all he was doin' was gettin' back at her through you."

"Did you love him?"

"Of course I loved him. But, lemme tell you, he was one hard man to love. I used to lay up and ask myself, 'Do I love this man?' I mean, he didn't know how to lighten up and accept nobody's love. All he knew was hard work and torment. And you gotta remember, son, that Papa was a Negro man in the state of Miz Sippy, and to get anything done you had to drive yourself and be smarter than white folks. But look like Papa never learned how to let up or ease up. The minute the photographer was done, Papa put his work clothes back on and hurried back out to the cotton fields. Bless his heart!"

"You know what? I kinda look like him."

Mama took another close look at Papa in the picture, then studied me.

"You favor your granpa a whole lot, son! 'Specially 'round the forehead and nose and cheeks. Yessir, you sure do!"

It took years for me to discover that I resembled Jordan Campbell in other ways as well. When, thanks to rebirth therapy, I fully became aware of this, it provided one of the keys I'd long been missing to open a few locked inner doors.

It was during a rebirthing session with a remarkable psychic in California—a woman who had studied in the Himalayas—that images of Papa kept cropping up, and the watermelon incident in particular. Although I, a somewhat professional rememberer, hadn't been conscious of it, the watermelon sequence had a galvanizing effect on me. Yet somehow I had managed to keep this early memory filed and forgotten in some old dark shoebox way at the back of the unlit closet of my mind.

What I ended up having to learn to do was to forgive Papa, pure and simple, just as I've had to forgive myself for harboring that grudge all that time; years that saw me always taking on more than I could possibly handle, the way I thought the oldest of seven children was supposed to do. It was a pattern that ran through everything I undertook, and that's a story in itself, a big fat novel maybe. But now that I can see quite clearly how I've spent a good chunk of my life trying to prove to my grandfather I could carry a watermelon, I feel free at last to let go of it all. Now I'm free to remember Papa fully and to love him that way, too.

Perhaps my favorite recollection of the man is from the last days of his life; that period from the late Forties when Mama was forever reciting that old adage that goes: "Once a man and twice a child." When he wasn't poring over the pages of the big home medical encyclopedia to read up on his health, Papa, in his seventies, would roam around the house and yard absentmindedly. Sometimes he would giggle to himself. It seems he had never gotten over June 22, 1938, the night Joe Louis got to be Heavyweight Champion of the World by knocking out Germany's Max Schmeling in the first round of their return match. Often I'd hear Papa muttering gleefully under his breath: "Joe Louis beat Max Smelin'! Yessir, old Joe up and whipped that Nazi!" Over a decade after it'd happened, the Brown Bomber's victory was still tickling Papa.

It tickles me even now to still be here to write a little bit about him, and to have on hand this classic photo of yet another moment illumined by the morning light of all pasts, all presents and all futures that will be forever flowing into the only time there ever is: the eternal now, which neither needs nor asks to be OK'd by anyone.

Boogie Chillen
John Lee Hooker, 1949

"One night I was layin' down," John Lee Hooker tells us while he lets his fingers do the walking along his guitar-strung street, a Hastings Street made of rhythm and memory alone. "I heard Mama and Papa talkin'. I heard Papa tell Mama to let that boy boogie-woogie. She said, 'It's in him, and it's got to come out!'"

And when Hooker came out with that record, he'd been playing house parties, but that was the end of that phase of his life. "The thing caught afire," he told *Living Blues* editors Jim and Amy O'Neal years ago, "It was ringin' all across the country. When it come out, every jukebox you went to, every place you went to, every drugstore you went to, everywhere you went—department stores, they were playin' it in there. I felt good, you know." Hooker quit his factory job in Detroit and never looked back.

After "Boogie Chillen," this blue-throated mesmerist recorded "In the Mood for Love," "Hobo Blues" and "Crawlin' King Snake." Like Lightnin' Hopkins, who worked out of Texas, Hooker recorded for everybody, under any pseudonym that popped into his head. As Johnny Lee he did "I'm a Boogie Man"; as John Lee Booker he made "Stuttering Blues"; as Birmingham Sam he did "Low Down Midnight Boogie," as The Boogie Man he did "Do the Boogie"; as Johnny Williams he did "Bumble Bee Blues"; and as Delta John he made "Helpless Blues."

I grew up with Hastings Street very much instilled in my consciousness. As a member of a family that had immigrated from Mississippi to Detroit, lived on the East Side, then made the jump to the West Side, I was forever hearing some figure of authority—usually my mother or an aunt—tell me: "Hey, straighten up! You act like somebody that was brought up over on Hastings Street or some place." What this meant is that Hastings Street was rough, possibly even rougher than Memphis' Beale Street had been, or Chicago's South Side. Hastings Street was hard to beat for boldness. You could go down there any night of the week and buy leg, dope, cheap bootleg hooch, hot merchandise, eat chitlins and ribs, listen and dance to the funkiest of funkybutt blues, and probably even get a contract out on somebody for $29.95.

Earl Williams the drummer lived up the street from me; we were at Central High together. His father, tenor saxophonist Paul Williams, had made a record called "The Hucklebuck" back in the Forties, which had been a colossal hit. Some say he'd gotten it from Charlie Parker (Parker's "Now's the Time" and "The Hucklebuck" happen to share the same melody.), but what whetted my curiosity about all of that was the way gutbucket and blues and swing and bebop and country stuff and doowop and gospel were all mixed up with one another.

Paul Williams had also recorded something called "Hastings Street Bounce," and when I'd go to visit Earl, I would see this clipping from a French jazz magazine Earl had on his bulletin board. Because I was a language buff, Earl was always trying to get me to translate it for him. When I did, with the help of a dictionary, it turned out that the French were paying tribute to Williams as an outstanding jazz musician. This mystified the both of us. The author of the article had actually made a pilgrimage from Paris to Detroit and straight to Hastings Street to gather background and color for the piece. He might have even dropped in on Henry's Swing Club (which Hooker on the record of "Boogie Chillen" pronounces to sound more like "Henry's Swank Club"). I've never forgotten the way Earl looked at me when he heard this. He looked at me and said, "You mean, a Frenchman came all the way over here to check out Hastings Street?"

"That's what it says here," I told him.

"Well, I'll be damned. My old man made all that money off that record, and he'd have a fit if he heard I was hangin' out or even giggin' over on Hastings."

And yet when Willie Mae Thornton came out with "Hound

Dog" in the early Fifties, it didn't surprise me at all to see Dizzy Gillespie, working in front of the Stan Kenton band at the Fox Theater, put his horn aside in the middle of some brisk number, push his hands to his hips and roll his eyes and cry out to the crowd, all gruff and rudimentary: "You ain't nothin' but a hound dog/Come a-snoopin' 'round my door." We fell out, every last one of us.

I'd heard John Lee Hooker as a child, but it wasn't until the late Fifties and the so-called folk music craze that he landed on my eardrums with both feet and full force. And what was he singing? Hooker was singing things like "Boogie Chillen," "Crawlin' King Snake," "Hobo Blues," "I'm Bad (Just Like Jesse James)," "Bumble Bee," "House Rent Boogie" and "Got the Mad Man Blues."

"You know," I heard him tell somebody during that period, "I been playin' the same stuff all my life, and they keep on changin' the name of it on me. Now they callin' it folk music, but it used to be rhythm and blues and just plain blues. No tellin' what they'll be namin' it next."

When I caught up with him again, in the Eighties, John Lee Hooker was living in Gilroy, California, which was where he said he had to go to get away from his wife. Giving her the car and moving from Chicago to San Francisco hadn't created enough distance. Crossing the Bay Bridge and settling into an apartment in Oakland hadn't done the trick, either. It wasn't until he'd made it down the Peninsula to Gilroy, a little town south of San Jose on Highway 101, that he finally found the kind of distance and solace he need. Anyway, that's the story he used to tell.

He was working with his youthful, all-white band at Keystone in Palo Alto. I decided I'd go down there that night. And when I got there, they were playing nothing but what Hooker calls "fast boogie" numbers all night long. A couple of times during the sets, Hooker would come forward and sit on a chair and play something solo, but mostly it was strictly rock and roll with a heavy blues backbeat. John sat up there on stage in his suit and tie and dress hat and listened to the band while he comped on guitar. It was as if he were saying: "Well, y'all got it and y'all can have it." The crowd, of course, was largely white, but there were a few black fans scattered throughout, older people mostly, people who probably used to actually dance to John Lee Hooker before the while folks had discovered him. Or so went the thoughts I was making up there on the spot.

During one of the breaks, I saw Hooker over at the bar and I made a point of going over and asking if I could join him, even buy him a drink.

"Sit down," he said, "but you can't buy me no drink; it's all on the house for me."

"How're you feeling?" I asked, alluding politely to news that he'd been ordered by a doctor, following a mild heart attack, to lay off performing.

"Not bad," he said. "I'm feelin' all right. I got to kinda, you know, take it easy."

"Well, you sure have given me a lot of enjoyment over the years."

Hooker acknowledged the compliment by giving me an automatic nod, then he sort of sat there with his hat on, drank some of his soft drink, and looked at me as if to say: "Say, Blood, can't you tell I don't feel like bein' interviewed or anything? I'm tired."

The take I got was that Hooker couldn't figure me. Maybe it was because, as Lonnie Johnson once put it in one of his Thirties blues, I was too old for the orphanage and too young for the old folks' home. Either way, I had enough respect for this world-class bluesman to leave him alone after that. Besides, there was a young woman loaded down with expensive cameras—a girlfriend perhaps—who came over and told him it was time for his supper, that his food was ready. She seemed thoroughly custodial. As she was leading him away, Hooker nodded at me again and shook my hand and said, "Pleased to meet you, sir. Thanks for dropping by."

It was after this that I read what he'd told Jim and Amy O'Neal in a *Living Blues* conversation when they'd asked him if he thought his music had changed since he went to California. "No," said Hooker. "A lot of musicians, they have to have a band—they can't play by theirself. But I can sit down and do it by myself and then I can do it both ways. . . . But we got so many young kids comin' up now, they want to dance, they want to buy records, somethin' with a beat to it. So I can make them kind and then turn around and make somethin' that's slow-goin' like folk blues. And then you get two different sales. So, I mean . . . sometimes you have to change with the times. If you want to survive. I play a lot of stuff now I really don't particularly like playing. You know, just all this fast boogie."

Everything I'd heard that night has boogied on back into being a memory, but as we close in on the 21st Century I'm still listening to "Boogie Chillen" and thinking how wondrous it is that Hastings Street played its part in inspiring such a record. In the Fifties they were still calling it slum clearance, and in the Sixties it was known as urban renewal, but now it's being called gentrification. Hastings Street was leveled and gentrified long ago. But the blues by any other name is just as bittersweet. People still get the blues, and people still boogie. The basic sound of John Lee Hooker is still around; it helps us keep in physical touch with our natural selves and the Earth.

Nostalgia in Times Square

Charles Mingus, 1958

In this Charles Mingus version of urban renewal, you can hear truck rumbling and traffic moaning and somebody's heart that seems to have gotten run over in the scramble. For me it's all so clear, not unlike the way life is when you've just turned draft age in a world laid out for one-way wandering.

No wonder I respond to the power of this music by letting my shoulders shake ever so vibrantly, and by letting my boodie move while my ears pick up the huffy he-bump and the shadowy she-bump that's busy dislodging itself in there. And like that crazy feeling my ears are picking up, I too refuse to grind to any halt that a city runner of red lights wouldn't. This means: There comes a time to sit down and recall in slow motion all this one-wayness, a process that seems to see each moment as one of a kind.

Even my deepest confusion back when this record came out often sounded so delicious it threw me. Take the days I was reading the New York papers in Spanish and hungering for the only friend I had in Manhattan at that point: a London-born under-grad I'd met at a gig in Oberlin. She was sophisticated, beautiful and spoke in lilac. Afternoons I'd drop by her East Seventies digs (her girlfriend's uncle's triple-decker townhouse) and, madly jabbering the only kind of jive I knew to put down—serious conversation—I'd land with her in the lovesick hotseat of their bottom-most deck and we'd pet like mink until the sky turned ink and we never bothered checking whether the stars came out.

One night we were walking to her place through Times Square—back before genitals and orifices were being packaged—and she turned to me and, letting go of my hand, shaped her lips to say something I sensed was going to be urgent and deep, but changed her mind.

It is this remembered silence of hers that has hovered for decades in a secret part of me that would come out sounding— were it ever orchestrated—like Mingus' subway-grounded, wounded slash-and-burn landscape of love. Sometimes, standing at the edges of "Nostalgia in Times Square" and listening to it without regard for history or time, this piece sounds to me the way God might've described how it might feel to go spirit-slumming and wind up sidetracked and unheard from on some festive backstreet. But I know I can always pull out of this mood because those choo-choo strains in the background of this blues come right out of Jimmy Forrest's "Night Train." I know I can always hop that load of freight and bum a ride home. Besides— and even Mingus will tell you this—it all started back there at the roundhouse with Duke Ellington's "Happy-Go-Lucky Local."

Love, where are you now? And what was that you were about to say before we were so hauntingly interrupted?

Perhaps

Charlie Parker, 1948

Dear Bird,

Sometimes it's hearing the blues in all the music of North America that makes me think of you again, that brings me back to your effervescent lines and soarings. Other times it's specific occasions that carry me back to you. This is one of those, for I'm about to be hired as the writer to write a movie about you that a British production company wants to make. They aren't half bad, either. To their credit, they've produced a couple of cinematic successes. *A Room With a View* is one of them, and *My Beautiful Laundrette* is another. These pictures are made first for showing on Channel Four Productions in London, then put into theatrical distribution. Yours would be one of those and, from the looks of it, they're serious about making this a good, honest movie.

Tell me, Bird, where should I begin? How should I structure this story, your story? Or is it your story, or a story at all to be told? Sometimes when I listen to Max Roach, who's a consultant on the project, when I listen to him talk about the things you used to do and say, I realize that you were and must have been at heart a very personable man. How else could you have gotten away with all that stuff they say you got away with? He told me the story about your knocking at some door late at night, in the wee hours, and when nobody would come and answer, you'd change your voice by lowering it, then knock harder on the door in a belligerent fashion and shout "Police, police!!!" Presently the door would open and a head would stick itself out and somebody would say, "Bird, is that you? What you doin', man?" And then you'd get the smack you'd come for, or whatever it happened to be. "That's a strange sense of humor," Max told me, shaking his head.

There's also the story he told about your dropping by his place at four one morning—explaining that you never slept and would often stop by friends' homes to nap in their easy chairs or on their sofas and sit up dozing and reading all night. That particular morning you went down the hall at Max's, according to him, to use the john. After awhile, he says, you yelled for him to hurry into the bathroom. "Max, Max! C'mere, you gotta see this!" And when he got there—and, mind you, you two weren't gigging together or anything anymore—he noticed, besides the evidence of blood in your stool in the toilet, he noticed you standing in front of the mirror with your clothes off staring at yourself. This would be the full-length mirror directly in front of the commode, according to Max, and you pointed and said: "Look at that, Max, just look at that, would you?" He said he looked and saw how bloated you were, your hands and feet and everything; how awful you were looking by then, which would've been just a couple of months before you disappeared.

"Max," he has you saying, "I done wore this motherfucker out!"

"So," I said to Max, "Bird was a spiritual person, huh?"

"I don't know about spiritual, Al. All I know is I'd never heard anything like that before."

What I like to remember about that story is what kind of vision it takes to see the body as something that can be worn out, and to know at the same time that there's something, some presence quite apart from the physical apparatus of a human being, that's capable of witnessing what the body experiences but without necessarily identifying with it.

They're playing Billy Strayhorn's "Take the A Train" on the radio at the moment, making me think about the time Duke offered you a job in his band, a story Mingus tells. Duke must've known what he was letting himself in for by doing that, but then again I have to admire the way he managed to bring all those gifted eccentrics together in one band, in a succession of bands for all those years—Johnny Hodges, Bubber Miley, Harry Carney, Cedric Hardwicke, Paul Gonsalves, Sonny Greer, Cat Anderson, Juan Tizol, Clark Terry, Jimmy Blanton, Ben Webster, and all the others—in a reasonably smooth way. Those who know the true ins and outs of that would doubtless tell another side of that story, but this is the way I see it from the outside. You would've fit into that band the way Duke would've wanted you to, but the catch, of course, is that you weren't the type—not past age 22 anyway—to do much fitting into anybody's bands but your own.

One thing I know: This movie will open with a flock of birds, city birds, fluttering out of some fountain, maybe around the old Times Square of the Forties during some early morning excursion you might happen to be on—unshaven, wiped, horn case in hand, wending your way some place or somewhere in a state of thorough fascination with what it is you're beholding as those birds fly off. Maybe they'll be pigeons. Heh, maybe they'll *have* to be pigeons.

There will also be an early scene that will catch people totally by surprise: a scene in which you do the unexpected, like walk out of some all-night movie house imitating the tones and movements of one of your favorite actors. You must've done a lot of that, going by the way you could come from out of nowhere with such lines as "Why, you cur!" or whatever it was Dizzy has you saying in his account of that fight that broke out in some club where some redneck sailor is hitting him in the face and you're standing there calling the dude a cur. Diz is wondering if the joker even knew what a cur was.

Maybe this scene could have something to do with a black crowd's reaction to hearing about some prizefight victory on the radio, even a crowd of musicians with a radio in the back room of some club. Or we could have you reading an article on Einstein or his theory of relativity or something like this. I have no doubt that you would've known a great deal about what Einstein was up to, just as he might've known about your existence. It's a safe bet, wouldn't you say? This opening scene could virtually involve you doing anything, for, if Art Blakey's to be taken at his word, you knew about everything: geopolitics, modern and classical art, Persian poet Omar Khayyam, Islamic culture, all the stuff Schoenberg and Berg and Stravinsky and Webern and all the avant-garde European composers were doing, chess, and so on.

Perhaps (and we'll work with that tune title too) this opener could encompass some of the experimental living that was going on in the American Forties, which was this country's true workshop period, not the Sixties, wherein we get a glimpse of how you might have viewed what was happening during the Cold War Era with the Rosenbergs or the Communist Party or something equally unthinkable to the average jazz fan or scene watcher who equates bebop with apolitical straight-ahead 4/4 time, or suchness.

It's a little on the ironic side, wouldn't you agree, that I should have written you so long ago under the influence of your "Confirmation" my feelings about the Hollywood film they were thinking of doing on you back then with Richard Pryor, and that I should now be the one sitting in the catbird seat, so to speak? The word now is that Clint Eastwood is going to direct a movie about you.

Chasin' the Bird. How's that for a movie title? Like it? Or do you think it sounds too much like J.C. Thomas' book on Coltrane called *Chasin' the Trane?* I'll do some more thinking about it, but I rather like the association of the duet you used to do with Miles and the title, which would sound good on the sound track. I must say, there's something altogether confirmative about the energy surrounding this project; it's been there from the beginning, since August, grave month of your departure in 1955. It's coming from something as simple as walking out of a SoHo artist's studio with Horace Ové, the Trinidadian Londoner who'll be directing the film, and whistling Miles' line, "Donna Lee," and having Horace say: "Oh, you know that one, do you? I grew up on Bird's stuff. Isn't it beautiful. 'Barbados,' that's the one I like. Do you know 'Barbados'?"

How many ways did you know how to play the blues, Bird? And this brings me back to beginnings, everything that's opening this letter and sustaining it and, for all I know—or will soon find out—ending it. My intention is not to make a movie about some junkie who happened to be black and a genius, but to make a movie about a sensitive genius of a musician who happened to be a junkie and all that stuff they like to celebrate, but stuff they leave out when they make official stories about Mozart, Chopin, Franz Liszt and all the others. My pal Betty McGettigan swears that Liszt must be the pre-incarnation of

Duke Ellington. "Just read Liszt's story," she tells me, "and then pick it up with Ellington in the late 19th Century, then tell me what you think. I think you'd be amazed."

Who were you the reincarnaton of? I'll bet anything you took time to look into occult stuff, too. As a black man, I *know* you did. The hidden, what's hidden, is simply a great part of the legacy. I know you hid more than anyone else can ever know. But you didn't hide the joy, thank God. I can hear it pushing its way out of you on all those old sides—from the beginning to the end.

I'm going to tape everything I can get my hands on, all your records and comments, and see where that takes me. The music should be the guide, agreed?

As always,
Al

I'm the Zydeco Man

Clifton Chenier and His Red Hot Zydeco Band, 1982

In the semi-reclusive autumn of 1982—on ice but alive and in-cubating in Texas—I went rather suddenly one night with poet Lorenzo Thomas directly from "Sound and Space," an avant-garde jazz concert performance by a Roscoe Mitchell ensemble out in Lawndale Annex to the Continental Zydeco Lounge in Houston's principally black, working-class Fifth Ward. Fea-tured there that Friday night was a threesome called the Sam Brothers.

I liked Cajun music, but only knew about zydeco largely through those early recordings of Clifton Chenier that music ex-plorer Chris Strachwitz had tracked down and produced for his marvelous Arhoolie label. Aside from one night when I'd caught Chenier's band during one of its swings through Northern Cali-fornia, an outpost for emigré Louisianans, and when I'd danced to their music until, it seemed, my body was going to melt and leave nothing hanging out there on the dance floor but infrared light molecules.

"What you got to eat?" I asked the tall, dark waitress once she'd seated us in a listening corner that reminded me of sections some of the jazz clubs used to rope off for minors and non-drinkers when I first started catching live music. As a matter of fact, "For Minors Only," trumpeter Art Farmer's brooding mel-ody, had been playing on the radio quite often that November, making me lonely for big bebop cities I rarely lived in anymore. It was a mood, it was a groove, and now the groove was zydeco and, while the patient waitress stood assessing me, I said, "You got any gumbo left?"

"Ain't nothin' left," she told me in a hurry, "but *boudin*—that's all we got."

"Hmmh, *boudin,*" I repeated, unfazed. "How much is it?"

"Three dollars," she said. "You want some?"

"Sure."

"And what to drink?"

"I'll have a beer."

I let Lorenzo and the couple we'd come with, a baritone sax player and his date, order their drinks before I asked Lorenzo, "By the way, what is *boudin?*"

Lorenzo laughed and said, "Just wait, you'll find out." He laughed again. "Gonna get you some *boudin,* huh?"

Because he knew everybody there, Lorenzo was up and at it on the dance floor in no time. Mike, the horn player, was quick to follow his example. I sat there with the beautiful woman, Mike's girlfriend, feeling awkward. She felt awkward too, so we focused our attention on the music and watched the sweating dancers in the half-darkened area right out there in front of the band. When one number ended, the dancers sighed or laughed or shouted, then the Sam Brothers, with an accordion at the lead, would glide right into another Cajun two-step or a bayou-flavored blues.

"They don't clap," Mike's girlfriend said. I want to call her Susan.

"No, it isn't necessary," I said.

"Isn't necessary?" she repeated, pushing a partition of blonde hair from her eyes to peer at me.

"No," I said, "Why should the dancers applaud? You might as well have the band applaud the dancers. I mean, it's the same thing; it's like a symbiosis."

All Susan did was continue to peer at me. I couldn't believe myself that I was coming on so pedantic. In a flash it hit me why the hostess had put us down there in that roped-off section in the first place; with the possible exception of Lorenzo, who was also sporting a tie and jacket, we probably reminded her of anthropologists. Two colored dudes and a white couple, college types, let's put 'em over here. Chances are good that the poor woman hadn't been thinking that way at all, but it was an all-black scene, and it was the Southwest, the underbelly of Houston, and it was pushing the wee hours.

After awhile, the impassive waitress came back with my order. When I saw the sausage-looking items on my dish, I knew I might've done well to do some checking around beforehand. I took a swig of beer and cut into one of the sausages.

"What's that?" Susan asked with her nose wrinkled up.

"Boudin," I told her, as if I'd been putting the stuff away by the plateful since early childhood.

"I don't know French," she said. "What is it in English?"

Laughing, I said, "That's what I'm about to find out."

It turned out to be a spicy, bready mixture—a little like turkey dressing—stuffed into a sausage casing. It wasn't bad; in fact, it was awfully tasty—but, really, three dollars?

I forked up a bit of it for Susan to taste, then Lorenzo and Mike came back to the table.

"Look at you, Al Young," Lorenzo said in jest. "Sitting up here studying this stuff. I used to be like you when I first moved down here to Texas from New York, but now I've cut all that out. Now I've just fallen on off down into this shit."

With this, Lorenzo loosened his tie and hit the dance floor again. Once the music got going, some perky little woman, who looked 16 at the most, actually walked over and asked *me* to dance.

What the hell, I thought, and proceeded to shed my coat and tie right then and there. It didn't take long to get back to that state I had experienced while dancing to Clifton Chenier in California. Soon those feelings of being on the verge of turning infrared or blue seemed only a matter of temperature and gyration. What was that old line about everything being one percent inspiration and 99 percent perspiration? It felt good to be moving with all those kids and old folks and people my age, people who had obviously come here to forget about the rest of the week and who weren't much for conversation at all.

"Where you from?" my partner asked.

"California," I said.

"Yeah," she said, "I knew you musta been from *some* place 'cause you don't act like nobody that live around here."

And that was the extent of the conversation.

When I excused myself to hit the men's room, I had to pass the jukebox. While I was waiting in line there at the back of the Continental Zydeco Lounge, I pored over the titles of the selections. It didn't surprise me to see that half the numbers on there were Chifton Chenier's. A framed, smiling picture of Clifton was hanging on the wall above the jukebox.

"You know what?" Lorenzo was saying. By then, Mike and Susan were driving us both home. "You notice how it took Roscoe Mitchell and Gerald Oshita and Tom Buckner and them all night to finally get around to the blues? You notice that?"

"Sure did," I said.

"And the Sam Brothers, they played the blues all night. They started with 'em and they finished with 'em. Now, how come it is that Roscoe Mitchell, the Chicago Art Ensemble, Ornette Coleman, Sun Ra—all of 'em, they're playin' the same thing, but it takes 'em *all* night to get down to it?"

"I know what you mean," Mike looked back and said.

"I thought they kinda treated me funny at first," I said.

Lorenzo said, "That's 'cause they aren't used to you. You keep going back, then they'll get used to you. By the way, how was your *boudin?*"

"I was disappointed."

"It was kinda late to be ordering food; that's probably all they had left."

"That's what the waitress told me. That was fun, though. We'll have to do it again."

"Yeah," said Lorenzo, "only next time, let's don't go to no art opening or jazz concert first."

When the Saints Go Marching In

Louis Armstrong, 1936

Like hang gliding, antique restoration, wine tasting or baseball cards, jazz listening and record collecting can turn into an exacting religion. And for many a born-again jazz crazy or zealous convert in the San Francisco Bay Area, the shop known as Jazz Quarter might as well have been one of the seven steps to heaven. Because of its placement in a Sunset District neighborhood that nudges, curiously, the northern entrance to Golden Gate Park, this shop, with its homemade ambiance, has always sparked my imagination at a supernal level.

For instance, after a wry, perceptive acquaintance—Kinnell Jackson, a Stanford history professor—told me that jazz people acted as if they and their heroes owned the Promised Land, I had no trouble picturing how a particular scene might play at the entrance to that other Golden Gate. I imagined how lanky, bespectacled Tom Madden—Jazz Quarter's proprietor—might pause to treat himself to one more 16-ounce bottle of Coca-Cola and another cigarette before facing St. Peter.

"Well, Tom," I heard St. Peter saying, "What's the word?"

"Louis Armstrong and His Hot Five; Lil Harding Armstrong on piano; Johnny Dodds, clarinet; Johnny St. Cyr, banjo; Kid Ory, trombone . . . Recorded for Okeh in Chicago in—"

"No, Tom," St. Peter might tell him, "exact dates aren't necessary. Just give me a few more potent passwords and you're in."

Mentally I can picture the way Tom might rear back, hook one thumb in the pocket of his corduroy vest, then upend his Coke bottle to swig the last drop. "With your permission, St. Pete, I'd like to quote Miles Davis who once said: 'You can sum

95

up the whole history of jazz in four words—Louis Armstrong and Charlie Parker.'"

"Cute," St. Peter would assure Tom. "All well and good, but I'm afraid you're going to have to be more substantial than that."

Now Madden would probably be wishing he had another Coke to uncap. Instead he might run his fingers through his longish, dark hair and—quite as if he might be scanning from memory the gallery of photos, posters, calendars, drawings and paintings that brightened his shop's funky walls back down there on Earth.

"OK," Tom Madden would finally say, "how about Duke Ellington, Lester Young, Billie Holiday, Art Tatum, Mary Lou Williams, Benny Carter, Tadd Dameron and, uh, Chu Berry and Coleman Hawkins and John Coltrane?"

"That's enough!" I can hear St. Peter crying with a wave of his hand. "Throw open the gate and let this man strut on through. Preferably with some barbecue!"

When Tom Madden opened Jazz Quarter in 1968 with John Fairweather as partner, it was the fulfillment of a personal dream. Although he appeared to be déclassé in a post-Beat Generation sort of way, San Francisco-born Madden liked to think of himself as middle-class.

"My father didn't have anything to do with jazz," he explained almost proudly. "But he did like Fats Waller and Gilbert and Sullivan. I discovered jazz at 14 and started haunting all the old used 78 stores, like Eddie Hoffman's across from Yellow Cab, and Jack's Record Shop, which Norman Pierce ran. Pierce was a neighbor of Kenneth Rexroth the poet. And I still agree with Pierce's definition of jazz: 'An unpopular form of American music.'"

Madden went to work for Tower Records when it was still barely more than a gleam in founder Russ Sullivan's eye. From 1957 to 1959, Madden had been a general arts major at the University of Oregon. It was there in Eugene that he took up painting and drawing, vestiges of which were still on permanent exhibit at Jazz Quarter. But it was while he was working for the legendary Bob Flynn at The Magic Flute, a haven for West Coast jazz collectors in the Seventies, that Madden's dream was formed.

From the outside, Jazz Quarter, in the late Eighties, looked very much like an old-time Fifties record parlor. No loudspeaker hung outside over its entrance to send the thump and groan and sigh and laughter of the music to the ears of passersby, but inside the store you would always find Madden ready to slide the shiny shrink-wrap from the sleeves of new albums—that is, if it was absolutely necessary—and center them on his vintage Thorens turntable, which was powered by a vacuum-tube-heated Scott amplifier. You sort of kept expecting somebody who lived out back or upstairs to bang on the wall and bellow: "Hey, hold it down, will ya, I'm tryna cop some Zs!"

Anywhere at Jazz Quarter was the best place to begin. You could start with the front window and its display of LP jackets, business cards and matchbooks from nightspots such as Bimbo's 365 Club, Kimball's, Wolfgang's, Milestones, the Kanzaki Lounge, Yoshi's, and Shoestring Records.

I remember especially the all-Lester Young display that graced one window.

It was fun to step inside and thumb through the racks and stacks of *Jazz News, Jazz Echo, Jazz Report, Jazz New England, Radio Free Jazz, Jazz Word Index, A Different Drummer, Music Maker, Cadence, Konceptualizations,* and other arcane fanzines. Or you could nut out poring over Jazz Quarter's ever-growing library of serious discographies, all of them European researched and prepared: Coleman Hawkins, Shorty Rogers, Wardell Gray, Hank Mobley, Kenny Dorham, Chet Baker, Kai Winding, Edmund Hall, Lee Morgan, *Ellington on Microgroove,* and on it went.

While Madden's pen and ink drawing of blues shouter Jimmy Rushing was tickling your eye, you might be drawn to all the old 78 rpm disks stacked on edge in boxes along one wall. Usually going for half of their marked price, there sat numberless afternoon or evening or after-hours portions of Big Band Jazz, Sweet Bands, Small Group Jazz (Mainstream), Traditional Jazz Vocals, with a scattering of Country and Western or even some Hawaiian thrown into the bargain.

Arriving at last at the alphabetized stack of long-playing albums, I got a kick out of beginning at the end, down there where the XYZs peter out, where I'd find myself in sections marked: THE OUTFIELD, INCIDENTAL MUSIC, and SHOWS & SOUNDTRACKS. Say you'd been on the lookout for the

Henry Mancini soundtrack to that ancient TV show *Peter Gunn,* the one that starred Craig Stevens in the Fifties. Well, there it was: played by Shelly Manne and His Men.

While Madden was busy late one Friday afternoon, cueing up, much to my delight, rare cuts by the likes of Nellie Lutcher, Jack McVey, Lionel Hampton, drummer Jo Jones playing bongos on some hard-to-find side, Sonny Stitt bebopping "Shine On, Harvest Moon," a young man in sweat gear—who looked and moved like a quarterback escaped from training—rushed over to us at the counter. Madden introduced him as Davis Jordan.

"David's a regular," Tom informed me.

Jordan, with several amazing finds under his arm, shook his head and said: "Uh-uhhh! I gotta get outta here! I'm almost up to $60 already, and that's my limit. I walked in here with $80. Tom, don't play anything else, man. I need to keep me a few bucks to get through the weekend."

But Tom Madden couldn't help taunting us with some tracks from an LP by a French band called The Anachronic Jazz Band of Paris. These were marvelous players who liked to take modern jazz standards such as Thelonious Monk's "Ask Me Now," Clifford Brown's "Dahoud," Charlie Parker's "Bebop," Dizzy Gillespie's "Salt Peanuts" and John Coltrane's "Giant Steps" and perform them antique style; that is, play those numbers the way they might've been tackled back in the Twenties or Thirties by Sidney Bechet, Fletcher Henderson, Louis Armstrong or Don Redmond. I was knocked out by the sound of them right away.

"But you'd be surprised," Tom Madden told me, looking like a highly sophisticated bad boy, "how many jazz purists get real uptight and want to punch me out when I play this record. 'How could they do such a thing?' some indignant guy told me once."

That's the kind of place Jazz Quarter was: relaxed, amicably unpretentious and so rich with surprises that self-imposed limits on how much time you were going to spend there were often in order.

"If it's Chuck Mangione or George Winston they want," Tom used to tell me, "they can track that down any place. I'm mostly here for collectors."

I once asked him when he was going to hang out a sign that said: BY APPOINTMENT ONLY?

Laughing, Tom Madden, handed me a squeezable plastic telephone in the shape of a Coke bottle. "They can always call first," he said. "I'm not that bad yet. Usually I'm open Tuesdays through Saturdays from two till seven."

"And how's business?"

His lively eyes darted momentarily heavenward. "Not bad," he confided. "Not bad at all."

The Mikado

(An Oriental Opera in Two Acts)
Gilbert and Sullivan, composers

It was the best of nights and it was the worst of nights. This is the kind of tale that could easily spread itself over the area of two cities: one of them touchable, palpable, dissolving at the very moment eyes and ears are registering it, and the other lodged almost entirely in the mind.

No sooner had my wife Arl and I sat down somewhere up near the front of Stanford's Dinkenspiel Auditorium than I glimpsed a young man stumbling through the forward exit off to our right. Right away I wondered, literally, where he was coming from, but when an entire evening of theater lies before you, the sky with all its stars is the limit.

He looked 30—a hard, down-and-out 30—and his style was good old Goodwill hippie in a military overcoat. He mumbled as he stumbled, and when he finally landed in a seat in front of ours I could actually smell the booze on his breath. And right away I sensed that this was one monkey who might very well be in both a position and the condition to stop the show.

"What's with this guy?" I nudged Arl and said, for even during the confusion and commotion of people scrambling for seats I could tell that he'd slipped in without a ticket.

"Shhh," she said.

But the moment the orchestra sounded the opening strains of the overture, this fellow went into action. He twitched and he fidgeted and he wagged his head excessively. His rhythmic groans and grunts were disturbing everyone around us. Several couples got up and found themselves new seats. When he turned around after I'd tapped him on the shoulder, I got a close look at his bearded, ravaged, drink-reddened face. I tactfully touched a silencing finger to my lips. All he did was blink at me and wobble his head to the music.

One thing was clear: the fellow might not have known the score, but he certainly knew the music. At several points during the overture he sat right up in his seat and flailed his arms as though he were conducting.

"Bravo, bravo!" he kept shouting. "Bravissimo!"

By the time the curtain was opening onto the courtyard of Ko-Ko, the Lord High Executioner of Titipu, this drunk and disorderly person was beside himself with glee. The bright colors of the quasi-Japanese costumes and stage set seemed to be exciting him all the more. The area around us grew sour and heady with his animated, alcoholic cries.

"Oh," he would shout, "this is fucking wonderful, wonderful! Can't you all see how wonderful this is?"

"Quiet! Pipe down! Shut up!" several members of the audience yelled at once.

"How can you just sit there," he yelled back, his hairy lips peeled back into the silliest of grins, "and not understand how fucking great this thing is?"

Arl turned to me and whispered: "Why aren't the ushers doing anything?"

Finally an usher appeared—well, a sort of usher—an usherette, I'd call her. "If you keep disturbing everyone," she told him, "you're going to have to leave."

This happened repeatedly. He would quiet down for a moment, then lapse back into his drunken muttering and gesticulating. The usher would return, and ultimately she came back with her boss, a tall young man, the both of them students, the both of them far too nice.

Finally a couple of football-player-size young gents in the row ahead of him turned to the drunk. One of them pointed his finger emphatically and said, "Listen, fella! We've had about as much of your shenanigans as we can stand. One more outburst and your ass is gonna get bounced outta here, asshole! You got that?"

I was as annoyed with this jackass as anyone there, and yet I had begun to even like him a little. There was something about his spirit that I found touching. Perhaps it spoke to the part of me that has forever looked through its fingers at the bourgeoisie,

a class whose life purpose has long baffled me. To make the
world a comfortable habitation often appears to be the bourgeoisie's sole and crowning pursuit. And since this drunk was
making us all so uncomfortable, didn't it stand to reason that the
only thing to do was to get him the hell out of there, whatever it
took?

There W.S. Gilbert and Arthur Sullivan were with tongues
poked way out in their cheeks, lampooning onstage the antics
and pretensions of Victorian society—indeed, with Nanki-Poo,
the Mikado's son, running around disguised as a second trombone and in love with a commoner named Yum-Yum—and here
we were all indignant and getting ourselves worked up to mur-
derous proportions over the tipsy enthusiasm some wino was
displaying over a show that he seemed to love and know by
heart.

I had been studying Ernest Holmes' book *Creative Mind and
Success*. Published in 1919, it stresses and discusses the mind-like
nature of creation. Not only did Holmes maintain that thoughts
were things and that our thinking controlled the conditions of
our lives; he further maintained that we all live within one
Mind. "There is nothing but Mind," says Holmes, "and nothing moves except as Mind moves it." Later Albert Einstein, referring to Newton's model of the universe, would tell us: "The
universe begins to resemble less a machine and more a thought."

Possibly because I'm a poet at heart who has spent a lifetime
whizzing about and strolling the vast cosmos of my own mind,
I'm a sucker for this stuff; I love this kind of giant, lofty thinking. And so, seated in the dark of that theater, basking in the
warmth of music and play-acting, I thought: "Well, Universal
Mind, Divine Mother, whatever You'd like us to call You, if
what Mr. Holmes says is true, that a change of thought can
bring about a change in circumstance, then let there be a merci-
ful solution to the problem at hand."

Over a century had slipped by since *The Mikado* was first produced at London's Savoy Theatre in 1885, but barely a moment
elapsed following my thought transmission before a quiet, white-
haired woman in suit and glasses made her way from the rear
and sat in the only empty seat there was, directly in back of our
boy. At first I wasn't sure what to make of her presence, but the
moment the drunk launched into a volley of spirited expletives,

she placed her hand on his shoulder very gently and said, "Shhh. . . ."

Seated where I could eye both of them clearly, it was all I could do to keep from laughing out loud when the drunk—no doubt feeling this strange hand on his shoulder and hearing someone shush him so flagrantly—whipped his head around and blinked at the woman. Her eyes remained glued to what Pooh-Bah and Katisha and Pitti-Sing were doing onstage, but that hand of hers was firm; even I could feel the density of its certainty.

"Holy shit!" the drunk yelled at one point. "Will you just listen at that!"

Again the woman's hand fell to his shoulder as the drunk swung fully around in his seat and glared at this little old lady. Watching him sneer and soften at the same time when he connected with her visually, I imagined that he must've sensed something maternal in her presence. I also watched frustration set in, for he didn't like being controlled this way any more than he liked having her touching him anywhere. But when the next funny line from a song winged its way to him from stage center, he was careful not to vocalize his reaction, choosing instead to gesticulate. As his arms went up in a wild swing, the woman behind him reached out and took hold of his right hand.

"Just take it easy," she said, "take it easy. There are other people here trying to enjoy this show too. You mustn't spoil it for the rest of us."

Unable to contain himself, the drunk asked out loud: "Who the fuck are you?"

"Now, that sort of language doesn't wash around here, young man. I'm in charge of all this, but it doesn't really matter who I am. You just calm down and enjoy yourself, but no more of these disturbances."

And so it went, right on down through the closing of the curtain at the end of Act One. Every time the drunk even looked as though he might begin acting up again, the little woman would give his hand a tender squeeze, bring a finger to her lip and shake her head from side to side.

I don't have to tell you how astonished and gratified I was. It is quite an experience to have two simultaneous dramas unfold before you.

While the lights were going up, the woman in the suit told the drunk, "Come on across the way to the Student Union. I'll treat you to a cup of coffee."

As though she had fully mesmerized him, the drunk got to his feet at once and, following her lead, off through the exit they filed along with a good half of the audience.

When intermission was almost over, just before the lights were dimmed, the handsome woman came back and sat in the same seat next to us. Arl and I kept waiting for the drunk to pop back in, but prospects seemed slim.

"What happened to our friend?" I leaned forward and asked.

"Oh," the woman said with the sweetest of smiles, "I left him over there at Tressider Union banging out Gilbert and Sullivan on the piano. After we'd poured a little coffee in him, he started to come around."

"Obnoxious," I said, "but he really seemed to know and appreciate the music."

"Oh, sure," she said, "but with all that alcohol in him, he was definitely O.O.C."

"O.O.C.?"

"Out of control. It's a pity he gets himself in that shape; he's a nice young man underneath."

Now it was my curiousity that was looming out of control. For all I knew, she was about to press a silver bullet into my sweating palm, adjust her mask and ride off into the sunset of Ko-Ko's Garden, the setting for all of Act Two.

"I must ask you," I said.

"Ask me what?"

"I watched you float from the back row and deal with this fellow as if you knew exactly what you were doing."

"I do know what I'm doing," she said, "I've worked with plenty of mentally disturbed people in hospitals. There are techniques for calming them; you have to be gentle."

"But it was . . . it was like . . . magic. What made you come up here in the first place?"

She took off her bifocals and pinched the spot at the ridge of her nose where they'd been resting. In the dark I couldn't make out the color of her eyes, but they seemed to pick up the silver of her short and softly coiffed hair.

Holding out her hand, she said, "I'm Rita . . . Rita Taylor, executive producer of this show. When I heard all the commotion this fellow was causing, I wasn't about to stand around in back and let him ruin a production we'd been laboring for months to bring off. Are you enjoying it?"

"Oh, yes," we told her. "It's beautifully staged and casted and choreographed. We know the violinist."

"Which one?"

"Elizabeth Breed."

"She's very nice. All of the musicians have been wonderful. Now, are you ready for Act Two?"

And with that, she turned to face the stage as the conductor tapped his baton and the "symphonious orchestra," as it was billed, took it from the top.

Like I say, it was the worst of nights and the best of nights. As it always must, the show rolled on, but I was surprised to find myself missing, for the moment anyway, all the sideshow dramatics that had helped make it so hellishly splendid.

Stormy

The Association, 1968

It'd been one of those days when everything seemed to be clicking into place. Motoring over to the shopping center to pick up a roast chicken at the deli for supper, you couldn't help but take pride in the way you were hitting those lights among El Camino Real. It was green all the way, no reds, not even so much as a tentative yellow. And it was one of those rare, glorious early afternoons in the middle of January when the sun was making a comeback, and the only song to be singing was "Blue Skies," all day long. But Thelonious Monk's variation on Irving Berlin's chord changes would do, so into the deli you stepped, whistling "In Walked Bud."

Ordinarily you paid no attention to the contest entry blanks on display by the deli window: WIN A FREE TRIP TO LAKE TAHOE, PLUS $2000; A FREE TRIP TO ACAPULCO, PLUS $2000; FREE TRIP TO HONOLULU, AND $2000. Maybe it was high time you filled out one of those goodies.

"Hey, got a pen I can borrow?" you ask the nice woman who's quartering your chicken.

"Sure. Feeling lucky today, eh?"

"Yep."

"That's the spirit. Betcha you're gonna win."

You scratch in your name, your address, your day phone number, your evening number. Then you stop and wonder why they need all this information: *Occupation, Occupation of Spouse, Current Combined Income, Places Where You Like to Vacation, Favorite Outdoor Sport, How Much Spent for Vacation? Do You Pay by VISA, MASTERCHARGE, BANKAMERICARD, Other?*—and on it goes until you feel your fingers cramping.

By now half the fun of feeling lucky's been pumped out of you. Thank goodness everyone's restricted to one entry only. You fold the square of paper and drop it in the little box stapled to the colorful display. Turning to pay for your chicken, you pause. "Hmmm," you think. "Maybe I should've folded that thing kinda special so when the judges reach in the box to make their drawing their fingers'll connect with an irregular edge, and they'll be sure to pull my slip."

But it's getting late. You've got other midday errands to run. Slow motion pictures of kicking around Tahoe, peeling off tens and twenties, even hundred-dollar bills, from that two-grand wad stuffed in your pocket play in your head as you see yourself shelling out for big-time meals or to play a hunch at the dice or blackjack tables. You can even hear yourself saying to someone: "Don't worry, there's plenty more where that came from!"

You can't wait until dinnertime when you'll be telling everyone about this trip you're going to be taking.

But by dinnertime, it's all been forgotten; the whole incident has collapsed back into that fuzzy pile of daily doings that somehow get buried in the laundry hamper of memory. In any case, it doesn't seem at all significant by the time night arrives.

In fact, days and weeks roll by. The rain returns. You fall back upon unspectacular days. Once again it's the red lights that're holding your whole life back, or so you think; the reds and the sneaky, unjust, arbitrary yellows.

Late one weekday afternoon, you finally make it through jammed-up traffic off Highway 280, only to find yourself the victim of yet another stoplight, a complicated one that keeps you waiting so long you practically fall asleep. Your mind turns over and over. A drowsy illumination creeps up on you: It isn't you who's negative; it's society. After all, how often have you ever heard anyone talk about the go-light? It's always the stoplight we focus on, isn't it?

At home, though, your spouse rather matter-of-factly mentions, in a voice bristling with annoyance, that somebody's called. "This person," she says, "from some promotional agency. Did you fill out a form for a contest or something?"

"What'd they say?"

"Something about a trip to Tahoe."

You can't help noticing how your heart thumps; not exactly fast, but there is a tiny rush that races through you.

"So what'd you tell them?"

"I told them you'd be in around seven. They'll call back."

When the phone rings in the middle of dinner—quite as if your callers were out there with a timer, saying, "He's gotta be exactly midway through his meal by now, so *dial!*"—you rush to pick it up. Calming yourself, you listen to the bright, feminine voice at the other end.

"Mr. Young? This is Marjorie of Blue Sky Holiday Home Promotions. You *are* the Mr. Young who filled out the entry form at Lugosi's Delicatessen to win a free trip to Tahoe and two thousand dollars, right?"

"Yes, yes, that's me!"

"It's my pleasure to inform you that your name has been selected, and you *are* a finalist. Congratulations!"

"Thank you, uh, I think."

"Oh, you're a cautious one, aren't you?"

"What's the catch?"

"No catch whatever."

"But, but what does it mean? What do I have to do?"

"OK, Mr. Young, here's all you have to do. We'll be holding a meeting Saturday after next with our other finalists at the offices and showroom of Blue Sky Holiday Homes in our Peninsula headquarters at two p.m. sharp. All you have to do is be there for the Grand Spin. You're already guaranteed to win one of the following prizes which we're obligated by law to award you and must present to you then and there."

"What are they?"

"You're going to receive either a one-week, all-expenses-paid trip to Lake Tahoe, plus two thousand dollars; a three-day and two-night stay in Tahoe, plus one thousand dollars; a six-piece set of designer luggage with a retail value of two hundred fifty dollars; or two days and one night in Tahoe, plus one hundred dollars."

"Those are the prizes?"

"Yes, but I must tell you that you *and* your wife must both be present to validate your eligibility."

"How come?"

"This *is* a promotion, so all our sponsor is really asking is that you be prepared to stay and hear the facts about our time-sharing vacation home offer. It'll only take a couple hours of your time. Have you ever engaged in or heard about time-sharing before?"

"No."

"You'll be delighted, Now, you'll have to spin the wheel—which is similar to the one you might've seen on the TV program, 'Wheel of Fortune'—and, depending on the outcome of that spin, you *will* be awarded one of the four gifts I've already mentioned.

"You're saying there's no way I can walk away without getting *some*thing?"

"Riiiiight! I'll be sending you a written notification of all this by mail, but if you haven't received it by the middle of next week, just give me a ring. My name is Marjorie, and you can reach me at this number in San Jose. . . ."

You're frantically scribbling all this down with a skipping pen on the wrongest piece of paper you could find. It's definitely a situation straight out of *Murphy's Law*.

Your son Michael, who's 13, says, "Whatcha win, Dad, whatcha win?"

You sit back down at the dinner table and try to read what you've only half jotted down, and you announce the prize possibilities.

Michael, with all the tactful aplomb of a budding teenager, says, "Oh, Dad, relax! You're gonna get the luggage!"

Less than an hour ago, none of you knew anything at all about any of this, but now that the odds have been spelled out, none of you can help zeroing in on the worst.

There's nothing left to do but cancel and rearrange all your plans for that upcoming Saturday. Grimly and lightheartedly, both, you settle down for Fate to have her way with you.

It turns out to be a gorgeous afternoon. You could be tooling down the Coast Highway to Half Moon Bay or Santa Cruz or Monterey or even Big Sur. Instead, you and your spouse are propped up in the Datsun, rushing down 101 toward Blue Sky Holiday Homes Peninsula Headquarters.

"We're fools, aren't we?" she says as your exit's coming up.

"I don't care what they're pushing," you say. "I intend

to sit still, keep my mouth shut, tough it out and collect my prize."

"And what if it *is* the luggage? We don't need any more luggage!"

"Look at it this way," you tell her. "They'll have us up there for a couple hours. Now, that could mean as much as one grand an hour for our time, or five hundred an hour, or fifty bucks an hour at the very least. Hey, that ain't bad for an easy afternoon!"

"Not unless we end up with luggage."

"C'mon, give it up!"

"We'll see."

When you see the other couples climbing out of cars in the parking lot and moving right along with you in the direction of that same gleaming office building, it makes you do a double take. You're thinking maybe there hasn't been any drawing after all. Rather, maybe all these so-called finalists have been selected by the dumping method; that is, all the boxes of entry blanks got dumped onto a desk for some overworked market research office crew to process.

Still running through your head is the memory of that smug afternoon at the deli, and how you might answer some of those questions differently now: *Occupation:* Professional writer. *I.Q.:* Dimwit, nay, dumb, very dumb!!! *Preferred Leisure Activities:* Yawning, napping, cat-napping.

But that's all becoming a blur. Now you've reached the top floor where you're greeted by a carefully groomed, eager-eyed receptionist whose demeanor reminds you of one of the cover stories you once checked out in a *Harvard Lampoon* takeoff on *Cosmopolitan*— "How to Giggle Like a Fool." She escorts you to the preliminary seating area, a kind of waiting room, as it were. The setup in this lavishly appointed suite is not to be believed. Suddenly the bottom of everything that's been keeping you halfway grounded drops away.

"What's going on?" you ask your spouse.

"Looks like television to me."

You're surrounded by several walls of TV screens. But what's that they're showing you? It seems to be a travelogue. You sit and blink at fleeting images of luxury condos, swimming pools, saunas, hot tubs, ski slopes, casino showgirls, running river streams and lakes and kicked-back, mellow types having fun in baseball caps and Pendleton shirts with fishing rods and reels in hand; shots of shiny, sumptuous meals on elegant tables, just waiting for you, yes, *you* to pull up a chair and dig in. You can't really hear what the off-screen narrator's saying, but gradually the imagery's shifting to Mexico, Spain, the Riviera, Tokyo, Hong Kong, Maui. You catch snatches of bullfight music, a wistful French ballad; Far Eastern and Polynesian melodies segué right past you before you can suck in your breath.

Glancing around to size up your fellow so-called finalists for this Grand Gimme, you take note of the demographic spread. You see couples that are young, middleaged, and older. All the obvious blue-collar aristocrats, office types, mosquito-league investment dabblers, technocratic elitists and yuppies are well represented. There's no denying it's an equal opportunity scam, and there's even a drunk in the crowd who looks mightily hung over from his Friday night debauch.

Presently the giggly receptionist appears again to usher you into a large, cozy, dimly lit room lined with rows of tiered, comfortable, TV studio audience style seats. Like everybody else, you plop down, still wondering which way is up. Then, just as you're folding your arms across your chest and tightening your smile, a lanky gent with neatly trimmed hair and beard, wearing a dark blue suit, bright tie and silver leather cowboy boots, walks into the room, moves to stage center and starts waving the palms of his hands around at you like some new comic who's just been introduced on the "Tonight Show."

"All right," he says, "let's see a show of hands. How many of you told your husbands or wives before you stepped in here: 'I don't care what they're pushing. I'm gonna look interested, not say anything, and walk outta here with the two thousand dollars!'? How many of you said that? Don't be shy, just raise your hand."

Of the forty people out in the audience, only two or three hands go up, including the wicked-looking drunk's. You elbow your spouse and clear your throat.

"Well," says the Warm-Up Man, "at least they're honest."

And so by degrees at first and then by leaps and bounds, this instantly likable, earnest-looking and studiedly witty fellow disarms us and gets us to laugh.

"If you don't think you've already participated in time-sharing," he says, "then think about the times you've split the fare with someone else in a taxi ride, or if you've ever flown on a plane. It's the same principle."

You shake your head when he explains how, by current rate of inflation projections, the cost of a single room at the Holiday Inn by the year 1999 will run $1000 a night. But $59 a night is all you're going to be paying to put up at your own vacation unit for the next 30 years, well into the 21st Century—that is, if you act right now and take advantage of Blue Sky's offer. Mind you, you're only paying for the one week or the two weeks you'll actually be using it. But you ain't seen nothin' yet!

"Say you don't always wish to spend your vacation in Tahoe," Mr. Warm-Up continues. "That might get pretty dull year after year. How'd you like to be able to exchange your place with some other Blue Sky time-sharing owner and take your holiday in Europe, South America, or Japan or Australia?"

"How about China?" the drunk blubbers out.

"We haven't made inroads into the People's Republic of China yet, sir. But we're working on it. The important thing is for you to act now, today, so you won't end up losing out like those shortsighted people who settled for the free toaster-oven back when condos were first being promoted the same way we're offering you a lovely vacation resort home right now."

On it goes like this until Mr. Warm-Up, rewarding us with his most polished, openhanded Ed McMahon guffaw, announces, "We're gonna show you a little video now about our product, which we're proud of and rightfully. When it's over you'll be greeted by your own personal guides who'll take you on a tour of a model of what you'll be buying. Relax, have fun, and enjoy the free drinks and snacks. And I thank you."

When the lights go down, you find yourself watching the same video footage that'd been running when you walked in the door, only this time the sound is crisp and clear. It all ends up with shots of Old Glory rippling in the breeze to the grandiose finale of "The Star-Spangled Banner."

But before you or any of the others can break out into emotional, uncomprehending applause, the door swings open and—just like at the Grammies or the Academy Awards—smiling faces pop into view, one by one and two by two, to read aloud from cards: "Luther and Jolene McNasty . . . Come with me,

pleeeeze! . . . Arthur and Diane Chu, right this way! . . . Al
and Arline Young, this is your golden opportunity!"

Around and around you're led, up one illuminated photo display and down another. Mrs. Rappaport, the woman doing the
leading, your personal guide, is ever so slightly nervous. She
asks about your family life, your children and, even though you
haven't asked, she tells you about her kids who're already in college. Over hot coffee, tea or bouillon, you chat about things,
anything, but especially about time-sharing. She keeps asking if
you have any questions and grows increasingly edgy every time
you shrug and shake your head.

"Sit down and make yourselves at home," she tells you once
you enter the model unit. It's a one-bedroom, with all-electric
kitchen (including a microwave oven), that sleeps five. It's also
got color TV, stereo, air conditioning, and a king-size bed. Of
course there's a communal sauna, tennis court, swimming pool
and even a darkroom for photography buffs. All you can concentrate on while she's making her pitch is the Laurel and
Hardy movie playing—not coincidentally, you suspect—on the
TV set that doesn't make a sound.

"Try the bed," she says. "Isn't that comfortable?"

It certainly is. You wouldn't mind kicking off your shoes, re-
clining and drifting into slumber. You're tired, terribly tired.
Those two obligatory hours have already slipped by and now,
two coffees and three Hawaiian Punches later, here you sit, still
allowing yourself to be tortured because you're so eager to get
your hands on that two thousand dollars you can practically
smell the bills and feel that sweaty wad clumped up in your fist.

"Isn't this a marvelous layout?"

You stifle a virulent yawn and, for what you hope will be the
last time, utter, "Yes, yes it is." The only thing, though, that
gives you the strength to go on is the sight of Stan Laurel and
Oliver Hardy, faking it as piano movers, letting that antique up-
right drop and tumble over an outdoor railing down a whole hillside of concrete steps into what appears to be a concrete patio,
totally demolished.

Back at the coffee area, things are heating up. Mrs. Rappaport has canned the chitchat and shifted quite gracelessly into
another mode. You can see that; Arline can see it. It's all coming

down to the moment of truth. Which unit interests you? What can you afford? Are you willing to buy today and pick up on all the glamorous tie-ins such a move would entitle you to, or are you going to be a drag and settle for the stripped-down, no-frills version of the deal? What deal? Nobody's even mentioned yet what kind of money we're talking about.

While the Muzak is working you over subliminally with a tune you recognize as "Stormy," doubtless calculated to make you feel insecure and vulnerable, your wife—altogether from out of the blue—begins to ask elaborate questions about Finland, of all places.

"What if you wanted to swap places," she says quite seriously, "with someone in Helsinki or some other part of Finland?"

You can't believe your ears. Even Mrs. Rappaport is confused. Obviously she's picked up on all the requisite signals. Everything her training's taught her to look for in a prospective buyer we simply haven't delivered.

"Finland?" Mrs. Rappaport sputters. "You mean, like, Finland?"

"Yes, Finland. What I'd like to know is—" And here you have to sit and listen to Arline meander into complex stream-of-consciousness inquiries and assertions about that north-central European republic, which you happen to know she's always wanted to visit, mainly because of her interest in textile manufacturing there, and the Marimekko plant.

What's going on? What's come over her? Maybe it's because the moon is in Mercury, or Milpitas. Maybe your egged-on brains have been scrambled by now to some point of no reasonable return. You know for a fact all the circuits of your brain have been fried. The view you have at the moment of the outside world through the window you're facing, where trees are waving enticingly in the breeze beneath a darkening sky, looks so inviting you're ready to get up, dash across the plushly carpeted room, and do a flying leap, feet first, directly into the tinted glass. Nobody else seems to be getting it; none of the other finalists, none of their personal guides, all crowded around these predatory tables, closing in for the kill. Freedom is only what any of us thinks we're about to buy or not buy. The real freedom though, you're thinking, is right here before us, all around us, waiting outside this stifling office building.

You can barely remain civil. Already you've suppressed so many yawns your neck and throat and the inside of your mouth are beginning to ache. One look at your spouse tells you she's momentarily crazed, simply zonked out on the effects of state-of-the-art motivational research and hype. Your own tongue feels the way it does after the dentist has done his pain-deadening job with Novocain.

Mrs. Rappaport, who can't look you in the eye any longer, says, "I can't really talk with you about Finland or the actual prices and terms because I'm not properly licensed or qualified to do so, but I can get someone over to the table who will."

Smooth and procedural, she waves across the room to some seasoned closer of deals who rushes at once to the table armed with clipboard, a ballpoint pen, legal pad and pocket calculator.

"All right," he says, straining to maintain the shallowest of smiles, "which package do you want?"

You really have to think about how you're going to handle this. It doesn't take much to see that this is the Hard Sell guy. He's glaring at Mrs. Rappaport and she's looking back at him in a way that makes you aware of the giant yawn she's been holding back.

Finally you say, "What would be the cheapest out possible?"

Mr. Hard Sell doesn't like your attitude one bit, but he's bound by law to act polite. "OK," he says, "you're talking studio unit at a one-week minimum."

Furiously he bips up digits on his calculator—buying price, monthly payments, financing, interest rates—and, muttering, he scrawls it all down in ballpoint ink on yellow paper even you can absorb.

"You'd be coming in at seventy-five hundred, which at these monthly installments financed at fifteen-point-six would have you paid up in full within five years. You already know about the annual maintenance fee, which is subject to change, and the fifty-nine bucks per night habitation charge, and the sixty-dollar-a-year fee for use of Blue Sky's vacation booking services, which is also subject to change. You want two weeks' vacation instead of one, you're looking at fifteen thousand basic buying price, got it?"

You've got it all right. It doesn't take a mathematical whiz to figure out that a buying price of $7,500 for this unit, available to

you for one week annually, would gross Blue Sky well over three
and a half million at a rate of just 50 weeks, and that's before you
even get around to financing charges. What a perfectly inge-
nious scheme!

"So what do you say?" Hard Sell wants to know.

You say, "Hmmm, got any literature I can take home?"

"What for?"

"You know, just something I could mull over in private."

Hard Sell turns to Mrs. Rappaport. "Boy, is this guy ever a
porcupine!"

At first you don't like the sound of this, but when you slow
down to picture it—an innocent little porcupine being menaced
by a wolf or a coyote or a crocodile, say—you rather like the
thought of those quills springing into action.

On second thought, though, you aren't really all that innocent. After all, you did come up here to collect that free gift,
whatever it's going to be. Mr. Hard Sell and Mrs. Rappaport
and Mr. Warm-Up know this, too.

"No, we don't have any literature," Hard Sell says. "We used
to, and it always turned up in the wastebasket downstairs or on
the elevator floor. Now, I know you professorial types need time
to reflect. And I'm willing to give you that time if you'll sign a
release saying we don't have to 'gift' you."

"You mean, no prize?"

"That's right. Because the minute you're 'gifted,' you can hang
it all up. There's no coming back. Besides," he adds thoughtfully,
glancing at his ally, "I've run a ton of people through this, uh,
procedure of ours, and I've yet to see the day when one of 'em
came back after going home and thinking about it."

"Yes," you hear yourself saying, "that makes sense."

"You just want the gift, right?" Hard Sell says.

You swap glances with your spouse before you say, "At this
point, yes, that's what we want."

The words are barely out of your mouth when you look up
and spot Mr. Hard Sell way across the other side of the room,
over there by the coffee urn, drawing himself a fresh, hot cup.

"You'll have to sign this release," Mrs. Rappaport dutifully
informs you.

"What does it say?"

"Says you were treated courteously your whole time here."

Each of you signs with trembling hands, madly, gladly. Mrs. Rappaport leads you down a narrow hallway to the wheel, which isn't anything like the one on TV's "Wheel of Fortune." Its cynical young attendant says, "What you gotta do first is spin this inner wheel and land on the red notch; there's only one red notch. That'll give you a shot at the outer wheel, and if you can get that to land on the red notch, too, then you win the week in Tahoe and the two thousand dollars."

There seem to be countless notches. They must be joking. Even Mrs. Rappaport has trouble keeping a straight face. "Yes," she admits, "it's terribly difficult, I'm afraid."

"And how do you win the thousand?" your wife wants to know.

"Same routine," the youngster explains. "There's only one white notch. You gotta hit it on both wheels."

"And if you don't?"

The young man's aggravated sigh strikes your weary ears as being almost soothingly appropriate. "If you miss," he says fatalistically, "you get the luggage. Everybody gets the luggage."

There's nothing left for you to do but laugh and spin the wheel. But the funny part is, now that you're pitifully in need of a vacation, you really could use the luggage.

Song for My Father

Horace Silver, 1962

Lately when I catch myself growing too tense about trivial inconveniences or tiny accidents, I let myself be whisked back inwardly to the morning my three-year-old son Michael knocked over a full cup of milk, and then made fun of me when I got upset about it. No sooner did the cup hit the floor, splashing milk in every direction, than I swept into my tiresome tirade.

"Michael," I yelled, "your mom just scrubbed and waxed this kitchen, and *now* look at it!"

"I didn't mean to, Daddy!"

"And you didn't *have* to either. Now I've gotta quit what I'm doing and start cleaning all over again. Why don't you pay attention to what you're doing?"

"I'm sorry," he said. I could tell really meant it, but that didn't soothe my indignation. What I was feeling, I suspect, had little to do with the spilled milk I was crying over.

Michael, who is never far from the edge of a smile or laughter, watched with beaming amusement while I mopped. I could see him wondering what made me tick. Or, for that matter, what was it with grown people anyway?

Once I had restored the kind of external order I lean on when the inside of my head grows unruly, my son broke his silence.

"Dad," he said, "I don't understand why you get so upset over something like that in the first place."

"I get upset, Michael, because it was something that didn't have to happen. You *must* learn to be more careful."

That's when I felt him tugging my trouser legs. I looked down. His face upset me; it was as serious and blank as mine must have looked to him.

"Here, Dad. I wanna show you something."

"Aw, c'mon, what is it, Michael?" Now I have no trouble seeing how heavily I must've worn that long-suffering, self-nursing take I had on family life, an outlook that can make the parents of toddlers so whiny on weekend mornings.

He led me to the dining-room window that faced the street. Pushing back the curtain, he pointed and said, "You see all those cars and trucks and houses out there?"

"Yes, I do. What about them?"

"Well, they aren't real."

"What do you mean, they aren't *real?*"

Clutching my hand this time, he tugged me into his room which was, as usual, so stacked and scattered with playthings it sometimes set my teeth on edge.

With a sweep of his arms, Michael turned and said, "You see all my toys and things?"

"Sure, and you need to be picking some of them up, too."

"Daddy," he said, "that's what I'm talking about. None of this stuff I'm showing you is real. My toys aren't real; these books aren't real; those cars and houses and TV antennas out there aren't real."

By then I could feel my chemistry changing. I stood in a hush as I stared at this little boy, my own son, who didn't seem all that small anymore. And whose son was he now? Even though I had lovingly watched him being born, I still wasn't sure, with all this playful wisdom he was imparting, just where he was coming from.

"You don't believe these things are real, Michael? Is that what you're saying?"

"Of course they aren't real," he said, quite as if he were standing at the head of some classroom, going over the lesson again to benefit an inattentive pupil.

Like the milk, all the irritation I had felt was being sponged away. My heart throbbed in my Adam's apple, and its beat quickened the moment I swallowed to get up enough nerve to say, "So, tell me . . . What's real, then?"

Michael laid his hand on his chest and smiled as he looked directly into my eyes and beyond. "People, Daddy," he said. "People are what's real."

The startling truth of what my child was telling me,

reminding me, hit home at once. I stood very still among the marbles and the teddy bear, the basketball, the puzzles, the hot-wheels tricycle, the Richard Scarry books, and looked all around. For a measureless moment it felt as though we were ac-tually suspended in space. And everything around us seemed to be fashioned out of nothing but solidified light. For all I knew, we could have been standing in ancient Egypt or Oz, or simply in the same house on the same street on the same morning, ex-cept from a perspective that had suddenly been joyfully altered.

As he has moved into his teens, I have told Michael this story, sometimes to his embarrassment. He says he recalls none of it. But for me it will always be one of the splendid interludes of my own coming of age, an incandescent reminder of that wise pa-rental glow children sometimes emit without knowing it.

Grazin' in
the Grass

Hugh Masekela, 1965

What always tickled me about Hugh Masekela was that album he put out called *The Americanization of Oogabooga.* That's one of the inspirations for my name: O.O. Gabugah.

Oogabooga was what they called that talk those natives from L.A. that used to be in those old Tarzan pictures would talk with one another. "Oooga-booga," they'd say, or: "Mmm-bawa." Hugh told me that when he first went to Paris and places where African dudes would meet up, they'd all sit at them outdoor cafés out there and put on the Europeans and tourists, talkin' that oogabooga stuff.

Cracked me up to hear him talk about that, the same as it cracked me up when he told about how in Johannesburg when he was in the fourth grade and they played this movie in school with Kirk Douglas called *Young Man With a Horn,* and it was after Masekela saw this that he decided he wanted to be a jazz trumpet player.

I must admit, though, that when "Grazin' in the Grass" came out, I was feelin' no pain. I had me a Last Poets kinda thing going and the revolution *was* being televised. But when I'd put on "Grazin' in the Grass," there was somethin' about that rhythm and ring and sway it had to it that made me wanna sit down and think about everything that popped up in my mind real slow. It was like a tranquilizer, you know.

My man Hugh Masekela and me, we got what you might call an affinity. We're both from places called U.S.A., except his stands for the Union of South Africa. That was the name of his band: the Union of South Africa. How's that for patriotism?

One day maybe Hugh—who has been persona non grata in his homeland for decades—can team up with Ladysmith Black Mambazo and Paul Simon, and they can be his bodyguard and he can be their long lost pal.

A Nightingale Sang in Berkeley Square

Stephane Grappelli, 1983

In one of the photographs snapped in the Thirties of the Quintet of the Hot Club of France, all five players—guitarists Roget Chaput, Joseph Reinhardt and his legendary brother Django, bassist Louis Vola and violinist Stephane Grappelli—are posed in formal dress on a Paris balcony overlooking a hushed and misty street. The brightest face in the lineup belongs to Grappelli who, as he leans over the iron railing with folded hands, looks positively resplendent in his suit and tie. In fact, with his dark hair combed back and radiant smile, he is very much the picture of sunshine and self-confidence. Serious yet cheerful— that's the expression, preserved in shadow and light, that distinguishes this Grappelli of long ago.

But it isn't so much the look as it is his sound that makes you feel as if you've somehow always known Grappelli. The hair has whitened and thinned and he has grown even more handsome with the years and yet, if anything, the man is playing far better now than he was more than half a century ago; he sounds twice as young. Anyone who doubts this possibility need only go back and dig up some of the early Quintet's classic recordings to hear the difference. Oh, the youthful Grappelli sounds ardent and inventive enough in his fashion—he never tried to be Joe Venuti, Stuff Smith, Eddie South or Ray Nance—but the deep feeling that fuels his playing today is what warms and steadies the heart. As is always the case with inspired improvising artists, Grappelli, with a knowing flick of his wrist, can spark fresh life into any worthy standard and make new songs seductively familiar.

Seductive too is his intermittent piano playing and his charm as a raconteur. Take the night in the early Eighties at San Francisco's Great American Music Hall when Grappelli, to a packed house, of course, gave his violin a rest and sat down gleefully at the grand piano to not so much knock out as expound a pithy and prolonged solo rendition of Richard Rodgers and Lorenz Hart's "Thou Swell." And then, as if that weren't surprise enough, he took to the microphone and, while his sidemen caught their breath, he slid into an unforgettable verbal introduction to the ballad that would follow: Britain's Eric Maschwitz and Manning Sherwin's "A Nightingle Sang in Berkeley Square."

"The war is beginning," Grappelli told us. "Django and I, we are playing in London when two men come into the club one night and during intermission they hand us some music to play. Django takes it and looks at it with a sigh, but Django is doing this because he cannot read music. I can read music, so Django asks me to play some of the melody, so I do. A big smile comes to Django's face; he likes this song. 'Tell me,' he asks, 'can you understand what it says, the title?' I tell him, 'Yes, I understand.' 'So,' he says, 'what does it mean?' So I explain the title of the song in French. So then, when the next intermission comes, Django comes to me and he says, 'Stephane, come, we must go.' I ask him: 'Go where?' But all he says is: 'Come, you shall see.' So we take a taxi and I tell the driver what Django wants me to tell him—that we wish to go to Berkeley Square. By now it is midnight. So Django and I, we sit on the bench and he smokes cigarettes and we sit very quietly and try to listen to all the sounds through the traffic. Do you know what we heard sitting there in this Square in the dark? We heard absolutely nothing. Django, poor Django, keeps shaking his head, for he is most disappointed. But that night we play the song anyway, and now I play it for you."

And it became obvious that time and its distances mean nothing to Grappelli as, night after night, he sails elegantly and movingly through many a musical sky—from Rodgers and Hart, Jerome Kern, Johnny Mercer, George Gershwin, Fats Waller, Sonny Rollins, Victor Young, Edvard Grieg, Duke Ellington, Cole Porter, Hoagy Carmichael and Django Reinhardt to Miles Davis, Sonny Rollins, Chick Corea and Stevie Wonder.

For all his soaring and gliding, though, Grappelli—at the level of pure, natural joyfulness—has remained well grounded in the playful spirit of those serious and imaginative musicians who have no trouble communicating with everybody lucky enough to have been born with ears that work.

THE FAR SIDE

By GARY LARSON

"Blow, Howie, blow! ... Yeah, yeah, yeah!
You're cookin' now, Howie! ... All right! ...
Charlie Parker, move over! ... Yeah!"

Nuages

Django Reinhardt, 1935

Monday struck me as being an unlikely day for a near-capacity crowd of 1,800 to shell out as much as $14 a ticket for a lecture and slide show, but UCLA's Royce Hall was packed to capacity. People of every age had turned up to catch Gary Larson, creator of "The Far Side," now syndicated daily in close to six hundred newspapers worldwide.

One enthusiastic ticket-holder, a bearded man who looked to be in his early thirties, was carrying a stack of paperbound books; all Larson titles. They included *Bride of the Far Side, Valley of the Far Side, It Came From the Far Side,* and *The Far Side Gallery.*

"I intend to get every one of these rascals autographed," I heard him tell a friend.

When I mentioned the story I was there to cover, he rested his books on a windowsill, pulled his finger through his beard, and broke out into a loose, sloppy grin. "Larson's so great," he said. "He takes me to another level, puts me in some other place. You know, it's kind of like music . . . like jazz. Gary Larson *draws* jazz."

All I could do was smile while I let that reaction roll to the back of my head. Remembering my early days of listening to jazz, early jazz especially, but also the music of people like Thelonious Monk, Ornette Coleman and Cecil Taylor, performing composers who play by their own rules, and with delightfully eccentric results, I thought I knew what this person meant. But then again, I'm never quite sure what anybody means when they use the term "jazz." They could have Spike Jones in mind, or Homer and Jethro or Martin Mull or any number of musical satirists. It sounded good, though, so I made a mental jot: *Hmmm, Larson draws jazz. . . .*

Larson's appearance had also drawn a crew from ABC-TV's "20/20." On hand, too, were George Parker, head of Andrews, McMeel and Parker, Larson's Kansas City publishers, and Vicky Houston, publicist for Larson at Universal Press Syndicate.

"They make him nervous," Houston said, referring to writers like me. "Gary doesn't even like giving interviews. But, face it, when you've got three books simultaneously on the *New York Times* bestseller list, it isn't exactly easy to hide."

Judging by the crowd, everyone in Los Angeles who cared seemed to know Larson was in town that Tuesday night to take part in the UCLA Extension series, "The Many Faces of Humor." Splitting the evening with Larson was comedian Jay Leno. As for previous guests, well, there was Victor Borge, Whoopi Goldberg, George Carlin, Patrick Oliphant, Gail Parent, Professor Peter Schickele (PDQ Bach), Dick Cavett, Chevy Chase, Mark Russell and David Steinberg. I was impressed, even though a New York friend, when I told him about it, snipped: "Wow, a college seminar on humor! Only in California!"

The theme for that night was "Laughter in the Eighties!" Addressing himself to this in a prefatory talk was Joseph Boskin, professor of history at Boston University and author of *Humor and Social Change in 20th Century America.* I couldn't have been the only one in the audience that night eager to laugh with Larson rather than be told about the humorous aspects of "scarcity and shared resentment in this decade of American disillusionment."

In his scholarly commentary, the jocular Boskin made a lasting point about humor itself. Automatically it slipped into the same mental drawer where "he draws jazz" had gone. "At its basic level," Boskin concluded, "humor wards off the darker side of ourselves and our culture by providing one of the most important elements of living; namely, a rewarding release and, through release, perspective."

I sat there in the darkness of Royce Hall, wondering why adjectives such as dark, bizarre, oddball, quirky, irreverent, surrealistic and whimsical always crept into discussions of Gary Larson's lucid, good-natured cartoonery.

My inner file drawer had no sooner slammed than the voice of

Harvey Mindess, the UCLA professor moderating the evening, reached me. It was showtime. People in the auditorium were clearing their throats and leaning forward. Our boy was about to be summoned to the podium. Sensing all the restlessness that had built up during Boskin's lecture, and knowing a little something about show biz, Mindess kept his introduction down to the length of a TV commercial.

"'Jiggs' typifies the laughter of the Forties," he offered. "'Blondie and Dagwood' the laughter of the Fifties, 'Peanuts' the laughter of the Sixties, 'Doonesbury' the laughter of the Seventies, and 'The Far Side' the laughter of the Eighties."

To rollicking, hero-worship applause, Gary Larson approached the podium. Then came the moment when I had to decide whether I wanted to join the people who were suddenly getting to their feet, quite as if Larson had already knocked us out in concert and we were avidly demanding an encore. Had he been Tina Turner, he would've gone straight into "What's Love Got to Do With It?" Or had he been Chick Corea, it would've been "Spain." I thought about the panel he'd done of a checkered-jacketed cocktail pianist saying to his fellow senior citizens, drink-clutching listeners gathered around the keyboard: "Hey, thank you! Thank you! That was 'Tie a Yellow Ribbon.' . . . Now, what say we all *really* get down?"

But Larson was charmingly himself: blondish, clean-cut, collegiate-looking, casual. He certainly didn't look 36. To me he was vaguely remindful, in manner anyway, of the early Dick Cavett. I could tell he was shy. In fact, he looked a tad stunned by all the uproar. All the same, there was something magnetic about his soft-spokenness as he peered out uneasily at the rows and tiers of well-wishers.

"A lot of people," he began, "think I'm going to be like someone who's stepped out of one of his own cartoons. And maybe I am. But I sure have a hard time analyzing it. I've tried to be introspective and ask, 'Why is this happening to me?' I never have been able to understand where the humor comes from."

What he had to tell us about how he does what he does sometimes made Larson lapse into a kind of dignified embarrassment, not unlike the bewilderment that blooms in the faces of improvising musicians pressed to articulate the fragile particulars and imponderables of their performing art. I thought about the diplomacy skills of someone like blues great B.B. King and all the times he's been asked: "Now, tell me, how do you go about constructing those marvelously expressive guitar solos of yours that reflect so poignantly the suffering and pathos of your people?"

"What makes or breaks a cartoon," Larson explained, rather tentatively, "comes down to an expression on a character's face. There are these nuances, and these tangible things. I just try to know when it *feels* right. I've drawn some things that have fallen very flat. Sometimes I'm convinced that one day I'm going to draw the cartoon that offends *everyone,* and that'll be the end."

Since its troubled, seedling beginnings in 1979 as a weekly feature in the *Seattle Times,* Larson's single panel cartoon—first known as "Nature's Way"—has flowered into a bona fide phenomenon. "The Far Side" is now read throughout the English-speaking world as well as in France and Japan. *The Far Side Gallery 2* is the third book-length anthology of Larson's dazzling panels to hit the *New York Times* bestseller list, where they've resided for a cumulative total of three years. But there are ten "Far Side" books in all, and the ever-swelling quantity of copies in print is currently well over five million. A line of products, designed around the peculiar appeal of Larson's panoply of unpredictable characters—animal and human—has emerged. Among other marketables, these include sweatshirts, T-shirts, mugs, posters, greeting cards and calendars. Screen director Alan Rudolph is even talking seriously with Larson about the prospect of making a feature-length "Far Side" movie.

As someone who had early learned to read sitting on my parents' laps and paying attention while they read the funnypapers, as we called them during World War II, I had grown up with an affection for comics and a penchant for cartooning. The opening decade of my life, in fact, saw me picturing myself as a comic-strip artist. Nancy and Sluggo, Mutt and Jeff, Archie and Jughead, Scrooge McDuck, Moon Mullins, Henry, Plastic Man, Li'l Abner, Snuffy Smith. Blondie and Jiggs were among my childhood favorites. When *Mad* hit the scene in the early Fifties and strips like Charles Shultz's "Peanuts" and Gus Arriola's "Gordo" began to make it big, I sensed, with all the glandular rebelliousness of a smirking adolescent who loved hard bop and cool jazz, that things were beginning to open up. My parents and other grown folks had trouble relating to some of that stuff—the first time around anyway—and so my pals and I were obliged to champion it. For me the fashionably scandalous underground comics of the late Sixties and early Seventies were strikingly like much of the shrill, cuss-and-tell avant-garde loft jazz of the period. The best of those artists survived and grew. Arguably the most influential cartoonist of that irreverent generation has been R. Crumb whose *Zap Comix* characters like Fritz the Cat and Mr. Natural have been imitated and ripped off the world over. Crumb's original vision and drawings fertilized and emboldened the cartoon world the way Ornette Coleman and Cecil Taylor helped change the way musicians and their audiences experienced "jazz." Around the same time in the late Seventies when supermarkets were beginning to flirt with bebop backgrounds, Crumb's "Keep On Truckin'" decals and bumper stickers had become entrenched in the national sub-psyche. The scene was set. It must've been a piece of cake, duck soup, or both, for artists like B. Kliban and Garfield's Jim Davis to waltz right in and get syndicated. That's how it seemed anyway.

But where did Gary Larson step into the picture? Where did it begin, this vision of his? How long had this process of transforming the usual into the unusual been "happening" to him before he went public with it? Individual "Far Side" readers are forever letting Larson know how surprised they are that anyone else gets what he's doing. Obviously his work—like superior humor and music the world over—is capable of blowing the lid off of some hidden, weeded over, back-alley regions of ourselves.

Take the "Far Side" world I've co-created with Larson. Sometimes it's a world of mature wives, mothers, aunts and grandmothers. Many of Larson's frowsy, no-nonsense women— astringent in their dowdy dresses, their upswept hairdos clamped glumly in place like helmets; eyeless behind opaque, oval glasses that waggishly exaggerate their long and drawn visages—are ringers for the relatives and neighbors of my childhood. From living-room couches they look on judgmentally, in dour disbelief, at buffalo scuffling to unstick themselves from "buffalo paper," or at cows encased like hamsters in rolling, see-thru plastic globes. Other times it's a world where laboratory scientists—usually physicists, biologists or paleontologists—play, childlike, with plastic models of prehistoric creatures, or study their own hangnails under the lens of an electron microscope. And always it's a world where animals interrelate facilely with human culture and with one another in ways as outrageous and uproarious as they are breezy and matter-of-fact. Larson's cows, for example, are eternally frustrated in a gadget-obsessed world that presumes the use of opposable thumbs.

"The Far Side" is a continuum of the unexpected; less a comic strip than it is a sort of laugh-inducing Möbius strip, where surprises are endlessly surfacing as No Big Deal. The look on Satan's face, for instance, as he routinely ushers a new arrival in Hell, a symphony conductor, to his digs: "Your room is right in here, Maestro." And through the opened door you see the roomful of grinning, pathologically jolly banjo pickers ready to have at the poor, startled fellow. And there's Carl Sagan as a kid, high atop a hill with a friend, gushing as he points at the nighttime sky. "Just look at all those stars, Becky," he's telling her, "There must be hundreds of 'em!"

The point, of course, is that Larson's work is vibrantly pictorial. Its humor is encoded in the offhanded magic of the drawings themselves. While this might appear to be characteristic of all cartoon art, the appeal of many of today's most popular strips and panels is surprisingly verbal. Garry Trudeau, for example, will think nothing of running a static shot of the Pentagon dome in "Doonesbury" for five straight panels with tidy balloons of dialogue puffing out of it to set up the situation. With Larson, it's the other way around. Often I catch myself laughing up a storm before I even read a word of "The Far Side"—if there happen to be any words to go with it that particular day. Years ago I worked with a fellow who would sometimes, out of the blue, look across the desk at me and say: "Man, you can talk about your Wonder Woman and your Barbarella and all the rest of 'em all you want. But there still isn't *anybody* can draw women like Al Capp could. I mean, he made you just wanna somehow travel up into the page and be a part of what was going on in Dogpatch. You know, get to *know* Daisy Mae."

Like the characters in Capp's "Li'l Abner," Larson's cave folk, ancient Egyptians, Vikings, Norsemen, Einsteins, slobs, couch potatoes, reptiles, insects and single-cell amoebas aren't easily forgotten.

In one unpublished panel, Larson has drawn a pair of smug houseflies motoring through traffic, their offspring presumably in the backseat. The yellow, triangular decal on their rear window reads: MAGGOT ON BOARD.

This is one of the ways Larson's humor achieves its off-balancing effect. By depicting casual, everyday 20th Century foolishness in capricious contexts, "The Far Side" throws everyday behavior into sidesplitting perspective.

Gary Larson admits that he sometimes has to restrain himself while he's at the drawing board expressing himself. From the beginning it's been necessary for him to acknowledge his own fearfulness about what might be going on out there in the world. He and his older brother Dan—the one who used to hide in the darkness of their closet at bedtime and play scary tricks—were reared in Tacoma, Washington by an office secretary mother and an auto salesman father. Larson describes his background as "blue collar" and his childhood as "normal."

When I told Larson at his home in Seattle about how my parents had taught me to read, he laughed and mentioned, as he often does, that his mother read to him nightly when he was small. His favorite book was *Mr. Bear Squash You All Flat*. Of course, Mr. Bear was in for a surprise when he went to sit on Mr. Porcupine's house.

"I drew a lot as a child," he said, "but I never pursued art in any serious fashion. I never took an art or drawing class. Then I stopped for about ten years.

"After junior high, I fell away completely from drawing. I was drawn to music, jazz mostly. I love it, swing and some bop. And girls. I was crazy about Herb Ellis, Joe Pass and Count Basie's rhythm guitarist, Freddy Green. I started on guitar and then—a horrible mistake—I went on to banjo for years. In fact, when I got out of Washington State University in 1972, I played music for money for a few years. That was before I took a job in a music store in Lynwood, which was probably the death of my musicianliness.

"After eight or nine months, I was very frustrated. So around 1976 I took a couple of days off and drew half a dozen cartoons. I took them down to a wilderness magazine in Seattle, *Pacific*

Search (now *Pacific Northwest*), and they bought them. When a check for $90 came in the mail, I was so happy! They'd bought all six at $15 apiece. I got inspired.

"Eventually I met a reporter from the *Seattle Times*, showed her my work, she showed it to her editor and, in 1979, the *Times* decided to run my panel, 'Nature's Way,' as a weekly. It ran next to a little feature called 'Junior Jumble,' a crossword puzzle for kids. That was quite a collision!

"After about a year, I took a trip down to San Francisco and showed the strip to the *Chronicle*. When I got back to Seattle I got the letter that the *Times* had to cancel me because they were getting too many complaints. It was two or three days after this that I got the *Chronicle* contract. I thought, 'Geez, that was real close!' If I'd gotten that cancellation before I'd gone to San Francisco, I know I would've said, 'What do I think I'm doing?' Of course I was scared to death when they said they wanted to do a daily; I had no idea whether I could. But I was too scared to say no. I've never been a very assertive person. I couldn't get that thing signed fast enough."

After giving it a new name, the San Francisco paper ran Larson's cartoon for three months before its syndicate, Chronicle Features, decided to promote it. Takers were slow in coming, but Stuart Dodds, Larson's British-born editor at the syndicate, wasn't discouraged.

"Stuart," Larson says fondly, "was the guy in the trenches. He was traveling around the country with it. And the strip was generating sparks—at least in editors' offices. Editors themselves were saying, 'I really like this, but our readers might not be able to handle it.' Newspapers would pick up on it, then drop it, then reinstate it. One step forward and three back."

In 1984 Larson signed with Universal Press Syndicate. "In the last three years," he said with a complicated laugh, "the thing has really mushroomed. It's still a weird cartoon, though."

Larson's laughter over his zigzag beginnings was as puzzling to me as the fame and admiration "The Far Side" has brought him. All of it makes him uncomfortable. My questions about his income seemed similarly disquieting. "I'd rather not discuss it," he said, running a hand over his sandy hair. "I'm doing OK." But when I later sat and calculated—and by the most cautious of estimates—Larson's share of the syndication fees daily and weekly newspapers pay to carry his cartoon, the sum I came up with suggests that success has made him very comfortable, indeed. And that wasn't counting royalties from the bestselling books or income from other "Far Side" marketables.

"Contractually," Larson said, "it'll take a while. But I'd like to see this line of products trimmed. I'm not real big on some of them—the T-shirts and stationery, especially. I never want to see this stuff get on keychains. I don't want to see it junkified."

Despite his uneasiness in the presence of fans—many of them acolytes devoted to what they regard as the deep, inner meaning of his drawings—and despite his press-shyness, Larson, not surprisingly, has an uncommon sense for providing journalists with lively copy. Several are well documented. There's the time his Plymouth Duster hit a mutt when a pack of dogs dashed across the road while he was driving to interview for a job with the Humane Society. There are also the practical jokes he and his close friend Ernie Wagner, curator of reptiles at the Seattle Zoo (Larson's old rented house in the Ballard district just happens to have been located right near the zoo) used to play on one another. One of these involved Wagner dumping a jarful of live whip scorpions into Larson's sleeping bag. After Wagner taped a scissor-snipped string of frozen mice tails intended as python food across the rear window of Larson's automobile, Larson vengefully dumped 50 pounds of rhino manure into Wagner's bathtub.

"That was before Ernie and I both settled down," Larson explained.

Having digested some of this hearsay beforehand, I had stepped into Larson's house expecting to find snakes coiled around the chandeliers, iguanas under the sofa, cupboards and closets writhing with other kept reptiles. But settling down, on Larson's part, has meant getting rid of the 20 individually caged pet king snakes he once kept, including one python from the Seattle Zoo. "She was 15 feet," he recalled, "and weighed 150 pounds when I finally woke up to what I had. The snakes just got to be too much."

The only prominent retentions of his abiding interest in the species are the breath-stopping paintings of prehistoric reptiles by Seattle artist John Altweis that animate the living-room and dining-room walls of Larson's two-story, three-bedroom home in Laurelhurst, the stately neighborhood overlooking Seattle's

Lake Washington. Larson still isn't sure what he'll do with the stuffed rhinoceros head that adorns the corner of one downstairs room. "I bought it from a guy," he told me, looking embarrassed, "who had it in his tavern and wanted to get rid of it."

"What's your interest in animals?" I asked.

"I was a biology freak from the ninth grade on," Larson admitted, seemingly comfortably enough with me by now to know it was OK to talk about it. "I squeezed in science electives everywhere; my brother was the same way. I loved to go to the neighborhood swamp in Tacoma, pick up salamanders, bring them home and try to keep them alive for a few days. I was always drawing dinosaurs—and gorillas and whales. I didn't major in biology, though. I didn't know what I would do with a four-year degree in biology, so I graduated in communications. In the back of my mind I was thinking of advertising, the creative end. I was going to save the world from inane advertising. I'm flattered by biologists' interest in my work. There's this panel I did about a mosquito who comes home to his wife from a hard day of spreading malaria. Of course I got these letters reminding me that it's the female who does the biting. So, besides being sexist in some bizarre way, I was also biologically incorrect."

Last year's recipient of the Best Syndicated Cartoonist Award, Gary Larson is an ardent follower of his colleagues' work. He prefers, however, the company of musicians and his Saturday morning basketball buddies. As admiring as he is of artists like Roz Chast and *New Yorker* regular George Booth ("He's great. Everybody loves his dogs, and his artwork is so critical to bringing that off."), Larson admitted—with more than a hint of "Aw, gee!" in his voice—that his personal favorites, those cartoonists who have most influenced and inspired him, are Gahan Wilson, Don Martin and B. Kliban.

"I like Kliban because he's morbid. With Don Martin, it's that surprise last panel and also the way he draws feet. With Kliban, well, he's drawing cartoons. But they come very close to being something real. And it's those nuances that can make or break a drawing. Booth is revealing in this sense. And Roz Chast is wonderful. Stylistically you can be influenced, but the actual guts come from the inside. Garry Trudeau is primarily a brilliant writer, but visually not too interesting."

Even though he feels he works hard at drawing his ideas five days a week in his upstairs studio—from late morning until early evening—Larson doesn't see his cartoons as having any kind of conscious message. "I just want people to laugh and enjoy themselves."

Working one month in advance of publication, he posts at least seven panels to his editor Lee Salem each Saturday after his basketball workout. "I send more if I can so Lee can pick and choose in case I get hit by a truck."

In the course of professional interviews, that interlude arrives when interviewer and subject know it's time to click off the Sanyo, and to simply kick back and get to know one another. Larson and I had clicked from the moment we'd talked on the phone.

"What other sort of writing do you do?" he asked.

"Oh, novels, poetry, essays, stuff on music."

His eyes brightened. "Music? What sort of things on music?"

"Well, a couple of volumes of my so-called musical memoirs are out."

Oh, yeah? Give me some titles."

"*Bodies & Soul* is one; *Kinds of Blue*, the other."

At this, Larson laughed, jumped to his feet, excused himself and raced upstairs. When he got back he was holding a copy of *Bodies & Soul* and beaming. "I've got it," he shouted, "I've got your book. A friend put me on to it. I read it; it's great!"

Tickled and embarrassed at the same time, all I could say was, "Hey, I figured since we liked the same music you had to be all right."

"Would you sign my book?"

"I'd be delighted."

"Come on upstairs to my studio."

And up we went, freed somewhat of the strictures of our previous journalist-celebrity relationship.

The first thing that struck me about Larson's cozy workplace—besides the placement of his cluttered drawing board by the window overlooking the street—were the bookshelves. They were packed with the likes of Ditmor's *Thrills of a Naturalist's Quest*, Robert Ardrey's *Venomous Reptiles and Amphibians,* and the Audubon Society's *Field Guide to North American Insects and Spiders.* His well-thumbed library also included literary classics, fine arts editions, a sizable collection of jazz biographies and discographies, and Norman N. Holland's *Laughing: A Psychology of Humor.*

Resting refulgent on its stand in one corner of Larson's studio was one of the five acoustical guitars he owns, all of them hand fashioned and custom built by the legendary Long Island luthier, Jimmy D'Aquisto, famed as the present-day Stradivarius of the guitar. On the music stand next to that particular guitar was a sheet of score paper upon which Larson had penned the chord changes to the evergreen jazz standard, "Nuages." "Clouds" is how we'd translate the title of this wistful, wordless ballad by Django Reinhardt, the fabled Belgian Gypsy guitarist.

It was also a cloudy afternoon in Seattle, even though Larson was radiant now that we were pretty much talking jazz, his music and muse. Everything around him looked classic: the stacks of virgin paper on his drawing board, the books and tapes and LPs, the sketches and pictures and notes pinned to the bulletin boards, even the sleek-looking word processor he'd recently purchased to give his cartoon captions "a professional look." More than anything else perhaps, it was rain-swollen Seattle I was glimpsing through Larson's barely opened window that looked so classic and timeless. Having once lived in that lovely, watery, Scandinavian-American city—just up the hill, in fact—I wondered about its lifelong influence on Larson. Instead of asking, which would've meant resuming our deep-talking-to-the-deep relationship, I treated myself to several hits of wintry air blowing through the window; air wet and ripe with the smell of fallen leaves.

It was the tinkle of chimes, door chimes, that broke my Seattle reverie. They were just soft enough and loud enough to change the mood of the house altogether. Who could it be? Maybe I was going to get to meet Larson's girlfriend, the one who had just accompanied him on a scuba-diving trip to Indonesia and Bali. No, impossible. Larson had already told me that she hadn't yet gotten back from Spain.

No, it was three ten-year-old girls—one blonde, one brunette, one redheaded—and they had bravely undone the front gate and sounded the doorbell. When Larson answered, softly surveying his nervy young callers, I watched the friendly squint of his easy gray eyes and could tell how perplexed yet relieved he was to see them. Relieved because all Ashley, Maria and Heidi wanted

were autographs. From the name on the mailbox, they had figured it out. This just had to be the house, *the* house! But Larson
knew weren't about to ask where he got his ideas or his theories
on the curative powers of laughter, or how much money he
made last month. He seemed perplexed, and later confided that
this sort of thing had never happened before, not here at home.

"Heidi," I asked, butting right in, "what is it about 'The Far
Side' you like?"

Heidi was the blonde. She ignored me and directed herself to
her hero exclusively, even though Larson was already busy sign-
ing the single sheet of paper he would presently tear into three
pieces.

"I don't always understand what your comics are about," said
Heidi. "But I like the pictures. I *love* the pictures."

"Well, thank you," Larson managed to say as he handed each
girl a signature, then excused himself. "I have to go now; I'm
being interviewed."

"Oh," said Heidi, all wide-eyed, while Ashley and Maria
stood by, looking scared. "Are they gonna do a bibliography?"

Respect

Aretha Franklin, 1967

It was Washington, D.C., more than 30 years after my mother decided not to marry Rev. C.L. Franklin and more than 20 years after his daughter Aretha, my old Detroit neighbor and schoolmate, finally switched from Columbia to the Atlantic label, slipped down to Muscle Shoals, Alabama and cut that unstoppable hit, "Respect," that was still filling the sunny May air of a late Sunday afternoon on my way, this time by taxi, to National Airport, which is actually in Arlington, Virginia.

Leaned forward in the backseat, watching the querulous, lanky driver's eyes connect with mine in the rear view mirror, I was thinking about Leon Russell's line from "A Song for You," the one that goes: *"I love you in a place/where there's no space/or time."* That so many years had already passed and that I'd soon be landing again at Chicago's O'Hare Airport in the time it would take to listen to a Leon Russell and an Aretha Franklin LP back to back had me thinking in rhythm and patterns and clusters and slices. If, for example, I were ever asked for some reason to draw one of those demographic, statistical pies sliced up to indicate how I'd spent my time on earth, there would have to be one thin, barely forkable sliver of pie to represent the entire one percent of my life I've spent making plane connections at O'Hare.

But this was National, a departure, and I wasn't in any hurry to be anywhere except perhaps at home asleep, for it had already been one of the busiest springs of my life. I could've sat in the back of that taxi for hours and listened to Aretha's earthy, life-affirming tones. The driver must've sensed this too.

"Where's home?" he asked.

"California," I said.

"L.A.?"

"No, up near San Francisco."

"Must be wonderful," he said, "I got cousins out there. I'm from Brooklyn, but I been here a long time."

"Oh, yeah?"

"Yeah, I had one of them mothers in Brooklyn don't too many people know about. Most people don't, but black people do. I had the kinda mother who raised four kids on $75 a week. I don't know how she done it. She was a good-lookin' woman too. Coulda had herself a sugar daddy, but it wasn't till I was 15 that I even ever seen a man kiss her on the cheek."

He zigged and zagged through traffic the way Aretha's voice was cutting through the heated lyrics and backbeat of "Respect" and, as he blew his story to me, it didn't take too much high I.Q. to figure out the height and shape of the volcano rumbling inside of him.

"Told her," he began, "I told her, I told that woman, 'If it wasn't for God, you wouldn't be here. No, you wouldn't be here, cause I'da *been* done killed you!' Coulda taken all day to do it too. And it was all on accounta them three dogs. Yessir, God kept me from killin' that woman, man. Fifteen years ago I was over in Vietnam, where it was my *job* to kill people. I got back here and people didn't treat me or any of the soldiers all that good. But that's just the way it is; I could understand where they were comin' from. But I couldn't understand where this Humane Society woman was comin' from. You catchin' this? I mean to say, I get tireda these people sit up and look at television and think and actually *believe* that's the deal.

"All she could say to me was: 'You were unkind to your dogs.' She kept sayin' that till I thought I was gonna scream! And check this, man; she wanted me to clean up my act and get myself together inside of two weeks. Two weeks! I used to be the kinda guy would go through $7,500 wortha drugs in six weeks, and she wanted me to do drug and alcohol rehabilitation in two weeks! You know? I'd just lost my mother, and I couldn't get *her* back, so maybe I could get my loves back. I loved my mother. I loved my dogs too.

"Listen, man, some woman, a neighbor, filed the complaint with the Humane Society. They broke into my place; broke the door down while I was out, and took the dogs, all three of 'em. I mean, I wanted to kill that damn Humane Society woman so bad it was all I could do to strain and hold back 'cause I was ready to spend the resta my life in prison just to teach her about respect.

"You know, here they are callin' themselves the Humane Society and tellin' me: 'You ain't takin' good care your dogs, so we gon kill 'em. I know that's all they wanted to do was gas 'em. That's all I had: them dogs and my mother. I didn't have no father. I mean, sure, I *had* one, but all I have are about four picture memories of my old man. He was killed in the Sixties.

"My mother, so she was all I had. Like I say, she coulda had her a sugar daddy or turned tricks, but she respected us kids and was lookin' out for us. I loved my mother, man, and I love my dogs. Sure, I didn't treat 'em all that well, and that's all that Humane Society woman could see. But, hell! Look what I was doin' to *myself!*

"So the Humane Society wanted me to clean up in two weeks, so I went over here to St. Elizabeth Hospital and got myself cleaned up. Then the woman said she couldn't locate me, couldn't find me. Well, man, you know, St. Elizabeth is in the phone book! Then she said she didn't like my apartment where I was keepin' the dogs; said it was too small and too messy, so I got another apartment, a whole new thing—six rooms—and she *still* wanted to take my dogs away and kill 'em.

"If it hadn't been for me lovin' my mother so much—oh, man! That's the only thing kept me from killin' that woman from the Humane Society. I called the city to find out what I could do and they said wasn't nothin' they could tell me 'cause they didn't have jurisdiction over the Humane Society. So then I called the mayor, and the mayor told me wasn't nothin' he could do 'cause he didn't have jurisdiction. I said, 'Then tell me, who in the hell does have jurisdiction over them people?' And he said, 'Hey, it's a national organization and way outta the reach of anybody in the District of Columbia.'

"Man, I mean, sir, the last time that woman come out to my place, wasn't nobody there but me and her and my girlfriend, and I know my girlfriend woulda got her told, but I wanted to kill her! She wasn't showin' neither me or my dogs no respect.

"So I'm tellin' you . . . All these people that lay up and watch TV and think life's the way it is on TV, they are sick!

Life's more complicated than that. These people on television be solvin' they problems in 30 or 60 minutes or maybe, at the most, in a coupla hours or in a few nights on a miniseries. You know yourself life is deeper than that. I loved my dogs, not as much as I loved my mother, but I loved 'em just the same. I was attached to 'em, even though at the time I didn't have myself together. I was sick. But do you suppose that, even for one minute, you think she respected that?"

I flew back into Chicago, thinking about all the molten feeling that had erupted from the volcanic action of that taxi driver's soul: human connectedness in a way I'd never thought about it before. And when, on the connecting jetliner to the Coast, I remembered my own departed mother's favorite adage—"Never forget that everybody is somebody's child"—I knew I would never be able to listen to "Respect" again without thinking about human connectedness and mutual respect, the glue of it all, in a light—the kind of light you only see from a car window crossing the Potomac at sunset—I'd never felt affect my solar plexus in quite the same way. Now when I hear Aretha sing: *"R-E-S-P-E-C-T/Find out what it means to me/R-E-S-P-E-C-T/Take care of T-C-B,"*—well, I'm ready to R.S.V.P.

(Sittin' On) The Dock of the Bay

Otis Redding, 1968

There were stories—and not even strange ones, considering the paranoid era that fertilized them—that Otis Redding had gotten too big for his show-biz britches; that the Mafia had somehow fixed his plane to crash when it did near glacial Madison, Wisconsin just when he was on the verge of making the leap into superstardom, whatever that meant or means. The truth is this: the man could sing. Although he was Georgia-born, Otis, in a sense, was a true Memphian. He grabbed hold of everything that floated down the river—Sam Cooke, Smokey Hogg, Ray Charles, Percy Sledge, any number of sub-American vocalizing gallants—then balled them all up into one big jolt of his own. Those early records of his on the Volt label went all through you the way electricity can make even the kinkiest of hair stand on end should you happen to be standing in a puddle of water and grab a live wire without thinking.

I hadn't thought about it before this record came out, but Otis Redding and Steve Cropper's tune—cut three days before Otis' plane went down, killing him and four of the Bar-Kays—conducted all the generative juice of my long ago West Coasting directly to my inner brain by way of vibrational touch. For me it was Berkeley. It was walking weekends down the pier down there at the Bay with my beautiful wife, gazing at the shimmering waters that mirrored the sun's glint of greeny-blue Bay-pull from a California Bay Area of the tide-flattened soul.

Even if none of that makes sense, I just want you to know I loved you, Otis, and still do. I love you for finding me with your thunder-coated voice. My choice was to stay in California, to never go home—not back to Georgia, where I wasn't from anyway—but to Detroit and the rolling and remembered light of orange and blue and black industrial fumes: symbol of loneliness as something generalized and motorly and catching.

Wasting time had always been the sweetest move I'd ever made for all those wandering, rambling years I'd spent getting down, right down to the real nitty-gritty, to living in depth as a way of sidestepping death.

Otis, your flow was the perfect advertisement for deathlessness, for bone-wearying loneliness just wouldn't leave me alone, either. Alone, alone, alone must be where we go to be cured, and for me it was the dark hickory dock of the Bay—a good kindergarten-to-high-school chunk of years before they built that restaurant known as Dock of the Bay, which has become Skates and will likely turn into something else again. Your song soothed a part of me that must have been in love with its own suffering.

Let go, your whistling wave of a song said, and go back where you really belong. When it came down to that, I didn't have any choices left; all I could do was face up to the truth, and the truth was this: Pacific Oceans don't know anything Atlantic Oceans don't.

All of this I had to learn over and over between June and October of that first year away from lake-and-land-locked Michigan, and it took a lot of longing and timing and forgetfulness, to say nothing of Rainier Ales and chilling mistakes and oversights. But finally I seem to have gotten it straight: "To thine own self be true." It turns out that Shakespeare, whoever he was, was trying to tell me something. Otis, your whistling at the end of that side surrounds me gently now, or however it wishes, like the shy warmth of coming to terms with oneself in these relatively benign climatic zones.

The point? I never got over either you, the dock or the darkness and its way of trying to pass itself off as actual, edible light. But, as a resident Memphian, who had been watching it all drift down the Mississippi, you knew all along what floated and what didn't.

Concert by the Sea

Erroll Garner, 1958

"I hate jazz!"

"You do, really?"

"I absolutely loathe it."

"What a brave thing to admit. I don't think I've ever heard anyone express that sentiment with such passion."

"Hope I haven't offended you."

"Not at all, but can you pinpoint what it is you don't like about jazz?"

I leaned forward to hear what the lively New York book editor would say; her reaction had genuinely surprised me. A moment ago I had mentioned being at work on a piece about the Monterey Jazz Festival celebrating its 28th year, and now she was squirming uneasily across the table, chomping the last of her luncheon salad, practically quivering with emotion. In quiet Vermont light, I watched her dark eyes narrow in her troubled face.

"The minute I hear the sound of jazz," she stammered "I wanna pull out a gun and shoot the people playing it, then train my aim on the people listening to it. Jazz is just, well, stupid, that's all. And let me tell you, jazz festivals are the worst. They bring out all the drunks and dope addicts and bad news people. Now, a classical music festival, or a film festival or wine festival, a cheese festival—those are fun. But a jazz festival, no way!"

Later, reflecting on her extreme attitude, it occurred to me that I should've asked this person what she thought about rock concerts, since she very well might have been confounding rock music with jazz. As anyone who's ever attended the Kool Jazz Festival can tell you, musical categories do get blurred, even ignored altogether. All the same, people tend to have fixed ideas about the way they're expected to behave in different musical contexts.

For example, I still haven't forgotten the night I sat in the press box overlooking the Monterey County Fairgrounds Arena and watched a young couple—evidently there on some journalist buddy's press pass—go formally bananas while I tried my best to ignore them and concentrate on Clark Terry's trumpet playing and Eddie "Lockjaw" Davis' tenor saxophone. But no; in the space of a single set, I had to watch these two rip, in dizzying succession, through reefers, pills and snorts of white powder. To top it all off, they were guzzling tequila. All the while, they chattered and squealed and clapped nonstop, stamping their feet out of time to the music, determined, I gathered, to get down, as it were.

Finally, irked beyond capacity, I turned to the person seated beside me and said in a loud stage whisper: "How high do they think they need to get, do you suppose?"

That's when the ruffled young man in his Brooks Brothers jacket, red-faced and red-eyed, twisted all the way around to get me told. "How come you're getting so uptight?" he wanted to know. "It's a jazz festival, isn't it?"

No one at a rock event, of course, is expected to sit still and actually listen to anything. Rock, after all, is about kinetics and uproar, volume, abandon and sheer physicality. Rock has its fans and groupies and freaks; jazz has acolytes. Jazz people tend to describe themselves as aficionados, devotees, enthusiasts, supporters, activists and authorities. While it may be permissible under certain circumstances to pat your foot discreetly, it's definitely considered uncool, even tacky, to climb onto your seat during a jazz performance and break into a spirited howl or a bump and grind. This isn't to say that jazz festival-goers don't sometimes carry on in just such a way; simply that it's unusual behavior nowdays.

But anybody who's dropped in on one of the Monterey Jazz Festival's Saturday afternoon sessions during the past 30 years knows a little about the Jekyll and Hyde nature of that crowd. What festival manager Jimmy Lyons politely calls "dancing in the aisle time" got underway back in 1964 when the brilliant singer and lyricist Jon Hendricks conceived the idea of filling that daytime slot with something he called "The Blues—Right Now." The first of these popular blues shows headlined Joe Williams and Lou Rawls, urbane and versatile vocalists capable of moving pop, jazz and so-called soul audiences alike. But it was the likes of Big Joe Turner (who recorded the original "Shake, Rattle and Roll" that propelled Bill Haley and the Comets to stardom in the Fifties), "Big Mama" Wille Mae Thornton (whose outrageous "Hound Dog" had done the same for Elvis Presley), country bluesmen Washboard Willie and Homesick James, and the saucy, barbecued bluesiness of the Hank Crawford Orchestra that satisfied earthier appetites. Talk about mass movement, people were jumping up and down, doing the Boogaloo, the Hitchhike, the Frug, the Pony, the Monkey, the Funky Chicken, the Broadway, the Watusi, the Hully Gully, the Swim, the Shotgun, and some other steps the most seasoned choreographer might have found unchartable.

Right then and there, in its seventh year, a Festival tradition was forged. And when this year's Saturday roster of blues wizards takes to the stage, you can bet that the woman who flies down from Seattle every year, the social worker who's had her name changed legally to Edie Rainbow, will be there on her feet, shaking her Afro-wigged head of many colors, goading the crowd to get up and boogie. The beat they'll be moving to will be laid down by Jay McShann, the legendary Kansas City pianist in whose band bop genius Charlie Parker sprouted wings. Co-performers will include blues belter Linda Hopkins and those impeccable jazz perennials: Buddy Tate, Claude Williams, Al Grey, Noble Samuels and Gus Johnson, Jr.

Tickets for that afternoon—for all five shows, in fact—were sold out last spring before any advertising was issued.

And what conclusion would our New York book editor reach about a three-day jazz festival that sells out all its seats, all 35,000, every year? What if I were to tell her that the average Monterey Festival patron is between the ages of 25 and 49, and is a professional in medicine, education, business, finance or marketing? Moreover—according to Fingerote and Grauer, the Monterey-based agency that handles Festival publicity—they come from all over the country, although mainly from the

Western states. Paul Fingerote further points out that the major- ity of these fans are "quality oriented." This means that they don't seem to mind kicking down $100 a night for lodging, which is the average inflated cost of a hotel room in the Monte- rey area for that good-time weekend. As for food and drink and additional entertainment, it's par for festival-goers to shell out another $500 to $750 between Friday and Sunday for that. Re- member, too, that these are people who have already dropped some heavy coin months in advance to snap up tickets, and I haven't even touched on transportation costs.

"We love it," Joan Pease told me. She manages the Monterey Peninsula Chamber of Commerce. "Back in the Fifties," she ex- plained, "there was strictly nothing doing after Labor Day once the old Bing Crosby Golf Tournament and the Sports Car Races at Pebble Beach ended. Now the summer season's a thing of the past; things go on right into Thanksgiving. The Jazz Festival started all that by dragging the season out well into September. And the beautiful thing is that the traffic's away from downtown because so many of the motels are on Fremont Street, so people can walk to the Festival. It's wonderful!"

Neither the Newport Jazz Festival, which takes place all over New York City these days, nor the touring Kool Jazz Festival can match Monterey for consistency and predictability. It's something people can count on to be there, in the same spot, year after year. In fact, many of the same people sit near each other at the Fairgrounds season upon season. It's probably only a matter of time before some anthropologist or social scientist makes a study of jazz festival attenders as a community or sub- culture. One observation they'll have to record is that the Mon- terey Festival always hosts a classy array of established musical artists.

This year, for example, between opening and closing nights of Friday and Sunday, September 20 and 22, listeners are being treated to the comforting if, in some ways, conservative sounds of the Modern Jazz Quartet, Dave Brubeck, Sarah Vaughan, Joe Williams, Gerald Wilson, and the Hi Lo's. Only the inclu- sion of Pancho Sanchez and the Toshiko Akiyoshi/Lew Tabackin Band make this year's nighttime lineup any different from the typical jazz concert I might have saved up paper route money to attend 30 years ago. Sunday afternoon, like Saturday, holds special appeal. That's when the annual California High School Band Competition takes place, as it has since 1970.

Even though the Monterey Jazz Festival's 15-member Board of Directors takes understandable pride in itself as a nonprofit organization that pours every cent it takes in back into "a highly acclaimed program of jazz education in the local junior highs, high schools and junior colleges," there are regular block ticket buyers who have nevertheless voiced complaints about the Sunday afternoon show.

"I can't knock those kids and their hardworking teachers," one Monterey repeater who prizes her privacy confided. "It's a tough job getting a band of teenagers to play with strength and precision. And I'm impressed like crazy with the young soloists who imitate Charlie Parker or John Coltrane or Miles Davis or Herbie Hancock. I know it's all about laying groundwork for the future of the music and all, but too much of the time the music comes out sounding too studied, too smooth, too clinical and academic and soulless. I'd rather pay to hear mature musicians expressing themselves. I mean, how about bringing in some fresh, under-recognized professionals for a change?"

She isn't the only one who's brought up the matter of the Festival playing it all too safe in its format and the acts it books. Longtime concert promoter and Bay Area media personality Sonny Buxton—whose elegant jazz club Milestones is currently San Francisco's newest—puts it this way: "The Monterey Jazz Festival has become Jimmy Lyons' personal house party." Buxton goes on to say that there isn't much he likes about jazz festivals in general. "All the intimacy between musicians and listeners that makes jazz work is taken away at a festival. But, in their favor, I must also admit that festivals—because they're held on spacious sites—can accommodate large numbers of people. Sometimes it's fun to get together that way with a bunch of old friends for a weekend."

It's partly for this very reason that I often catch myself feeling like the late arrival at a party that's been going on for years when I visit the Monterey affair. Often it looks and sounds as if music is the last thing on the minds of the people in the audience around you.

A warm and breezy night comes to mind when I was straining to hear a gifted singer, Carrie Smith, sing "Take the A Train."

An illustrious house quartet was backing her, and yet when I play back my memory tape it isn't so much the music that I recall. Somehow the song has been blotted out by the nitwit exchange of two whiskey-throated gents sprawled behind me, who chatted all the way through the performance.

"Hey, yeah, 'A Train'! How about that?"

"Whew, when Duke wrote that one, it *stayed* wrote, didn't it?"

"Duke? You mean, Billy Strayhorn. I'm sicka Duke getting all the credit for Strayhorn's stuff."

"Well, whoever wrote it, it's a classic. Only can't nobody sing it like Betty Roché."

"Who's Betty Roché?"

"Man, I thought you were supposed to be some kinda jazz buff! Betty Roché's the singer cut that number with Duke on his *Ellington Uptown* album, one of the first truly great hi-fi recordings, for jazz anyway. And Betty can sing rings around anybody else tryna do it."

"Oh, yeah? How much you wanna bet?"

"Now, you're telling me you know somebody can sing 'A Train' better than Betty Roché?"

"That's right."

"But how can you say that when you haven't even listened to Betty Roché, and never even heard of her till I mentioned her just now?"

"C'mon, chump, lighten up! That's like last year when we made that bet about trombone players—and you ain't paid me my money yet."

"Paid you your money! You been sitting up here for two nights straight, hogging up my Jack Daniels, and I'm supposed to—"

"C'mon, admit it! You lost the bet. I played you that cut where Frank Rosolino is playing trombone faster than J.J. Johnson ever did."

"I wasn't convinced. I happen to know from hearing J.J. in person that he *is* the fastest trombone player alive, still to this day."

"Hey, I played you the record. Far as I'm concerned, you still owe me fifty dollars. Now here you come with Duke didn't write 'A Train' and all this Mel Torme jive."

"Mel Torme? You're goofy! Gimme back my Jack Daniels!"

And on it went, interspersed with bursts of neighborly laughter, until someone close by shushed the two of them by name.

"In the audience at Monterey," Jimmy Lyons has said, "we have little clusters of people, all been sitting next to each other for 10, 15, 20 years. All been sitting in the same seats." Lyons calculates that repeaters, as he calls them, roughly make up 60 percent of the audience these days. Divorced couples have been known to squabble over who'll get the front box at Monterey, and the heirs to season tickets have been designated in wills.

Fred Brown, a Palo Alto cabinetmaker, who has followed Northern California jazz doings since the Thirties, took time to point out to me the high proportion of Louisianans who haunt the Festival. "I swear," he says. "I was with some Louisiana friends one night at that big hotel across from the Fairgrounds, and nobody was even thinking about catching the show, even though they all had tickets. They were partying from room to room. It was like those people that hang around in their vans and RVs at the football game and spend the whole time partying in the parking lot. And everybody's room we stopped in at to have a drink was from some part of Louisiana. See, these are people who're heavy into spectacle. Mardi Gras, Carnival, that sort of thing. I would go so far as to say this is one of your core groups at the Festival."

In his provocative autobiography, *The Pony Express,* brought out by J.A.S. Publikationen, the German publisher Jurgen A. Schmidt in Frankfurt, saxophonist and singer Norwood "Pony" Poindexter writes about how Jon Hendricks hired him in 1960 to appear in "Evolution of the Blues Song," one of the most dramatically memorable presentations in Monterey Festival history.

"Jon," writes Poindexter, "had lined up an all-star cast, including Jimmy Witherspoon, Miriam Makeba, Hannah Dean backed up by a hip gospel group from Berkeley (The Andrew Sisters), Ben Webster, Big Miller and me, plus the Ike Isaacs Trio. Out of all those people, I was the only dude from New Orleans. And because of this, I was presented with the golden opportunity to narrate before a large audience at the most prestigious jazz festival in the country. The show was to be covered by several California radio stations and also by the Voice of

America and the Armed Forces Radio. The plan was to have 20 to 30 children seated on stage and the story of the blues narrated to them from the beginnings in Africa, when the people that were to be slaves were rounded up, put on ships, and taken to America. . . . The show was a big success. . . . CBS decided to record the show. We had some offers for TV. And most important for me, I became a member of the Lambert, Hendricks and Ross group as a singer/saxophonist."

I heard *Evolution of the Blues* back in the Midwest, in Ann Arbor where I was an undergraduate at the University of Michigan. I was touched by it and associated it with another Monterey-connected LP, also a Columbia item, which had already become one of my all-time favorites: Erroll Garner's *Concert by the Sea*. This live recording, a bestselling album for that astonishing, self-taught pianist, was made in 1958 when Jimmy Lyons, then an independent promoter, had booked Garner into one of his wintertime outdoor "Jazz at Sunset" concerts in Carmel.

Even now when I go for a walk by Monterey Bay or visit the beach at Carmel, I often imagine I hear in the roar of the waves or the wash of the surf the exhilarative sound of the crowd on the record applauding Garner's rollicking, joyful, cascading intro to the prestidigitatious "I'll Remember April" that opens the concert. It was a performance so enthralling that even in 1985— when time seems to have leaped forward the way a nick in a phonograph record can cause the needle to skip suddenly from the middle to the end of some selection—I can still experience the gentle rush I felt as a teenager eager to fly the cooped-up Midwest and set down by some ocean, preferably the Pacific. The thought of all that remarkable music just waiting out there for me to sun in and get wet by under the stars seemed positively unreal, given as I was by then to hearing jazz played almost exclusively in stuffy auditoriums or smoky clubs. Just the notion of being near the ocean with thousands of other music lovers, outdoors, was practically otherworldly.

It must have seemed that way to Jimmy Lyons, too. He clearly enjoys reminiscing about the Monterey Peninsula he fell in love with 35 years ago, back when he and jazz columnist Ralph J. Gleason—who, like Lyons, had been at Columbia

University in the Thirties—were looking for a fresh and relaxing setting to stage the music they so adored. The Monterey that Lyons fell in love with back in 1950 was the Monterey that serviced the GIs at Fort Ord; a place known primarily to the outside world as the picturesque fishing village immortalized in *Cannery Row* and other John Steinbeck novels.

"It was a pretty sight," Lyons wrote in his memoir, *Dizzy, Duke, the Count and Me,* the book about the Monterey Jazz Festival that he wrote with Ira Kamin. Lyons and Gleason wanted to see and hear jazz played in benign surroundings. "We wanted it in the middle of a meadow," he says, "outside, in the wind, under the sky where it belongs."

A former advance man for the Woody Herman Band in the Forties, Lyons, born in Peking, China of missionary parents, hosted in the early Fifties a popular San Francisco radio program known as "Discapades" Its night-owl listeners were treated to jazz records in general, but the show eventually came to serve as a sympathetic and pioneering venue for a particular sound, blossoming just then, that came to be labeled West Coast Jazz. Shorty Rogers and the Giants (with sidemen like Art Pepper, Jimmy Giuffre and Hampton Hawes), the pianoless Gerry Mulligan Quartet with Chet Baker and Chico Hamilton, and the unstumpable Dave Brubeck Quartet, which featured the lyrical alto saxophone artistry of Paul Desmond.

"There isn't much I wouldn't do for Jimmy," the garrulous Brubeck told me from his home in Darien, Connecticut. "He was one of the original boosters of my career. Even before the Monterey Jazz Festival got off the ground, he had my quartet down at the Fairgrounds, playing in this place that was like a cross between a barn and a shed, years before we all got famous." The group was featured at the first year's Festival program on Sunday, October 5, 1958, performing "Summer Song" and "G Flat Theme," accompanied by nothing less than the Monterey Jazz Festival Symphony under the direction of Gregory Millar. Other symphonic-tinged performances were presented on that maiden occasion by former Festival music director John Lewis and the Modern Jazz Quartet. With a grand finale of Pete Phillips' "Toccata for Jazz Percussions and Orchestra," featuring drummers Max Roach, Joe Morello and Shelly Manne, even my New York book editor acquaintance might have been impressed. It was a period when jazz was straining for respectability.

What happened between the middle and later Fifties to make the Festival dream a reality? Jimmy Lyons had gone out and approached the business people of Monterey, those who, in his words, "would benefit most: the hotel and motel people, the restaurants, the Chamber of Commerce. And then we had the professional people, doctors and dentists, lawyers and people like that, people who thought it was a good idea. Finally, in 1957, we got everyone who was interested together in a restaurant on the wharf. We told them what we planned to do and offered two-year, no-interest notes to anyone who would put up $100. We wound up with 67 donations—$6,700—which we paid back within a year." Fund-raising continued to be a problem for years. "We muddled through," says Lyons. "I went to my friends, Brubeck, Paul Desmond, the Modern Jazz Quartet, and asked them to come play." When the Festival extended invitations for corporate support in 1983, Michelob Beer and Apple Computer accepted and, a year later, Western Airlines joined them.

I moved to California in 1961 and almost right away landed a disk jockey slot at FM station KJAZ. But it wasn't until 1966 that I finally walked through the Fairgrounds gate for the first time. Within minutes, the Charles Mingus Sextet (with my old Detroit chums altoist Charles McPherson and trumpeter Lonnie Hillyer) had me sailing into peaceful, whipped cream skies. Then Thelonious Monk and His Quartet took over, followed by Mingus' childhood sidekick Buddy Collette leading the Festival Workshop Ensemble. From then on, I was a goner.

"Festivals," in singer Joe Williams' opinion, "bring together people in the performing arts who might not otherwise come together. We're all tripping around in New York, London and Paris, doing our thing. . . . Then all of a sudden we're snapping pictures of Louis Armstrong, Wes Montgomery, Leonard Feather, Bill Evans at a Newport 'Tribute to Alec Wilder' at Carnegie Hall."

Williams, who is both timeless and tireless, a favorite of no less a jazz fan than Johnny Carson, is as high-spirited now as he was when I first interviewed him one Sunday morning on KJAZ close to 25 years ago. He still hasn't gotten over the time he was visiting Turkey in 1979 for the State Department. "Somebody snapped on the TV and there I was with Duke and Woody on a videotape shot at Monterey. From the first time I was with the Basie Band and we drove up there from L.A., I've been knocked out by Monterey. The Monterey Peninsula is a dream. You know, my wife and I seriously considered moving there years ago. I love that Festival. I love jazz festivals."

Dave Brubeck agrees. "I last saw my friend Joe Venuti the violinist at a festival, and Cal Tjader. There are these little moments where we're crossing each other's paths backstage. And you never know. It just might be the last time."

Mundell Lowe, the impeccable guitarist who has been its music director since 1983, sees Monterey as "the granddaddy of jazz festivals, and still the best. Lowe, a 12-year veteran of the Festival, spoke affectionately of Joe Williams and other singers who have graced that stage.

"A singer," he says, "with a big band or four or five pieces will make it every time. It's tough for instrumentalists, trios especially, because it isn't easy for them to get across those footlights. But, you know, everybody identifies with singers. Everyone figures they can sing. A singer like Bobby McFerrin can hold the whole stage by himself."

Lowe went on at some length about how he'd like to see some new and younger faces at Monterey—'Some Wynton Marsalises and Stanley Jordans and Jon Faddises and Bobby McFerrins" in addition to the high schoolers. "The kids are better off now than when I was coming along," he thinks, "because they get educated musically early on. But that isn't enough. They need to go out in the world and get their corners knocked off and bleed some before they're ready. I remember when I was working with Mary Lou Williams and Coltrane hit New York. Even he had to pay some dues before he was really ready."

Hate jazz? How can anyone hate jazz? Especially anyone who's been at Monterey and watched Ramona and Kenny Crowell selling Dizzy Gillespie for President T-shirts? Or watched Horace Silver, as dapper as a preacher, walk across the Fairgrounds, looking as if he's just unearthed the Fountain of Youth? Or seen Queen Ida, without her Bon Ton Zydeco Band, seated on the shoulders of some husky young man, puffing aristocratically on her cigarette as if she were, indeed, a Creole monarch? Or caught the John Handy Quintet with guitarist Jerry Hahn and violinist Michael White the year they made history with their blistering performance of "Spanish Lady," causing Columbia Records exec John Hammond to rush up as soon as the set was over to hand them a contract? Or watched the heavy-duty Mingus gobble down two tacos, simultaneously it seemed, at a Fairgrounds snack stand?

How can anyone who's ever danced in the rain at night to the salsa sounds of Tito Puente's Band, or gazed at the rhythmic blueness of the sea at Carmel in April, or listened closely to the festive, heartbeat sound of the ocean breaking on the shore hate jazz?

Bobby McFerrin
And Tandy Beal

Live and In Concert, 1985

If something marvelous doesn't break loose at Cabrillo College in Aptos, California when singer Bobby McFerrin and dancer Tandy Beal perform there together December 27 and 28, then alchemy is strictly Dark Ages stuff, spontaneity means running stoplights and, to quote the late Little Willie John, "eggs ain't poultry/grits ain't grocery/and Mona Lisa was a man."

"What people can expect to experience," Tandy Beal told me by phone from Salt Lake City, "is a wonderful celebration. Working with Bobby isn't just a thrill; it's fun and uplifting. He's one of those very rare artists who transcends the difference between entertainer and artist."

At the time, Beal, who has danced and taught dance all over the world, was rehearsing with Salt Lake's Ririe Woodbury Dance Company for a premiere ballet performance of Darius Milhaud's *La Création du Monde*. Salt Lake was where she and McFerrin first met. "He sang and played piano for a class of mine about ten years ago at the University of Utah."

Born in Hollywood—"Somebody had to be!"—and raised in New York and Connecticut, Tandy Beal has been based for some time now in Santa Cruz where she has her own studio. Both her parents were actors; her mother Helen Craig for the stage, and John Beal, her father, a film and TV favorite. Not surprisingly, most of her work is theatrical. "My home is theater. I see things always visually. Somehow I found dancing and it gave me great joy. The things I'm planning for the concert with Bobby are visual ambiances. The dancers will be framed references, but it's improvised. We'll rehearse quite a lot, but in a very different way than we prepare for a normal concert. This is unusual for dancers; it's more like jazz musicians. Dancers rarely work improvisationally."

When they joined energies last February at Cabrillo, McFerrin and Beal's performance ran longer than scheduled—two hours and forty-five minutes in all—and the audience was enthralled. "We had a great time!" Beal recalled in breathless telephonic tones. "I mean, it was one of the high points of all of the dancers' performing careers." She expects that there will be as many as seven dancers in the troupe this time around: six men and three women.

"Visually," Bobby McFerrin explained over waffles in San Francisco, where he lives with his wife and two young children, "movement helps sound. It also helps the imagination."

Everything you can imagine about the inner recesses of Bobby McFerrin—the physical, the emotional, the spiritual—is there in his music, which he sleeps and breathes.

"It wasn't until I was working with dancers in Salt Lake City," he said, "that I consciously decided to become a singer. And then all of the resources I had been gathering from day one to year twenty-seven came to my aid."

McFerrin seems to have been a natural. Born in New York to parents who were professional classical musicians, he early grasped the relationship that exists between discipline and spontaneity. And although he is the recipient of this year's *Down Beat* Readers' Poll Award for Best Male Jazz Vocalist, McFerrin refuses to pigeonhole himself musically. It's classical music that he listens to most of the day, but those who've listened to his Elektra album, *Bobby McFerrin*, or his Blue Note LP, *The Voice*, or his guest appearance on Manhattan Transfer's *Vocalese* album on Atlantic—on which he not only sings but doubles as bassist and percussionist as well—know how formidably eclectic he is.

The essential Bobby McFerrin, of course, is the live one who can walk out on stage—maybe even straight from the shower—and mesmerize audiences, as he has been doing constantly throughout North America, Europe and Japan, with nothing more than the sound of his voice. The power of that voice is so revivifying, so nourishing, and the spirit that informs it so jubilant that audience and performer at a McFerrin concert often blur beautifully into one. A thorough virtuouso, as tuneful as he is rhythmic, Bobby McFerrin is as much at home with Dizzy Gillespie's "A Night in Tunisia" as he is with Lennon/McCartney's "Blackbird" (in which he once vocalized, between lyrics, the flapping of wings in flight) or James Brown's "I Feel Good" or Sam Cooke's "You Really Got a Hold on Me" or, for that matter, a Bach cantata.

"I was working with a band three years ago in London," he said, "when I decided I wasn't going to plan anything anymore. We were filming. The TV crew *insisted* on a set list, so after a lot of hemming and hawing I wrote out a set list; we performed it and it had no heart at all. Because we weren't ready to perform those tunes in that order. So I *vowed* I'd never make out a set list again. When I'm working by myself, I don't plan anything. That's why Bach was so good; that's why his spirit is all over the place because basically he was improvising."

When I asked McFerrin what the audience could expect at the concert at Cabrillo, he smiled and said, "Of course, we'll have to rehearse a lot of that, but it'll be live. And in a live moment, *that* concert becomes so special that in order to regain the feeling you have to bring it up from within yourself."

So devoted is McFerrin to the flow of the moment that he doesn't particularly like recording his music since the very process is an attempt to freeze those special moments, so that audiences come to hear him already conditioned to expect that he'll simply perform his "hits" again and again for them, precisely as that material has been captured on record. "I almost wish I didn't have to record," he sighed.

"Tandy and I are going to have a piece of fabric designed for the performance, some kind of costume that'll allow us to either be strapped or attached to one another so that when she moves, I'll move. I'll be dancing with her on stage; I'll *have* to! The other possibility is the audience actually accompanying a dance, which was something that happened spontaneously the first time we got together. That had an astounding effect on me because here we were, dancing and singing, with an audience collaborating on something that hadn't happened before. Everyone was involved. It just wasn't an audience sitting back and watching it happen. I like to see audiences involved. It gives me a chance to even rest, take a breather. Lots of times I'll give the audience some parts and then I sit out in the audience and relax and check it out. I'm hoping it'll happen again at Cabrillo."

Not only did Beal and McFerrin and the dancers deliver, but that night at Cabrillo was filled with joyfulness from the moment the dancers first stepped out on stage until the close, a number that left the auditorium filled with balloons. McFerrin variously sat in a chair or on the edge of the stage. Usually off to one side, and extemporized music and lyrics while Beale and her dance troupe enlivened the sounds—many of them unbelievable—this amazing vocalist projected.

Something that McFerrin also does well is to involve audience totally in whatever he does, so much so that it isn't unusual for him to invite members of the audience up to the stage—divvying them up by vocal range, say—and teach them some round or contrapuntal melody rich in elements of call-and-response that he's usually composed right there on the spot. And at one point, he actually did sit out in the audience to "check it out."

It was a thrill to work with him several months later as part of the Cal Poly Summer Arts Festival at San Luis Obispo. This was a setting that combined music, dance, film, video, graphics, sculpture, photography, literature and theater. On the Wednesday night that Bobby McFerrin was performing with the marvelous dancer Lynn Simonson, who should happen to be sitting behind me in the audience but trombonist and cellist and composer and jazz educator Dave Baker. At one point, while McFerrin was whining an achingly doleful line of blues for Simonson to animate, Baker, who had been expressing all along his awe and enthusiasm for the performance in uncontrollable remarks and bodily reactions, abruptly leaned forward and whispered, "He's kinda out there, isn't he?" This cracked me up so much I almost lost it right there in the next to last row of the theater. And when I remembered that we were listening to the son of Robert McFerrin, the baritone who used to sing with the Metropolitan Opera (that's his voice you hearing coming out of Sidney Poitier's mouth in the movie version of *Porgy and Bess*) and who is married to operatic soprano Sara McFerrin, I did lose it, laughing so hard in seemingly the wrong place that people around me turned to stare.

Later, hearing that McFerrin and Simonson would be giving

a late afternoon workshop in voice and body movement at one of the illustrious old barns at the edge of that scenic, mountain-surrounded campus, I stopped by to see what would happen and ended up on stage with a few dozen others while they taught us everything they could in the space of two hours about music and movement and the discipline that is part and parcel of being spontaneous.

I felt so good afterwards, so warm and loose and opened up, that I went back to my room and started writing poetry.

It didn't surprise me to snap on the TV a few months later and catch McFerrin's unmistakable voice singing a cappella about Levi's and how they were "good for my body." Nor was I surprised to reach my movie seat, my popcorn still warm, just in time for the opening credits of French director Bernard Tavernier's *Round Midnight,* over which McFerrin chimes Thelonious Monk's timeless melody. Nor did it surprise me when he picked up a Grammy Award.

What surprises me is that it's taken the world so long to catch up with Bobby McFerrin. But that's the way it's supposed to go, isn't it?

"What I'm trying to do," McFerrin has said, "is to restore the vocal instrument to its status as the first, original instrument. I've heard people say that the dream of all vocalists is to imitate a horn. Well, that's not my dream. I want to be a good vocalist."

Giant Steps

John Coltrane, 1957

When John Coltrane cut this side for Atlantic on May 5, 1959, I was an undergrad busy studying *Don Quixote* for Sanchez Escribano's graduate level Spanish lit class at the University of Michigan, Ann Arbor. I was several steps ahead of myself and delighted that Professor Escribano had even let me into his advanced Cervantes seminar.

In his memorable liner notes to the Atlantic album, *The Art of John Coltrane,* the venerable jazz historian and commentator Martin Williams stated: "'Giant Steps' is perhaps the full expression of Coltrane the harmonicist. An ingeniously constructed obstacle course of chord changes for the musician (and an almost perfect instruction piece for the student), it is also a gracefully exciting experience for the listener. Coltrane explained when it was recorded that 'the bass line is kind of a loping one. It goes from minor thirds to fourths, kind of a lopsided pattern in contrast to moving strictly in fourths and half steps.' Notice also the openness which Tommy Flanagan, a virtuoso pianist when he wants to be, wisely uses in his solo as a contrast to what Nat Hentoff called Coltrane's 'intensely crowded choruses.'"

Even though Trane's attractively laddered melody has become a jazz standard, recorded subsequently by the likes of Woody Herman, Rashaan Roland Kirk, Phineas Newborn, Joe Pass, Chaka Khan and Kenny Barron—to lightly skim the surface— my favorite version will always be the one my boy Michael used to do when he was two. While he enjoyed his nightly bath, laughing as he played with his tub toys—his rubber duckie and his boats and plastic people—Michael would gurgle the "Giant

Steps" melody to the rhythm of water running or the sound of his own splashing.

"I like that one, Daddy," he told me more than once, his eyes afire, humming zealously the part of the melody that rises so beautifully as it moves backwards then forward in successively higher progressions—giant steps.

Of course I was struck by how a mere child could pick right up on something so intricate yet as fundamentally singable as this exquisite piece that for me runs all the way back to my teens. I can almost paint the never-decaying light of how it all glistened, bath bubbles and all, from memory.

In the lobby of the Michigan Union—upstairs where I'd buy Greyhound bus tickets to go visit all my homefolks in Detroit—I used to collapse in one of those big old cozy leather chairs and style or pose or wait and sometimes doze. To this day, I'm convinced those chairs were either guarded by Morpheus or some other deity, some minor god of naps. Once I'd plunked down for my round-trip bus ticket to the Motor City, I would settle back of, say, an early Friday evening and pretend I was a college boy; the real thing, like all those kids from Grosse Pointe, Bloomfield Hills, New York, Bucks County, Long Island, Silver Spring, Shaker Heights, and the city of Paris, France. Leaning back, resting my tired eyes just enough to to keep peripheral, squinting vision of what was going on outside my head, I would dream about all those writers whose work I valued; where they'd gone or hadn't gone to school, and I would imagine myself as each of them.

But I would also dream of all the many musicians I wouldn't have minded being at the time, either. When the bus finally pulled up, I'd either be asleep or numb with fantasy. When the driver would ask my destination, I'd say: "Going home to Detroit." But actually I was never sure. Buzzing through my head were other questions: Where was home? Where was I really headed? Where had I been? Where was I now?

There's no way to get around having to take these giant steps; at least if we're lucky. My son keeps taking them; I can't keep up with him. My grandmother, who was born in 1892, told me on a recent New Year's Day: "Just try and keep up with yourself, son. It's so easy to get ahead of yourself or behind yourself. The best thing to do is stay right with yourself. That's not easy to do, but can you understand what I'm saying?"

I think I understood.

This much is clear: There are steps and there are steps, but it's that slow, dumb moving through the world of shadow and act, emotion and stealth, hunches and hits, that propels every single one of us forward toward home—no matter how round-about the path may be.

As Time Goes By

Dooley Wilson, 1942

It was Ralph Waldo Emerson who spoke of the single day as the perfect measure of eternity, a notion that very few lovers of San Francisco would question. Locating the eternal San Francisco in palpable time and space, for instance, needn't take any longer than a day, even allowing for a full night's sleep.

Sparked as always by live music—this time on a Friday night at the Casablanca Restaurant, snuggled neatly between Polk Gulch, the Marina and Russian Hill—I began to recount all over again my own reasons for loving that city. And why, I also wondered, should the Casablanca be the catalyst to ignite, like kindling, all those tender, splintery backlogs of warming San Francisco memories I've been stacking up over the years? After all, as its name suggests, the Casablanca is timeless. It takes its theme and décor from the 1942 movie.

Bob DiFranco's Casblanca is a friendly, solid-feeling room; there isn't a fern plant in sight. A couple of old-fashioned, well placed potted palms and slow-whirling ceiling fans are all it needs to suggest a cinematic North African setting, not unlike Rick's American Cafe. Gold-framed stills of Bogart and Lorre, Bogart and Bergman, Bogart and Greenstreet illumine the walls, dramatically completing the picture. But it's those shots of the genial, brown-skinned Dooley "Play-It-Again-Sam" Wilson quietly slipping us his piano-vocal version of "As Time Goes By" that nudge me softly again and again in the direction of to- tal recall.

While I'm busy being moved by how the past is always blos- soming out of the present, my attention is warmly reclaimed by what's going on right in front of me. Across from where I'm perched at the bar, Merrill Hoover, the city's outstanding veteran pianist, has woven a delicate, filmy jazz intro for singer Laurie Antonioli to begin her own version of "As Time Goes By." Suddenly it's as if I'm some movie-goer at a matinee who has just tiptoed through popcorn from his aisle seat up onto the screen to get in on the action, like one of Woody Allen's characters in *The Purple Rose of Cairo*.

"You must remember this," this singer begins, *"a kiss is just a kiss, a sigh is just a sighhhh. . . ."*

It works. At once I start remembering the textures and contours of a long day that seems to have begun 25 gleaming years ago—although I know it was only that morning—in the wet sand and windblown light of Ocean Beach. Huddled there by a sand cliff for warmth, I understand why those surfers I see bunched up along the shore are always in wetsuits. Here the Pacific is icy! It's like wading around in a vast repository of refrigerated water on the rocks. In the days when the movie *Jaws* was very much on summer beach vacationer's minds, there was little chance of any but the most valorous of waders getting chewed up by sharks at Ocean Beach. And you're getting this from a wader of discretion.

Thoughts I've been weaving to the music are broken by the actual tinkle of ice cubes being dropped into a glass. I twist on my stool. The gentleman on the stool next to me is an acquaintance: an elderly, bright-eyed New Yorker, a retired social worker. We last talked music a few years ago when we were introduced by a mutual friend in the lobby of the Hyatt Regency, which at that time featured live jazz every Saturday afternoon in its lobby. But it's as if no time at all has passed.

After making a joke about the alias-sounding ring of his name, Joseph Smith, Perrier drinker, turns on his seat and says, "You know, San Francisco's got everything New York has, except without the dirt and overcrowding."

"Yes," I say, "and you can always come back here and find what you remembered and wanted to see again, even it's been a while." I glance aroud the Casablanca again. "This place feels about the same, doesn't it? And look at Merrill over there; he hasn't aged one bit, has he?"

Joseph Smith is excited and eager to talk San Francisco versus Manhattan, but he can also tell how caught up I am in the song being sung at the moment. He settles back politely and waits. A white-haired, alert looking man, the relaxation in Joe's face tells me he's neither given to worry nor hurry; that he is, so to speak, a patience millionaire.

Laurie Antonioli eases and oozes into the ballad, sounding a smidgen here like Ella Fitzgerald, a tad there like Anita O'Day, but mostly like herself, like someone who has lived out the experiences encoded in the song's hypnotic lyric. Diners lay down their forks and knives. Supper table chatter subsides. Even the festive birthday group celebrating the pianist's Norwegian wife's birthday way at the back in a distant far corner is enveloped by the hush.

"... *The fundamental things apply,*" Laurie Antonioli carries on, *"as times goes by."*

From Ocean Beach, where the Pacific itself roars and sloshes and churns forever in a fundamental rhythm that connects California with Hawaii, Hong Kong, China, Singapore, Japan and Australia, the way the hipbone's connected to the kneebone and the legbone's connected to the anklebone of the mammoth dinosaur skeleton in the lobby of the California Academy of Sciences, memory of my leisurely day jogs me pleasantly back to Golden Gate Park.

Today I was in no mood to take in all the attractions that are regularly available at the Academy alone—the North American Hall with its exhibit of large American sea and land mammals, the Mineral Hall, Steinhart Aquarium. And this isn't to mention the beautiful stops within the park itself, which include the Arboretum, the Garden of Fragrance, Speedway Meadows, Stow Lake, Spreckels Lake, Rainbow Falls, the Music Concourse, the Japanese Tea Garden, the Equestrian Field, the Buffalo Paddock (where actual buffalo roam.) Mind you, I have nothing against all this undivided splendor; it's rather that today I was hungering for quiescence and contemplative space.

Morrison Plantetarium is where I ended up again, at the very back row of that concentric circle of cozy seats, nestled there with my eyes turned to the dazzling imitation of the heavens revolving on the domed screen overhead. Even though I *know* these stars and shooting stars and constellations and planets and suns and moons and nebulae and Milky Ways and galaxies are being projected from the device that spins on its carefully programmed course in the center of the circular theater, the effect is invariably magical. Always, in some unexpected way, the narrator can be counted upon to open me back up to the mysteries of space and time. This time he does it by reminding us that we are relative specks in the context of eternity; that we are experiencing the light and heat we get from the sun that is already eight minutes old. When it comes to the Milky Way, we're looking at 100,000 years ago, and 40 billion years for those vast, remote galaxies discernible to the eye-like ears of only the most sophisticated radio telescopes.

Or course it's all too much to fathom or grasp, and soon, because the program's begun with the sun going down, the sky ripening with darkness as the heavens inch by degrees toward daylight, it isn't long before I've grown so relaxed that I catch myself sinking directly to the bottom of a dream. Embarrassed when I come up out of my nap to the gentle sound of the taped narrator's concluding tones, I stretch and smile at everyone around me, wondering if I'd snored while I dozed.

I'm in for a treat, however, for in real time there's plenty of unused daylight still out there for me to soak up. Motoring through the rest of the park to Fulton and over to Civic Center takes less than 20 minutes. Parking downtown is another matter. For fun, I check in at the Fifth and Mission Garage, an economical public facility, and from there take public transportation and good old shank's mare for what's left of the afternoon.

It's always fun to walk from that particular parking garage to the Emporium, less than a block away. There, entering the back way, I like to walk through that cool department store keeping a sharp eye for sales, then exit at the front onto fluttering Market Street, where you're liable to see anything, anything at all. Despite decades of continuous remodeling, restoration, beautification and renewal, this rambunctious thoroughfare, one of San Francisco's vital nerve arteries, often feels to me like it's still 1905. I have no trouble imagining what it might have been like around there in the heyday of the Southern Pacific, the Spring Valley Water Company and the Market Street Railway. I can even picture San Francisco's erudite, cultivated mayor, the smooth and mustachioed Abraham "Boss" Ruef, making a speech at the corner of Market and Montgomery, say. That would put us somewhere around the turn of the century, and not far from where his parets operated their prosperous, expansive dry goods store in the 1860s. To manage this, all I have to do is stand reasonably still while I feel the tempo of the street. There's no other downtown street quite like it, not in North America.

"You know," Joe says, as if he's been tapping into my thoughts, "there's something awfully European about San Francisco."

"I agree."

"Really," he says, "I was thinking about it in North Beach this evening while I was having dinner at little Joe's. In a sense, North Beach is Times Square, only a great deal more sophisticated. The people aren't as on edge here as they are in New York. I mean, I've never been to Italy, but I loved my stay in Portugal and Spain; people were warm and friendly, just like here."

"Yes," I said, thinking about poet Lawrence Ferlinghetti's book, *A Coney Island of the Mind,* and his poem about a very earthy yet intellectual dog who trots freely around North Beach, looking at moons on trees, ants in holes, "chickens in Chinatown windows,/their heads a block away," walking past the Ravioli Factory and Coit Tower. I think, too, of the leather-skirted barker outside topless Big Al's just after I'd driven past City Lights Bookstore in that part of town. So now, I thought, they're hiring female touts. Well, the more things change around this town, the more San Francisco they become.

Like miniature divining rods, Merrill Hoover's fingers hover above the keyboard before floating down and spreading themselves to make the perfect minor chord. Now we're all ready to take Antonioli's unhurried vocal boat ride along the river-like ballad, "Lazy Afternoon." Again, the contemplative mood descends on me like smoke from the cigarettes of the couple holding hands at the other side of the bar.

By now, by subjective time, it's still late afternoon and, having done some leisurely shop crawling, I'm listening to the young sidewalk musician got up in an immaculate tuxedo across the street from Macy's Mens Store. Urbane and obviously conservatory trained. All puckered up, he fingers the keys of his flute and blows Antonio Carlos Jobim's "Wave," a bossa nova classic. I can tell by his exquisite manner and sound what a genuine flute player he is; not just another uppity flautist. And then,

as I go to drop a handful of small change into his elegantly in-
verted hat, I'm so taken by the sight of all the crisp notes already
deposited therein—mostly ones, but several fives as well, and
even a ten—that I go back in my pocket and pluck out a dollar
bill to go with the small change. Undaunted, the flute player's
nod is barely perceptible as he submerges his breath and heart
into the melody's throatiest reaches. It's if he might be assuming
I've already read about him in Herb Caen's *San Francisco Chronicle* column.

Since the downtown shopping district is flanked by the Tenderloin, I decide to take a brisk stroll through that part of the
city, where adult bookstores and X-rated movie houses and
peepshows appear to be on the wane. Flashing neon signs and
lighted marquees shine in the gray, watercolored afternoon. It
doesn't take long for me to register that something curious is
taking place in the Tenderloin. Here and there the district's
shabby streets and dingy storefronts are being perked up by colorful boutiques, grocery stores and other shops that have lately
been popping up, run by the area's newest residents: the Vietnamese, the Cambodians, the Laotians. The streetwise children
of this latest wave of Bay area immigrants, residents of the run-
down hotels, now play on the Tenderloin's impoverished sidewalks that have always been peopled with winos, junkies and
other derelicts. But slowly, as their enterprising, self-sacrificing
parents and elders adjust to the pressures and tensions of their
new surroundings, the Tenderloin will increasingly reflect the vi-
talizing impact that this new family life is having there. The re-
sulting change in appearance is dramatic and heartening. "This
neighborhood ain't what it used to be," I overhear a longtime
derelict resident say. "And, hey, you know what? I'm glad."

A cable car ride? It's been time, so why not? Indeed, Mayor
Dianne Feinstein has done some heroic maneuvering to keep
this quaint yet expensive to maintain mainstay of San Francisco's municipal transport system refurbished and restored. A
controversial and endearing tourist attraction since 1873, when
Andrew Hallidie, an enterprising English-born engineer, de-
vised and tested the first one down Clay Street from the top of
Nob Hill, cable cars have long been a touch-and-go political issue in San Francisco, going all the way back at least to the Forties. I even have misgivings sometimes about them myself, but

it's hard to resist the cheerful crowd queued up to board the next arriving car on the Powell-Hyde Line up the hill to Chinatown. We stand making friendly small talk—as friendly as talk among strangers in a city can get—while the tracks at our feet and the cables above go on humming like the sound the lifeblood of a city might make if you amplified it coursing through her arteries.

Joseph Smith smiles at me while we're applauding Hoover and Antonioli; two wonderful jazz crazies dizzy with the wine of time and the rhythms of life.

"I should've moved out here," Joe tells me suddenly.

"Oh, yeah?"

"I'm from Baltimore," he explains, "so when I left college, I moved to New york to be close to my mother."

"Do you regret it?" I ask.

"No, it was the right thing to do at the time. How long you been here?"

"Most of my life now," I tell him. "Twenty-five years. I came here right after college. When I left Detroit I had my choice of either going to New York or coming out here."

Treating me to his gentlest avuncular smile, Joe says, "I'll bet you're glad you did." He sighs and laughs. "I could talk about San Francisco and the Bay Area all night. Bet you could, too."

It's midnight. Through the window I can see soft rain beginning to fall. I think about the couple from Dublin I'd sat next to on the cable car. Learning that I was a writer, they'd spent the rest of the ride to Ghirardelli trying to urge me to move to Ireland, where writers don't have to pay taxes.

With the sight of the Bay shimmering brightly in the mist at the bottom of the hill we were riding, and 360 delicious degrees of pure beauty surrounding us at that very instant, I really hadn't known what to tell them.

To Joseph Smith that night at the Casablanca, all I can answer is: "Of course, I love it here; I'm crazy about the Bay Area."

On a napkin he writes out his phone number and address for me and says, "Look me up when you hit Manhattan. But if I don't hear from you, I know we'll probably run into each other again, maybe even right here, because I definitely plan to come back again."

We shake hands good-night, and as I descend the hill to my

auto, I notice that images of cable cars are blinking like neon inside me. For all these seasons they've been swooping and chugging along the margins of my consciousness, and I've just now gotten around to realizing how amazing and exciting cable cars can be. A famous musician pal once told me how he had to travel all over the world to keep from being known as "just another one of them local dudes."

What is there to say about a ride that lifts and plunges you so thrillingly and rapidly into the vitals and along the peripheries of so many inviting worlds and half-worlds? Maiden Lane, Jackson Square (once known as the Barbary Coast), Chinatown, Fisherman's Wharf, Pier 39, Ghirardelli Square, Union Square, Russian Hill, Embarcadero Center, Nob Hill: some of them are clearly explorable at once, *somewhat*. But most of these special San Francisco realms are only completely discoverable in the full measure of time, which could turn out to be an eternity.

Passion Flower

Billy Strayhorn, composer

Listening to Duke Ellington's band deliver this Billy Strayhorn beauty, how can you not be taken back to the very childhood of spirit by Johnny Hodges' sound?

You know exactly where you are. You don't need no map, no compass, no geography lesson. The men moving around you now are, every last one of them, you. They're all dressed the way you thought, in the Forties, you were going to have to look when you grew up, with one of those big-lidded detective hats on your pomaded head, to top it all off. And the women are all you too: lovely, slightly perfumed and fanning themselves, their hair piled high, Lena Horne high, and sloe-eyed.

You know exactly where you are. You're in heaven. And the moon of your return to earth is as full as it'll ever be. Something sails past: a thought, a notion? The peace of mind that's coloring in the spaces on this blissful map of yours is so all-assuring that you can barely make out what it is. Surely it might be there in the breeze by itself; in the magnetic wind of roses that keeps pulling and drawing the soreness from your lopsided sorrow like a kiss or a lyric or a lark.

You can talk about your skylarks and your nightingales and doves, but when it comes to sonic ecstasy, Johnny Hodges will beat a jolly, doleful songbird, wings down, every time.

Listen to the way Hodges plays with time; kneading the years like cookie dough, and making us laugh and weep that they be brought back, but only in the Johnny Hodges/Billy Strayhorn/Edward Ellington fashion. Flowering yet never flowered, and always fragrant with passion.

Improvisando Jazz

Tito Moya y su Conjunto, 1963

It had been 471 years since the Moors and their Jewish allies had been run out of Spain in the wake of the Inquisition, and I was stepping around Madrid on a rainy afternoon in early autumn. All of 24 years old, I was thin, thirsty, lonely, impetuous, almost broke and dream-ridden. I kept big and little notebooks and liked to read everything, especially signs and long complicated posters and announcements in Spanish. The bestseller you saw in all the bookstore windows that fall in Spain happened to have been a history of the Spanish Civil War by Generalíssimo Francisco Franco. It was getting smash reviews.

Actually I didn't know what Spain I was in. I would walk the main boulevard, José Antonio, El Gran Via they called it, nights and pretend I was back in Lorca's Spain, or sometimes I'd turn a corner and there I'd be in the backstreet world of Benito Pérez Galdós, or I would be sitting up in some park or public square in the working-class outskirts of town, wondering what Carmen Laforet was really trying to tell us about life in postwar Spain in her sparse little novel, *Nada*.

But that afternoon I was enjoying the rain so much I wanted to get out of it for awhile so I could look out at it. Sometimes it's fun to dry off just so you can get yourself wet all over again. There was this little bar not far from my pension, El Galápagos in Calle Hortaleza, so I dropped in to have a beer and gaze back at the drizzle.

Some hometown stranger, a bright, young madrileño, a kid maybe 13 or 14, but even poorer than most, was sitting at a table behind me. This young man—Mario, Enrique, Manuel, I

forget—took me at once for an American, which I didn't at the
time think I genuinely was. Watching while I sat and sipped my
cerveza (thair-VAY-tha), he followed me to the jukebox and lin-
gered while I dropped my pesetas in the slot, then paused to read
all the complicated, punchable selections.

"Any suggestions?" I asked him in my most relaxed Mexico
City Spanish, pointing out a title at random.

"Ese no," he said, *"toca este."* Nah, not that one, play this one
here. He mashed the button, grinning as if he had just done me
a big secret favor that I would never quite grasp. While I stood
there, eager to hear what was going to come out of the machine,
I couldn't stop thinking about how "to play," as in "to play music," and "to touch" share the same verb—*tocar.* And since poets
don't know when to leave well enough alone, I even took it a little further. I thought about the letters themselves and saw *to car*
as a possible English verb, as in "to transport someone or something." Oh, you have no idea how writers clutter up the insides
of their heads, especially when they're just coming along, with
such silliness.

But when the music came out, that is, when it started pouring
and tumbling from the jukebox in great tides of Latin-like Afro-
Cuban rhythm and the robust Dexter Gordon sound of the tenor
player, whom I presumed to be Tito Moya himself, reached my
homesick ears, I wanted to hug this kid. How could he have
known that this was exactly what I needed to hear—a little hit of
North American/South American salsa with some brooding bebop stirred in to bring a little heat to the beat?

"Le gusta," he said to me.

"Me gusta," I told him needlessly.

I bought him a grande de Coca-Cola and we sat there at
the table and talked about the weather and did some solemn rain
watching; then he told me he had to get going. I couldn't figure
out what he had been doing in a bar in the first place, except he
did seem to know the bartender, and could have been related.
Such connections didn't trouble me in the least.

I dropped more coins into the jukebox and listened to some
hot local vocals before punching up Tito Moya again.

Why the incident was of consequence at all, I still don't
entirely comprehend. But our journeying on Earth leads us

inevitably to such exotic yet all too familiar locations and subtle situations, where one heart reaches out to another to touch and play and listen and transport the feeling of the moment elsewhere.

Summer Sequence

Woody Herman, 1950

COOLED BY REFRIGERATION was how the old banners read that you'd see hung up outside movie houses, restaurants, department stores and other serious palaces of commerce. The ice-blue lettering would always be frosted over with brittle, snowy icicles, and you couldn't wait to get inside, out of that breezeless heat of high summer, in order to enjoy what some of the denizens of Houston, Texas still refer to as "a freeze."

Sometimes my shiftless buddies and I would hang around the entrances of such architectured iceboxes just to savor the vaporous, momentary chill that spilled out into the melting streets when anyone exited or rushed inside for cover. And that's where Woody Herman's fabulous *Summer Sequence* comes in, for this lilting piece of music covered this experience for me. But it was the soothing cool of autumn—celebrated on the record by the throaty whisper of tenor saxophonist Stan Getz—that to this day continues to surface in my mind as the way things actually were then, when I was 15 and 16 and 17, rather than as musical conceit. And back there too, back there in the solar plexus of the Herman band, among all the others, was Bill Harris, keeping the whole sound toasty and profound with his balmy trombone sound, which, like the title of the ballad he wrote, went "Everywhere."

There was something about the way air conditioning in public places worked in those days that draws this lovely Ralph Burns suite back to heart so clearly. I'd slip the sapphire needle into that little jewel of a ten-inch Columbia LP—one of the truly early LPs, no pictures on the jacket, just black print on a blue and white background; a little like those uniformly designed editions of Penguin paperbacks I saved up to buy, the plays of George Bernard Shaw especially, for 35, 40 and 50 cents—then I'd post myself by the window in my attic room at the house on Edison Street in Detroit and watch summer parade past down there on the sidewalks of 12th Street. And once I'd gotten wise to earphones, that listening and watching the promenade would last long into the sticky, steaming night.

Yes, air conditioning. There was something about the Herman band of that era that had Ellington stamped all over it. Perhaps it was Ralph Burns, whose arrangements and compositions they were, who'd fallen under Duke's spell. All I know is that, tonally, *Summer Sequence* took me all the way from the school's-out jubilance of June clean on down to the wistful fake-out of September; that is, from that part of the cycle where it took some doing to tell spring from summer to the interlude where early autumn catches fire as a smell in the leaves people would be burning all up and down the street and all over town, and sometimes there was Nat King Cole intoning: *"La de da/de la de la/'tis autumn."*

But it was summer and the promise of summer that always sent a thrill through the hearts of all the kids I knew then, just as it still does. *Summer Sequence* seemed to have the goods on everything that was going on around that time of year; Ralph Burns and the Herman band had gotten the whole draggy, bubbly dream of summer down pat, one delicious version of it anyway. Certainly it was easy for me to imagine, while I was raptly tuned in and under the music's sway, those next to naked nights in that industrial city where sheets stuck to me in July and August, when I was endlessly turning my pillow over and over, opting for the cooler or coolest side and knowing I'd never uncover it until dawn turned up.

In that hot house of ours, I longed for any kind of air conditioning, even though I was partial to the real old-fashioned kind that wasn't muted or subtle or energy-saving the way air conditioning later became. I dreamed of the kind that was virtually freezer-like; exaggerated in its glacialness like those fictitious Good Humor bars they used to feature on the sides of ice cream trucks: chunky ice cream bars, armored in chocolate. And there was always one toothy-sweet vanilla bite missing that you could taste and feel as it chilled your mouth and throat going down.

Summer Sequence still goes down, even now, at the close of the 20th Century, the way a whopping scoop of chocolate or vanilla fizzles in a glass of wild cherry soda or ginger ale, reinforcing my addiction to the seasons. When I play it for myself sometimes in January or March, it's to check to see if I can still remember that exotic time of year when the sudden thought of a snowball fight is a dream.

Things Ain't What They Used to Be

Mercer Ellington, composer

"That was 1941. I had been demanding that I get some more songs, some more tunes written and arranged and on record. I'd been very fortunate as it was; Pops had let me do 'Blue Serge' and a few other things, like 'Jumpin' Punkins,' 'Moon Mist,' and so forth. So all of a sudden the BMI-ASCAP ban was going on, so Pops couldn't do any of his things for recording or for broadcasting. As a result, Strayhorn and I had our big opportunities at that point.

"So now to settle an argument, Strayhorn begins to get an edge on me. He gets more tunes done, and one that came in about that time was 'Take the A Train.' I beat my butt off to Pops about not getting the opportunities. And Ellington was very, very, well, somewhere between wise and tricky would be the best description for him. He generally kept track of my movements from time to time. People would always be telling him what I was doing. Seemingly he was a disinterested parent, but that wasn't really true. He had his various cronies and people around watching to see that I didn't to get in trouble; following me around, and so forth.

"This particular night, he knew I was drunk as hell. He called me at four o'clock in the morning and said, 'OK, you wanna put a number on record? Well, have something for me at nine o'clock in the morning. We have a record date and I need a fourth side.' He figured, 'Well, this is a great chance to get him; he's in no shape to write nothing, and now I won't have to listen to all that noise and flack he's been giving me about wanting an opportunity.'

"At nine o'clock that morning, I had this song ready. I knew what he was doing, so I just fast-talked something so I could see if I had it, and everything that I had heard from anywhere and everywhere—if it came to my ears at all—I just threw it in there. Johnny Hodges swears I stole it from him, and there's a whole bunch of other guys with all these various riffs and stuff. But I mean, this was like things that came outta jam sessions and so forth, and we just put it together on this one thing. And that was 'Things Ain't What They Used to Be.'

"In essence, the first arrangement was mine because that was just for a small band—Johnny Hodges, Harry Carney, Cootie Williams and Lawrence Brown. Then later Ellington did an arrangement for a big band; it worked out successfully. He liked it. And even further, he wound up seeing to it that it got put into the picture, *Cabin In The Sky,* with Ethel Waters and Lena Horne. He had his role in the picture, but I don't give a durn how big you are, you got another boss somewhere, and so they asked him to audition certain numbers to see what it was they wanted to use for some of the scenes. And he made sure he played my thing, 'Things Ain't What They Used to Be'—and sure enough it *was* picked. So that was it.

"Actually, if it reflects anything, it reflects the fact that it was something that was born of happiness. I had a lot of great friends, wonderful people that I had met in Los Angeles; that I've been close to for my entire life. I don't believe there's any place else that I met or knew as many people as I knew in that era in Los Angeles. We had so much fun, and it was all kinds of gangs and things we did to enjoy each other, you know.

"It was just one of those things where you look for something. I wish I could say I was wise enough to come up with some really great deal, but no; the title just happened to run across my mind and that was it.

"The whole thing, it was one big blur. It was just something that passed by; something I did and was intent on doing. There was no great musical inspiration, or romantic, uh . . . I never went to bed. [Laughter] That's what I'm saying: I came in at six o'clock and that's when he caught me on the phone. It was almost like he was watching me go through the door. That was the Dunbar Hotel, Central Avenue, Los Angeles. The Club Alabam was next door to it.

"It gives me a great deal of pride. Financially, the money that came out of it helped me to a buy a house I put my family in. That was before I went off to the army. Soon after—about six months after that—I was in Los Angeles and the cops stopped me one day and asked me for my papers. Shortly after that I heard from my draft board. But it was proof that I *belonged.*

"This was one of those things where I had to fight all the time; not fight being Duke Ellington's son, but fight belonging to the group of people we were around. We had some great minds at that point. Luther Henderson was there; Calvin Jackson come up from Philadelphia; Billy Strayhorn had come in from Pittsburgh. Lots of kids were no slouches; some of 'em just didn't happen to gain a tremendous amount of fame, or whatever. Another one of the piano players that hung with us was Carmen McCrae. And so here we are, kids in the latter part of high school, and going into Juilliard and just hanging loose and— although I didn't know him that well—Miles Davis was also in that era, going to Juilliard. We had to try to compete and sort of carve out a place of respect in this group we traveled in. I wasn't trying to prove anything to the public nor my father; I just wanted to make sure we could look 'em . . . I was like sitting at the Round Table, you know, knights and all, and you had to have your deeds that you'd accomplished yourself. So this was why 'Things Ain't' represented such a thing of importance.

"It taught me a lesson that I had to become highly educated in order to be able to appreciate; and that many times there can be and is a greater appeal in ignorance than intelligentsia; the fact that these things were just done as a normal response, as a result. A lot of the things that I did with great study, trying to make the world's greatest number, didn't amount to a hill of beans, according to a lot of people. But no matter where you went, 'Things Ain't What They Used to Be' could have a good reaction on whatever crowd—young, old, society-like, you know."

Black Magic Woman

Santana, 1970

"Amerikanski?"

"Da."

At that point the driver pushed the Santana cassette of "Black Magic Woman" into the car stereo of his taxi.

"Where you from?" he asked in Serbian English.

"San Francisco."

"Ah, eez beeyootiful, veddy, veddy beeyootiful. You like Beograd?"

"I'm enjoying myself, yes."

"You are . . . You are poet, da?"

"Yes."

"You are Al Yahng."

"Da."

"I know thees, becawz I see you on tele-veeshun." And, turning up the music while he whisked his head round for a glimpse of me, he said, "So, tell me, how eet eez going, theez long poem you are riding about moon?"

Recently I had been on Belgrade radio and television, and among the things I'd talked about were the Moon Poems I'd been composing as I traveled through that lovely, complicated country as guest of the Yugoslav Writers' Union. My acquaintances, Djórdge Ristič—an ex-jazz singer turned painter—and his schoolteacher wife Lubica, called it the Science Fiction Republic of Yugoslavia (jocularly reinterpreting the nation's initials of S.F.R.J., which actually stand for the Federal Socialist Republic of Jugoslavija).

What happened during the months I spent there in the mid-Eighties would stack up quickly into a hefty novella, maybe even a novel, but for now we're talking anecdotes; we're talking "Black Magic Woman" in a Belgrade cab taking me home to the Street of the Unknown Soldiers out there where I was rooming with a widow named Vera Cvijovič and her two sons, Djórdge and Vuk, not far from where President Tito used to live.

It was midnight, raining, and I was leaving the Writers' Club Restaurant and a night of being so homesick that when Brano Prelevič, a poet of Montenegrin origins, had introduced me to a visiting student from Mexico City, a young woman named Cristina Barajas, who was as far from home and as disoriented as I was, I choked up with emotion and, forgettig how rusty my Spanish had become, spoke ardently with her about everything that came to mind all evening long. At one point, Ivana Milankhova, my Serbian translator and a poet herself, recognizing the state of mind I was in, had said to me across the after-dinner table in English: "I know what it is you are experiencing. When I am in Los Angeles, I meet a Polish man from Warsaw and I cannot stop the tears that pour from me like rainfall."

Anyway, it was raining and I was eager to get to Neznanog Junaka, my street across town, but the driver was bobbing his head and saying, "You like thees music, you like eet, yes?"

"Yes, I do." And I did. The sound of Santana in Belgrade was enough to turn anybody's wistfulness around. It turned me all the way back around to the summer of 1969 when I'd last vacationed in Mexico City and Pátzcuaro in the state of Michoacán. And, while the tape played, I thought too of my mother, who hadn't long passed away. I had last seen her alive during visits to Mexico, Baja California, where she'd gone for laetrile treatments. And I thought about my wife's cancer and my actor brother's recent suicide. There was lot of stuff going on in that taxi as it rolled me momentarily homeward.

Just as I was getting reacquainted with the snappy, salsa rock of Santana, the driver ejected the tape, then pushed in another; this one of Aretha Franklin singing, "Chain of Fools." Whew! The driver's emotion-filled response to that number gave me new insights into the meaning of those lines in the song that go: *"My doctor said:/'Take it easy . . .'/All of your lovin' is much too strong . . . /I'm talkin' to you. . . ."*

"I love theez black singers from your country," the driver said suddenly with the purest of feeling. "They are reminding me of the music here, of our Serbian music. You are hearing what I am telling you, yes?"

"I hear you talking to me," I admitted, thinking secretly of "Hear Me Talkin' to Ya" and of Louis Armstrong who'd written that blues and Gertrude "Ma" Rainey's version of it.

"They have in their voice that cry," said the driver. "Ees the same as in our music. Ees sad, ees, how you say? . . . Ees from the heart for the heart. My English ees not so good, but you understand, da?

"I am loving too your B.B. King and Sam Cooke and all of thees women who sing bloos."

"Hvala," I told him in baby Serbo-Croatian, *"mnogo vam hvala."* Meaning: "Thanks; thanks a lot."

It didn't make sense to be saying that, but why the hell not. I felt inexplicably happy and wanted to break out into song myself. When I did sing a line or two along with Aretha— *"Chain, chain, chain/Chain, chain, chaaaiiinnn/Chain, chain, chaaii-yaiiinn-yainnn-yainnn-yainnnn/Chain of foo-ooools"*—the reality of what that song had been trying to tell us broke inside my head like thunder over the Danube. And I'll always believe from the driver's laugh that he must've heard it too. It was a chain reaction. We drove home that way, laughing.

Prelude to a Kiss

(Duke Ellington, composer)
Ben Webster, 1953

TAKE 1

In foreign streets, just beneath closed eyelids, horns squawk
and traffic melodizes itself to Ben's gruff, glistening whisper, and
there's no telling what always went on underneath that tight-
fitting hat of his.

The Brute, as he was called, hardly ever went bareheaded.
You'd see him in the Negro nights, eyelids fluttering as if in a
dream. What is this thing called color? It's hard to imagine any-
one but Ben Webster coming up with that sound, *that* "I Got It
Bad and That Ain't Good," *that* "Sophisticated Lady," *this*
"Prelude to a Kiss."

In the darkness of a five a.m. vision, you picture the very
sound he's wrapped around the luminous layer of your being;
the other body, visible only to seers, just as Ben's country glistens for listeners alone.

TAKE 2

Barely touched elegance. This is what jazz is, this. You grow
up with your elbows sticking to jam left on a kitchen table set for
peanut butter and jelly sandwiches kind of sound, and then
somebody lets you taste something that makes you into a gour-
mand for the rest of your music-hungry life. Didn't your grandmother tell you where it said in the Bible that the eye isn't filled
with seeing, nor the ear with hearing?

Finally you're seductively reduced to essences, and then to

essence. Since Ben Webster's come to your drowsing ear more than once in a dream, the world is a lot more bearable.

You know Ben was a bear of a man, prone to violence, people who knew him will tell you; always looking for a fight after he'd gotten himself a snootful. But what does this smattering of information matter? All he plays is what he loved.

In foreign streets—Stockholm, Copenhagen, Amsterdam, Munich, Tokyo, Nice—just beneath closed eyelids, horns squawk and traffic melodizes itself. That kiss Ben's been helping you work up to is now becoming as unnecessary as a midnight splash in the sea.

You drift back to that movie house where Ben played piano in that silent movie house in Amarillo, Texas. Staring at that screen, you listen to the story he plays of how he'll go and be gone with the wind; working early with Dutch Campbell's band (Did he know he would settle decades later in Holland?), then it was W.H. Young (Lester's Dad), Jap Allen, Blanche Calloway, Bennie Moten, Andy Kirk, Fletcher Henderson, Bennie Carter, Duke Ellington, Jay McShann, Jazz at the Philharmonic. But it wasn't harmonious; Ben couldn't make a living, so he flew the coop and emigrated, sort of, and departed to foreign soil.

You enter this giant's castle a brute, and come out tingling like a poet; in time to be flown back home for a giggly snooze and surrender all your crowns and your thorns. And the fluttering, which runs deeper than eyelid-level now, goes on and on and on.

Jazz and Letters: A Colloquy*

Al Young, Larry Kart, Michael S. Harper

YOUNG: My father was a professional jazz musician in the Thirties, back in the days when the tuba held down the rhythm section, along with the drums in the jazz aggregations. It wasn't until a man named Jimmy Blanton came along with the Duke Ellington Orchestra that the string bass, the acoustical string bass, became the bottomizing element in swing and jazz music. I grew up in a household where records abounded. In fact, my mother used to get very upset with my father, who worked as an auto mechanic, because when he got his paycheck, he would stop by the record shop and pick up a bunch of records before he ever got to the house.

So I grew up with all these records and later played tuba and baritone horn myself and trumpet in junior high and high-school bands and took music as just a very natural part of life. Because I had been interested in writing from the age of six, the two always went together for me. I never made those distinctions between the arts that a lot of people make, despite the differences in practical approaches to various media. As a teenager I would go to the Detroit Institute of Arts to look at paintings and sculpture, visual and plastic arts. I always carried that same idea about all art with me into that experience. I would look at paintings as a form of music, poetry and literature. I would learn an awful lot of things from the painters when I'd go to museums, and bring it back into my writing, and project those things into the music that I'd listen to. And I think I was very fortunate to

---

*Presented as a panel at the annual meeting of the Associated Writing Programs, in Chicago, April 12, 1986.

189

grow up in the late Forties and during the Fifties when there was sort of a ferment in American culture that eventually rose from subterranean level to become a very evident public factor in shaping, I'd say, even the art that we find around today in all media. In the Fifties, when I was at the University of Michigan, the phenomenon of poetry and jazz became very bankable, as they would say out in Hollywood. And you had people like Kenneth Rexroth, Kenneth Patchen and others. Langston Hughes even got into the act, although Langston had been doing the poetry-and-jazz thing way back in the thirties. But they were making national tours with jazz bands and making records and everybody would go and experience this synthesis, myself included.

That was also the period, you have to remember, when abstract expressionism was king. Jackson Pollock and Franz Kline and all these people were holding court and, if you can recall the New York poetry scene at that time—"San Francisco East"—as somebody called it once, you would note that the painters were actually running the show. All the other artists, the musicians and the poets, all looked to the painters, circa 1954–55, for cues as to how to proceed. So that if you talked with somebody like Robert Creeley or LeRoi Jones (as he's calling himself again) they would tell you that they checked out the painters first, before they went on and wrote their poems. And if you look at, say, the poetry of Frank O'Hara, who was very powerful in those days and held a position at the Museum of Modern Art, you'll see that it was very jazz-conscious and very painterly-conscious, and it was a very exciting period when all of these people's ideas were flowing together.

I was a kid then and I was paying attention to this in a very intense way, as you can only do when you're about fifteen, sixteen years old. You're much more serious then than at thirty-five or forty because, like Jan Carew was saying yesterday, those are the days when you can sit up in the tree house and go through five or six books in a day, or certainly in a week, and really think about them and absorb them. Well, I was doing all that. I was absorbing everything at once. Now the writer who emerged on the scene nationally and internationally and turned everybody around—and I find people in English Departments still don't understand how this happened—was Jack Kerouac.

Jack Kerouac, Lowell, Massachusetts, 1967. Photo by Stanley Twardowicz, courtesy of Gerald Nicosia.

Jack Kerouac came out with *On the Road* in 1957. There had been excerpts from it in *New Directions* as early as 1956. There was a lot of noise about the Beat Generation and Kenneth Rexroth was writing all these long manifestoes and there was a very exciting groundswell taking place. Everybody I knew in Ann Arbor, Michigan was reading *On the Road*. Copies were dog-eared, and people didn't want to lend you a copy because they were afraid they wouldn't get it back or it would come back with beer stains on it and jelly and bacon grease and all that. And it wasn't so much that the writing was "good," whatever that was supposed to be, but it represented an alternative to what we'd been getting. I think that one of the things that the Beat Generation did was to take art out from under glass. I had been brought up in grade schools and middle schools and high schools where we were taught that art was something that was unapproachable. It really didn't have much to do with your life. It was something you had to learn in order to become a more expanded person, acquire good taste and all that. And one of the things that the Beat Generation did was to restore poetry and literature to the people. The people went out and attended poetry readings. Dylan Thomas had come through town—there were a lot of factors in this—had come through in two or three national tours and given people the idea that you could actually get up and read this stuff aloud and people would respond to it, instead of sitting around underlining it late at night in dormitory rooms. So that all of that excitement seemed to coalesce in the pages of *On the Road*.

Now, I don't know how many of you are familiar with Mr. Kerouac's techniques of writing. But he published a very influential manifesto of his own in the pages of *Evergreen Review* in 1958, which is called "The Essentials of Spontaneous Prose," in which he attempts to articulate the way in which he himself worked. He proposed, for example, that you not think about what you're going to say, just picture in your mind what your objective is going to be on the page. And then just blow. That kind of thing, like a jazz musician. You've got to remember that he, as much as anybody else, was under the influence of things like abstract expressionism. I mean those canvases that Jackson Pollock achieved by getting up on a scaffolding and just taking the paint and just—to the uninformed eye or to the people who didn't know the vocabulary of modern art and all that, it would look as if—like if my Uncle Billy saw it, he'd say, "That man is just splashing paint on the canvas. You call that paintin'? I can do that!"

But there was a very elaborate, articulated esthetic that accompanied it that said that process to the abstract expressionist was more important than product. Those painters themselves were highly influenced by jazz. If you went down to the—what's the name of that place they used to hang out? Tenth Street— aren't there any old-timers around here?

VOICE: The Cedar Bar.

YOUNG: Cedar Bar. If you went to the Cedar Bar, they were all talking about Charlie Parker and Miles Davis and whatever was going on in the jazz world at that time and they were trying to recapture the spirit of jazz, the spontaneous spirit of jazz in their work. When the Zen Buddhists turned up during that period, because people like D.T. Suzuki and Alan Watts were also publishing in the pages of *Evergreen Review,* they brought that spirit of Zen spontaneity which enhanced this whole idea that art was supposed to be something that came from the spirit, that for all too long, certainly in the West, it had been dominated by what somebody in those days called the "form freaks," people who were more involved with product and form than they were with content and spirit. Now as a kid I got the idea that still persists with me, that when we look at any painting or piece of writing or listen to any piece of music, what we are actually doing is searching for the human spirit. There's a spirit that accompanies a piece of art that we're usually not aware of except perhaps in a subliminal way. But if it isn't there, it can be the most clever work, it can be perhaps a masterpiece formally and all that, but if it does not have that spirit, if it doesn't swing, as they used to say in antique jazz parlance—what was it that Duke wrote?— "It don't mean a thing if it ain't got that swing." So I got the idea that it was better to sacrifice form if necessary for content.

I was also reading people like William Saroyan, who would sit down and knock out three and four stories in a day and publish all of them. As a kid, you admire this kind of stuff. You think that this is the way it should be; that it should be fun above all else. And jazz always represented this for me, as I think it did for the majority of Americans who were looking beyond everyday, quotidian American values for some meaning to life. I think that jazz mythology has always affected American intellectuals and artists when they were looking for a way out of what Artaud once called "the bourgeoisification" of everything in life. You see these guys who lead odd lives, quite often they have odious habits, personal habits. They stayed up all night, died young. They bared their souls and gave us some pleasure and some insights into a way of life that can be very interesting.

When you look at jazz itself, you see some interesting divisions historically. The early jazz musicians, for example—this is very rough—the early jazz musicians of the New Orleans school, if you want to call them that, the Dixieland people, were heavy drinkers. You go into, even now, a Dixieland bar, it's very difficult to be depressed because they're stomping that stuff out; and they're drinking that juice, and *rum ta da ta da da dum,* and it engenders a kind of spiritedness that, I don't know, may be artificial, but it's kind of a happy music, happily oriented music. This persisted on over into swing, which was a dance music, and people forget that during the Thirties and early Forties certainly—I'd say from the mid-Twenties up until World War II—jazz was the popular music of the United States because people didn't say, "Oh, I like jazz," they just liked Benny Goodman, they liked Count Basie—they danced to this music, it was a *social* music.

It wasn't until the advent of World War II and the postwar years that musicians tended to switch from alcohol into heavy pharmaceuticals, and became very introspective. Among Afro-American musicians you had this intense awareness of themselves as artists and they took themselves very seriously. Those of you who followed mythologized jazz history would get the stripped-down idea that jazz was invented in one night in Minton's up in Harlem when Thelonious Monk and Dizzy Gillespie and Charlie Parker decided to come up with a music that white musicians couldn't steal because they wouldn't be able to play it.

Much is made of that, but of course that's very distorted. You talk to people who were around and you see that this music evolved over a long period of time. But the jazz spirit has always been solidly grounded in technical ability and in the spirit to

Charlie Parker. Photo by Howard Morehead, courtesy of the Institute of Jazz Studies.

soar. In a book called *The Interpretation of Music,* Thurston Dart, who's a musical historian, points out that in Western European music prior to the middle-to-late 19th Century, room was always left for the soloist to express himself or herself. Composers would leave whole sections open for a gifted soloist to come out and improvise, and that was regarded as the apex of a musical performance—somebody not reading the notes, just standing up there playing from the heart. That went out of Western European music when inexpensive ways of reproducing musical scores were arrived at—so that what Mr. Dart calls "the tyranny of the composer" set in. Every note, every speck, every sound, every silence was written down on the page. And the drummer Max Roach, who's a professor of jazz these days at the University of Massachusetts, has said, "I wouldn't be in a classical orchestra for anything, because that's like working at the post office. Go there and sort that mail; you get no chance to do anything on your own."

People always gravitate towards where the spirit is. And when jazz in the late Fifties and early Sixties got to taking itself so seriously, sealed itself off by being available only in clubs where a lot of the young people couldn't get in because they didn't have money or they weren't of drinking age, whatever, then of course rock drew them over. They always go where that beat is and where there's the freedom to say something on your own. Sure, learn your instrument, be firmly grounded in what's gone on before, but have an opportunity to contribute something of your own.

How does this function in writing? It functions for me in a very interesting way. Whenever I sit down to write these days, I always begin by free writing. That is to say, a typical morning for me is to get up and to record remnants of dreams, if there's anything that's taken place in my dream-life. I sit there and I just put some paper in the typewriter and I pay no attention to what's being written, whether it's good, bad or whatever. I have no idea how long it's going to run, and I just start going! And I put all these things in a notebook, and that notebook has become one of the most interesting books in my library, because all this writing hasn't been consciously done, but over the years you've been writing for so long it's hard for you to really write anything bad at a certain point, the same way that it's very difficult for an improvising musician to play anything bad. You might catch a musician on a night when she or he is not so inspired, but their professional level is such that they can be proficient even when they're not feeling well. It's rather like those old Zen painters, who used to look at a tree for 15 years and meditate upon it and in 30 seconds they'd sit and with pen and ink and just go *brrrrrrr* and get the whole spirit of that tree. I think this is attractive to people the world over. It's no wonder that jazz has been called the music of the 20th Century. We're probably less aware of that in this country than people would be in a lot of, abroad. Whenever I travel abroad, I'm always amazed at how aware people are of American music.

In conclusion, I thought I would read something from a series of books that I've been doing, something very short. There are two volumes of this that have been published so far, and there's one more coming out next year. They're called musical memoirs. The first volume was called *Bodies & Soul*. The second volume was called *Kinds of Blue*. And the third will be called *Things Ain't What They Used to Be*, which is an old Mercer Ellington title. What I tried to do in these books was to take a piece of music and conjure in prose in one form or another what the music meant to me. It's a difficult thing to do because even though music is powerfully evocative, sometimes it's so private, the experience that it evokes can be so private, that it's difficult to communicate this to anyone else. And so the problem here—and you need a problem when you play jazz—people aren't just up there blowin'. They know the chords, they know 16 different versions on record of what everybody else has done to this and they know it's going to count if they can do something that's original, that hasn't been stated before. That's the problem for me. How can I say this so that everybody will understand what I'm talking about and at the same time make it, keep it, meaningful? And I experiment each time I write one of these things. Probably the most experimental I've been, and with this one I really let go. It's a form that I'm inventing as I go along, so to speak. And so each time I sit down to do it, I say, "Wait a minute, you know, I've already done that. Do I want to do that all over again? Let's try something new." So I depend a lot on intuition. In the Sixties, later Sixties, Herbie Hancock, a very different Herbie Hancock, wrote something called "Maiden Voyage,"

**Herbie Hancock. Photo by Sulaiman Ellison, courtesy of the
Institute of Jazz Studies.**

which was one of those milestones in contemporary American music—in fact, one critic says that everything that's been produced since "Maiden Voyage," every original sounds like "Maiden Voyage." And I was so taken with this that even though Herbie Hancock came out with it in 1969, I used it as a metaphor for an actual maiden voyage, my first ocean trip that I took in 1963 when I sailed from Brooklyn Harbor to the Azores and to Portugal on an off-season freighter. And this is how that piece begins. I'll just read a page of it and get out of here. But I tried to—the music was playing in the background as I was writing, and it sort of fired my thoughts as I went along:

Maiden Voyage/Herbie Hancock, 1969

Shhh. Listen. Can you hear it? Listen, listen. Shhh. It's like a soft whispery splashing sound. Symbolic. Cymbalic. It's a cymbal tap. The sound of wood barely touching a cymbal. The drummer's poised and ready to slip up on it and the moment Herbie Hancock drops his fingers to the keyboards. Reeeal pianissimo. To sound that lovely dark chord and four bass notes in tricky off-accent time. We'll be on our way. It's still astonishing, isn't it? What is time? I'm laying this down, you're picking it up. Everything happens at the same time. Ask any quantum physicist the kind of dancing that goes on inside atoms, if you get my drift. This time we'll be drifting over and across the Atlantic, sailing away from the Brooklyn pier like an easygoing recreational blimp in an amazing, if not exactly good, year. It just happens to be the very year they shot Medgar Evers in the back; the year they bombed that church in Birmingham and killed those little girls; the Russians put a woman in space; the year they marched 20,000 strong on Washington, D.C. and Martin Luther King and other black leaders met with the President; the year Defense Secretary McNamara and Diem started taking over the headlines; the year they were singing, *"Ain't gonna let nobody/turn me round,/turn me round,/turn me round./Ain't gonna let nobody/turn me round/in Selma, Alabama."* The Governor was shouting, "Segregation forever." It was the year they shot Kennedy down like a dog in Dallas and when they started beating those little white kids, especially the girls, beating them

with those billy clubs the way they've always done colored people; you knew the American century was coming home to roost.
Shhh. Herbie's just mashed down on the go-forward pedal.
George Coleman is sounding the ship whistle. the waves are
churning all around us and if you look closely, you'll see me, a
little brown speck of a speck in eternity, standing on the desk of a
freighter pushing off from the Brooklyn pier. It's the 28th of August, sunny and hot. Standing on the deck waving at the work-
ers on a ship from India docked next to ours, I'm growing a little
bit sad and joyous at the same time as I picture myself atop the
timeless ocean pondering the vastness of my animal-wrapped
soul and vision which I know I must cleanse of false learning before I can go the infinite way of Atlantics and Pacifics, Indian
Oceans and Bering Seas. I stand there watching the Statue of
Liberty grow greener and tinier in the fog beginning to roll in
now. "Roll with the boat," I'm remembering hearing somebody
say. "Roll with the boat, don't fight it and that way you won't
get seasick." We're rolling along right now with the beat, which
isn't easy to pin down and measure, and all the ghosts outside
our porthole ears seem to be portholed ears carrying on in Por-
tuguese. Timelessness, meanwhile, is enfolding me and washing
me clean on this maiden voyage. Who am I? What am I doing?
Where are we going?

KART: That's a tough solo to follow. I'd like to begin by bouncing off one of the first points you made, which was how you
came to the music and, in effect, how Americans manage to decide that something that has the label "art" is theirs. My circumstances were a little different, but I think the process was
similar, similar enough that I think there's a general principle involved here. Music was a little bit around me as I grew up, but
not jazz. Because the music around me and the literature
around me were clearly, at least as I felt, not mine, I was looking
without being aware of it, for some way to find something that
had the qualities that I knew art had, so that I could say, "This is
mine." And it hit me in about adolescence. I think it hits a lot of
people in adolescence, and that's another interesting point. Jazz
is a music that includes the world. And not until you're an adolescent do you begin to think of yourself as a being moving
through a society. Before that, it's the family, or you don't even

Jackie McLean. Photo courtesy of the Institute of Jazz Studies.

know that there are other people. But when it hit me, I was about age 12, which is 31 years ago. I think it was maybe a recording by Jackie McLean. I'd heard some jazz before that, but something about Jackie McLean, who's a wonderful alto saxophonist, spoke directly to me; and when that happened, it was like a covenant had been made, a bond that he wasn't of course a direct participant in; but I thought I had made a bond, and 31 further years have convinced me that it was for real. The process of making that bond and coming into contact with all the music I readily identified as jazz, all the qualities that it had, enabled

me to come into contact with, and make mine, or believe that I
could make mine, all kinds of other art. And I think that's one of
the basic problems that any young American, black or white,
has. How do you deal with this culture which, when you're born
into it, seems more or less alien to you, and how to say, "Yeah, I
have a role to play in here"? Maybe as a responder only, maybe
as a full-time participant, either with a horn or with a pen. I'm
convinced that the notion of covenant is crucial to it, and I was
reading something last night about Moses in Egypt, which was
where the covenant was first formed, and then was renewed
when the Ten Commandments came down. This guy explained,
very interestingly I thought, that the word "exodus" in Hebrew
has the meaning of liberation *and* covenant, and that because of
the story of the exodus from Egypt, the idea of liberation takes
precedence. But they're one thing. The point I'm trying to
make is that, in one way or another, and I think it can be fairly
specific a lot of times, jazz is a music of liberation, spiritual liberation. There's a wonderful book that Sidney Bechet wrote, his
autobiography: *Treat It Gentle*. And there's no doubt on his
part—I can't remember exactly how he puts it. I didn't think to
bring that with me.

YOUNG: He says at the beginning of that book that things
were—you had this tension in New Orleans between the blacks,
the Creoles and the whites, and it was a fixed race, and he said
about some other musician they were talking about, "You know,
if we developed this music right, it'll be something that'll slip in
on these people."

KART: Do you remember the part where he says that the music
arose after an actual physical liberation, the Emancipation Proc-
lamation and all that followed in its wake, but that the music had
the role, whether or not the people who made it and the people
who were on the receiving end were conscious of it, of teaching
the people what to do with the freedom they now had, that they
didn't have before. I think that strain in the music has been
prominent all the way through, and it can be felt, since a certain
kind of liberation is what we're all striving for. It can be felt
down through the whole history of it. And I knew that when
I listened to Jackie McLean and lots of other people and re-

Robert Creeley, Mallorca, 1955. Photo courtesy of Gerald Nicosia.

sponded to them the way I did, that I was using that music in an attempt to define myself.

Another point, to switch horses a bit, about the literal connection between jazz and specific writers. You demonstrated how vital the connection is between the music and your writing, and it runs all through Michael Harper's work. But I remember once listening to Charles Olson read on a TV program. I'd always been fascinated by what I thought his rhythms were, as I read

Charles Olson. Photo by Johnathan Williams, courtesy of New Directions Publishing Corp.

them on the page. When I heard him read them live, or live on
TV, I said, "He sounds just like Sonny Rollins." He swung in
just the same way. It was frightening. And then sometime later, I
ran across this collection of letters that Robert Creeley and
Charles Olson exchanged. Creeley, who was very much involved
in jazz in Boston in the late Forties, was trying to sell Olson on
listening to the people that Creeley was interested in. In this one
letter he quotes what became one of Creeley's most important
poems: "Le Fou," which is, I believe, the breath. I guess I'll try
to read it:

Le Fou*

for Charles

who plots, then, the lines
talking, taking, always the beat from
the breath
          (moving slowly at first
the breath
          which is slow—

I mean, graces come slowly,
it is that way.

So slowly (they are waving
we are moving
          away from   (the trees
               the usual   (go by
which is slower than this, is
          (we are moving!
goodbye

And then in the letter Creeley has in parentheses added in pen-
cil, "Thank you, Charles Parker. Et tu, Thelonious Bach." It was

---

*From *The Collected Poems of Robert Creeley* (Berkeley, Los Angeles: University of
California Press, 1982).

so natural. I mean, you get the lists of the guys he's trying to tell Olson to listen to. It's Bud Powell, it's Dizzy Gillespie, it's Al Haig, it's Monk—I mean, it was natural to them. They knew it.

A third point that intrigues me is that the connection between jazz and literature might be that jazz has more or less spontaneously developed in the course of its life musical parallels to preexisting literary forms. I've always thought of the typical good jazz solo as being more or less a lyric poem. It's a way of stating and elaborating your personal identity, as they say in show business, "in one." You're up there; you are you. You don't have a costume on; you're not playing a role. If it's going to be any good, it's your story. I mean, it's almost a truism of jazz that when somebody gets up there and plays well, the reaction of a fan who responds in kind is, "He's a good storyteller." The literal storytelling, the personal lyrical storytelling, just goes without saying.

There's also a sense that orchestral jazz particularly is dramatic. A typical Duke Ellington piece, like "Harlem Airshaft" or "Sepia Panorama," is a play. And the soloists function both as people who are expressing themselves and as actors who have specific roles to play. Ellington casts them in those roles because he knows who they are and what they have to say and he gives them this framework. He says, "OK, Johnny Hodges, I know what you can do and you're going to be—oh let's say, the lover—in this play. And Cootie Williams or Tricky Sam Nanton, you're going to be maybe the sarcastic commenter on it. And then Ben Webster, you're going to be another kind of romantic lover, maybe one who's a little rougher than Johnny Hodges— maybe it's the male and female principle going on there." But a definite dramatic context, one that includes the lyrical element.

Then there's a way in which over the course of his career the accomplished jazz musician is either compiling an historical account or writing a novel, because there's no doubt that jazz takes place in a specific society in a specific chunk of historical time and it is about, to some extent, being a person in that world over that period of time. John Coltrane would be a perfect example, or Dexter Gordon. Any great player, their music changes over the years, and it changes because of inner musical impulses and psychological impulses, but it's also an accumulated body of knowledge about what it means to have been that person over that period of time. And I think that's not a bad definition of what a novel is. Another way to look at it is that it's autobiographical. But the interesting thing to me—and Kerouac comes in here—is that as jazz musicians have, without necessarily thinking about it, made those literary/musical forms their own, put their own spin on them, they also have affected certain kinds of literary artists. There are techniques about the way jazz musicians state things, state the self, the way they incorporate their history in what they're doing, in response to which various writers have shrewdly or innocently said, "I can use that." I mean, you just did.

YOUNG: Old tunes, man!

KART: In Kerouac's case, I think there's a lot of doubt about how honestly such things were done. I admire his work sometimes, but did he know enough about the materials to use them as high-handedly as he did sometimes; was he a tourist? I think that's one of the problems the music poses to anybody who either writes about it or just comes to it for pleasure or personal enlightenment. Are you part of it, or are you a tourist? Because being a tourist with it doesn't feel good. And it doesn't feel good if you suspect you are a tourist; and if you are one and don't know it, then you're making a big mistake. I wrote a piece about Kerouac and jazz that I brought along, thinking I was going to quote from it, and I guess I am. But I don't know now if I can find a chunk of it that will work. Kerouac tried to do it in two ways. One, he consciously said, "I'm going to try to imitate in my prose and in my verse"—and I think it worked better in his prose than in his verse—what he felt to be the core structure of a jazz solo. "I'm going to get up there and improvise." What was the name of that essay again?

YOUNG: "The Essentials of Spontaneous Prose."

KART: I think there's a fair amount of evidence that he rarely, if ever, followed those principles, that what really counts is just the work on the page. Does it feel, does it have the joy of spontaneity? Whether he actually labored over it or not. I think he did a lot of laboring over things. Which is fine, as long as it works.

And the other thing was that a lot of the furniture of his life was jazz. Some of it got a little creepy, for my tastes. I'll quote some things, if I can find them, that will make anybody's hair curl. Let's see. Here's a line from *Visions of Cody:* "I am the blood brother of a Negro hero." Or he refers elsewhere to "good old-fashioned old-time jitterbugs that really used to lose themselves unashamed in jazz halls." And he also refers to "wishing I could exchange worlds with the happy"—oh man—"the happy, truehearted, ecstatic Negroes of America." I mean, you just go, "Wait a minute, Jack." Although you could say in some of these cases, that's a narrative voice, maybe that narrator is supposed to be a little bit of a fool at that point in the book. But a lot of times that doesn't work. He was going all the way with it.

YOUNG: But he's speaking—if I could intrude on your time . . . Black readers were always aware of that tendency in Kerouac, but it was no different than when I would go with white friends at college to see a Marx Brothers movie and you'd have a sequence where Harpo would go down into Niggertown and everybody'd be dancing and singing and he'd be playing the harp and all that. And my friends would say, "Are you embarrassed?" And I said, "No, I'm not embarrassed, because I know who's making this movie."

KART: It's a good point, because I guess the person, or kind of person, who would be most embarrassed by that would be somebody in my shoes. But also in the back of my mind I'd be thinking, when he's doing something like that: What would his contact with the music be, compared with someone like Al Cohn or Zoot Sims or Bunny Berigan or whatever? Measure it that way. I mean, there's something, there's a strength in the one kind of contact and something presumptuous or weak in the other.

YOUNG: Remember—I haven't talked about this—he was in the hipster tradition, the tradition of the white hipster, which attempted in large degree to turn middle-class white America on its head. If his folks didn't like it, then he liked it, you know.

KART: I'll end with that passage from my piece on Kerouac and jazz, which begins with a quote from his *Book of Dreams:* "I wish [tenor saxophonist] Allen [Eager] would play louder and more distinct, but I recognize his greatness and his prophetic humility of volume, his, 'quietness.'" Eager, by the way, was an excellent white disciple of Lester Young, and his music and his example obviously meant a great deal to Kerouac.

Then, after the quote, I go on to say [reading]:

Listening to Allen Eager or Brew Moore, one knows what Kerouac meant, a meditative, inward-turning linear impulse that combines compulsive swing with an underlying resignation—as though at the end of each phrase the shape of the line drooped into a melancholy "Ah, me," which would border on passivity if it weren't for the need to move on, to keep the line going.

Of course there are other precedents for this, which Kerouac must have had in mind, notably Whitman's long line and Wolfe's garrulous flow. And I wouldn't insist that Kerouac's prose was shaped more by his jazz contemporaries than by his literary forebears. But that isn't the point. For all his moments of softness and romantic overreaching—his "holy flowers . . . floating in the dawn of Jazz America" and "great tenormen shooting junk by broken windows and staring at their horns"—Kerouac's desire to be part of what he called the "jazz century" led to a prose that at its best was jazzlike from the inside out, whether jazz was in the foreground [as in much of *Visions of Cody*] or nowhere to be seen [as in *Big Sur*]. And perhaps none of this could have come without the softness and the romanticism, the sheer boyishness of Kerouac's vision.

"These are men!" wrote William Carlos Williams of Bunk Johnson's band, and he certainly was right, as he would have been if he had said that of Louis Armstrong or Coleman Hawkins, Benny Carter or Thelonious Monk. But there *is* something boyish in the music of Allen Eager and Brew Moore and in the music of Bix Beiderbecke and Frank Teschmacher for that matter—a sense of loss in the act of achievement, the pathos of being doubly outside, that is an essential part of their grace. When he was on his game, Jack Kerouac knew that too.

Count Basie. Photo by Bill Mark, courtesy of the Institute of Jazz Studies.

HARPER: I have been internalizing this dialogue between these two gentlemen, and I'm going to try and respond. I come out of a very strange background culturally, and I think that's very important in the way in which we define ourselves as Americans. The whole question of self-definition is the American problem, and the way in which you locate yourself in this very strange terrain is a question, of course, of voice. And I've had some considerable difficulty communicating with my peers on many levels, mostly at the level of assumption. So I'm going to be rather tedious for a moment and go through a few principles of my own way of approaching this self-definition process.

Everybody begins with a notion of autobiography that sometimes expresses itself as sensibility, sometimes in terms of the constructions of what I call "work," which is to say the way in which one gets inducted into the culture. Oftentimes this happens by accident; sometimes it happens by geography—the notion of black people in particular being forced to migrate because of all kinds of economic concerns. And something which doesn't get talked about very much but which I'm going to bring up, and that is the notion of terror. Black people in this country have been under a continuous assault, and the response to that assault has a great deal to do with the vibrancy, not to mention the rigor, of the artistic expression.

I'm reminded of a review which I recently wrote for the *New York Times* of Count Basie's autobiography, as told to Albert Murray. A man called me up on the phone and I said, "Well, send it to me," and he did. I looked at it and I wrote this review. And then I saw the review in the *New York Times* on Sunday, and I was amazed at what they'd done to it. They had cut out all of the illustrations of how the tradition gets extended through people, through circumstances and events, particularly events having to do with economics and war, and the kind of continuity which was necessary to understand something about Count Basie's minimalism, his refusal to overplay, and the way in which he developed his "charts," particularly after he got some exposure on the radio. I'm a little bit tired—and I don't want to start throwing stones here—but I'm a little bit tired of people assuming that John Hammond discovered Count Basie. The question is: Who did John Hammond bring Count Basie to? And the answer is: To the job market of New York City, publishing and the control of the markets which brought that music to a wider audience. Now this is typical American technological commercialism. But Count Basie was already somebody in his various communities, and the Blue Devils band was wonderful.

I began my review by talking about an incident which took place and seemed to be of no significance. Basie is in Tulsa in 1925 and he's got "a head," which is to say he's drunk himself into sleep. He's a young man and he hears this music, which he assumes can only be Louis Armstrong, the quality of the playing being such. And he wakes up and he says, "I gotta find out who that guy is that's playing. You know, it's gotta be an album. Somebody in here's playing a record." And he wakes up and stumbles downstairs and he runs into some people who are advertising on the back of a wagon and it is the nucleus of the Blue Devils band, including Hot Lips Page, and a number of other people. This is Basie's introduction into the standard of what he has to live with, in terms of artistic excellence. And the narrative begins with this little episode and then it goes back to a kind of chronology, that is, in Albert Murray's handling of the story of Count Basie.

Now it's important that we understand something about the Tulsa riot, because I thought I was just making a kind of aside, but a woman from the *Philadelphia Inquirer* called me on the telephone and said, "By the way, what are your sources to the Tulsa riot?" And I said, "Well, why are you asking me these questions?" And she said, "I'm just interested, because you said it was the first instance of aerial bombardment on any community in the modern world." And I said, "Yeah, well, that's true." She says, "Well, I'd like to know about your sources." So I said, "Well, you know, one of the sources is the *New York Times*," and I gave her the date. I got the sense that she was trying to solve political problems, because those of us who know anything about Philadelphia and MOVE, for example, know that that community was decimated by a certain kind of technological temper tantrum which burned down a whole city block and ruined a neighborhood, a community. And that attitude, I think, is as American as apple pie.

I want to take you back to Tulsa for a minute because it is there that the beginning of the story of Count Basie is framed. Tulsa was a place which had a very burgeoning middle class.

The black community was right next to the train station and the community was full of entrepreneurs. The white community was very angry about this because it seemed to be that with the discovery of oil, black people just had too much. They had too much of a frontier enterprising spirit, and they'd gone out to Oklahoma and carved out, among other things, a way of existing with the Indians. And you could oftentimes go into all-black communities or all-Indian communities very much as you do in Narragansett in Rhode Island now. But when the Indians get together—they have a big powwow—and they all look like bloods. I mean, you'd be looking around saying, "These all look like brothers!" And they call themselves Indians, and they are Indians. And so the amount of interchange at the cultural level, not to mention the bloodline level, is long and extensive. The reason why I tell you this is because Basie came to have a standard of playing simply because he ran into some musicians who taught some things that he could have never believed were being done. So the first question I would ask is: Who taught these people how to play like that? I'm talking about the Ben Websters and so on. Somebody taught them, and the people who taught them were people who were invisible—the people who came out of communities and believed in discipline, who knew something about the arts, who knew something about expression and who knew something about living, how one had to make a life. And the communities out of which these people came were black communities, they weren't white communities—and it was kind of a surprise to John Hammond, among other people, that this kind of music had been in existence for a long time.

Now all you have to do is get the albums and listen to the Blue Devils band and you'll know what I'm talking about. That became the nucleus of Count Basie's band. I tell you that because it seems to me that we have this ongoing dialogue—I think that Ellison said it best in an essay where he corrected Irving Howe for approaching his particular novel (that is, *Invisible Man*) in the wrong way. He said that he was in "a continuous antagonistic cooperation" with Mr. Howe and others. I think that that is a good expression for our use here—"antagonistic cooperation," which is the willingness to disagree about the way in which we see what we call reality.

Which brings to me to some compositional questions. I as an

academic—I characterize myself as an academic because I've spent too many years in American universities explaining— oftentimes to people who don't deserve the kinds of explanations—the complexities of what it is to live one's life, and saying that one does not live one's life exclusively out of books and that one has to have some experience and background. This is a visceral question and has to do with one's attitude about all kinds of things. It has to do with my attitude about composition when I was too stupid to know any better. Which is to say that when I was taken through my paces in courses, literature courses, I was critiquing my teachers at the same time that they were evaluating me.

I'll give you a couple of examples. I remember when we were studying O'Neill. I had seen, because I was a kid who would go to the library and just read randomly, that, for example, in the undergraduate school that I went to, the novels of Richard Wright had never been taken out of the library. Never. No one had to read the books. No one had read *Native Son.* Nobody had read *Black Power.* Nobody had taken these books out. So I was the first one to do this. I mean, the books were there, but one had to read them. I tell you this because when we got to talking about *All God's Chillun Got Wings,* one of O'Neill's plays, we found Eliot had done a review of it. I was amazed at the way in which Eliot could be so much "on time" when he was talking about Dante, when he was talking about tradition and the individual talent. But the minute he started talking about brothers, his whole expertise, his formal training, just went to hell. I asked myself: How come? What happened all of a sudden with T.S. Eliot? At that time, Eliot was the high priest. He's still that, but there are some other voices now. But at that time everybody was hung up on the New Criticism and so on. I just listened to these white folks and let them say anything they wanted to tell me and I did what they asked, which included writing villanelles and sestinas and Petrarchan sonnets and Shakespearean sonnets and Miltonic sonnets. And they always assumed that you were doing this by accident; you were kind of stealing this. What they didn't know is, they didn't know anything about my life.

I left school and went to the post office. I heard this riff about the post office and I ran into many young men and women who were advanced people, who had gotten an academic degree, who knew more about Melville and Shakespeare, not to mention the Russians! Now, take Gaines. Mr. Ernest Gaines writes about his rural community of Louisiana; has used the framing devices he has learned from other people who have studied peasant communities, like those Russians, so that he could exalt his own and give the speech rhythms, the modes of discussion, the communal interests and values, a kind of relief which hasn't been seen before. People just think that Gaines is somebody who's got a good ear, walking around with a tape recorder, you know. I mean, this is madness. At that same time, there are people walking around with their biases, their attitudes. I was taking a course from Christopher Isherwood, who would come to class sometimes and not say anything, he would just walk in and say, "We're going to have my colleague read to us." And I would look over—I was the only black person in the class—I'd say, "Damn, that looks like Auden." He would read for about 45 minutes and then he'd stop and say, "Well, are there any questions?" and I'd raise my hand and say, "Well, I wonder if you'd read the memorial poem for W.B. Yeats?" And he'd recite that, and then I'd ask him to read other things. And when we'd walk out of the class, the girl who sat next to me would say, "How did you know that that was Auden?" And I'd say, "Well, I'd seen his picture on the cover of a poetry book, you know." She thought it was kind of magical that anybody black knew anything about anything else.

And she always used to talk to me about Langston Hughes. "Well, are you going to be the next Langston Hughes?" I don't want to be mean now, but I'm kind of reminiscing now, and it's interesting to know about how people develop. She used to drive a bread truck to school and she'd pull this damn bread truck up, and you know, it had a lot of charisma. She'd get out of this bread truck—it didn't say "Wonder Bread," but it said something like that on the side—and she'd come into these seminars, and she assumed that I was a black person and that the best way to get in touch with me was to talk about black people. Well, I didn't share with her my great love for Langston Hughes. I grew up in a household where Langston Hughes' poems were framed and were on the steps going down into the basement which, as you know, is the real solid part of the house.

All right. So that gives you some sense of the kind of antago-

W. H. Auden, 1958. Photo courtesy of _Poetry_ magazine.

Langston Hughes, 1923. Photo by Nickolas Muray, courtesy of Oxford University Press.

nistic cooperation that goes on in this long dialogue in this country, which begins even before the Declaration of Independence, over the American tongue and who's going to control it. The American tongue is something which I think is extraordinarily important and we owe musicians a great debt because musicians were always at the frontier of what we call "parlance," the way in which they express themselves to other people. And by the time the hipsters, the Kerouacs and others, caught on to what black musicians had been talking about, black musicians had gone on to other things. The language was revivified and revitalized as the result of these particular men and women living their lives at literally the margin of destruction from one time to another.

I tell you that because I think we have to have a respect for the historiography of this culture and the lack of memory. There are terrific losses in America that are taking place. And many people don't even know they're there, because nobody took the time to write them down. Or much of the memory is in black periodicals. I'm talking about things like the *Chicago Defender* or the *Pittsburgh Courier* or whatever. And who reads them? I mean, where are the archives on these newspapers? There aren't many, but there are a few. And out of that memory and out of that loss comes a kind of ritual content, which is to say the framing of the experience and the presentation of the experience, which I've spent some time dealing with.

Now I've been asked to tell a few tales. I'm glad to do that, but I want to say a few things first about the interrelationship of the arts. I would speak to you about Romare Bearden, for example, who, in the process of putting together a theory of collage, can manage to give a social context, a social feel and an artistic expression simultaneously. This is something which he learned as a result of studying the technical innovations of collage and modern painting. But his heart and soul lives in the black community and the black community has never been looked upon as a resource for art at the level of cosmetics, of decorating appeal—which is to say black figures which hang on the walls of people's homes. Richard Yard told me a wonderful story one day. He said, "You know, Michael, people love my paintings, but they don't want them hanging on their walls. Too many black faces in there." And I thought he was making a little joke.

Lester Young, 1957. Photo courtesy of the Institute of Jazz Studies.

Then later on we came to do a little project together, and he had done something on the Savoy Ballroom, making these figures which are about four feet tall in the attitudes of dance as one would run into them playing in front of Chick Webb's band in 1938. This looks like a dance hall of some sort, and in its better days it probably was. If you went to the other end of it, you could just imagine these dancers spread out in various ways, and they were painted in the attitudes of dance. And the musicians up on the bandstand were responding to the dancers—you could imagine Lester Young, for example, who was getting his energy from watching somebody do the Lindy. This is important cultural iconography, and I tried to capture it in an essay.

Now Sterling Brown wrote a poem called "Cabaret 1927, Chicago." It was about the era of Prohibition and it was probably Fletcher Henderson's band playing to a segregated audience. In it, Sterling Brown, in the manipulation of voice, criticizes the lyrics of Irving Berlin, and he has as a backdrop the lyrics of Bessie Smith singing about the Mississippi Flood of 1927, with James P. Johnson on piano. It was James Baldwin who talked about taking that record to a small village in Switzerland so that he could write *Go Tell It on the Mountain*. Now I think that we owe Bessie Smith and James P. Johnson a debt, and the way in which I pay it back is just to say what happened. And maybe to say in either one of their idioms, maybe both combined, that the business of making a poem is a complicated matter.

I ran into Hayden Carruth recently and he was just sitting in the audience and I was there to give a concert with two musicians: a man who plays cello named Abdul Wadud [Ron DeVaughn]—some of you who follow contemporary music might know him—and the other Julius Hemphill, who plays with the World Saxophone Quartet. We were playing to a small library in Scranton, Pennsylvania, which is a depressed area, and we got up and we put together this program in two parts. It was a wonderful evening and it was right next to a church and the acoustics were terrific and we were glad to see one another and to talk about all kinds of things, old times, and there's Hayden Carruth sitting in the back. So he comes up to me at the break, and he says, "You know, Michael, you ought to write a book on jazz." And I said, "Well, there's some people that are

Hayden Carruth. Photo by Cynthia Day, courtesy of New
Directions Publishing Corp.

writing books on jazz." And I mentioned Al Young's name, because I've known him for years, and other people. And he says,
"No, your stories are just as important as their stories."

He says, "If you don't write them, they'll never be down.
The poems are fine."

I say, "But nobody's going to read the poems."

He says, "You and I know that."

I say, "Poets only read one another's work."

He says, "And by the way, I liked your book."

He says, "I always do this when I go to people to find out
whether they got any heart. I read the last poem in the book;
turn to the last page."

He says, "In your recent book, *Peace on Earth* [which is a takeoff on Coltrane's great song, 'Peace on Earth'], I read that poem
and I knew I wanted to read the whole book."

Hayden Carruth knows a good deal about jazz and has written about it wonderfully. He's a fine poet, and he's also an eccentric. He knows that you carry the legacy and the resonance of
your experience with you no matter where you are. Certainly
musicians do this, and this is why they're all my heroes. I can't
imagine a greater tribute than a person who is tired coming into
a town and getting up on a bandstand and singing about "love,
oh careless love, oh aggravatin' love." And making those particular people who are either on the dance floor or in the audience
transformed. That's the hardest work I know, and for people
who do it day after day is just beyond me. And so I think we owe
them a tribute.

Now, I'm trying to write a poem for the ear as well as for the
eye. The New Criticism and postmodernism has forced us away
from the ear in large part. I don't think that we can get along
without our eyes, but we still need aural quality of poetry. And I
remember when Etheridge Knight was talking the other night,
when he was talking about his belief that no matter what, as long
as he could say a poem to somebody; that somebody could hear
it; that was pre-technological and pre-textual in the written
sense; that that aural quality was very important. And for him to
stand up on the bandstand and sing gives me some idea of what
it means to be terrorized in a real sense and at the same time to
not be totally inarticulate.

Which brings me to a few of my notes in conclusion. My education was rather scattered and what I would call in the vernacular "habit" of putting together disparate things to make a kind of collage. That's certainly my education and it continues to be that way. I have to go back to the University of Iowa in about a month, and I have to lie. I have to say to Paul Engle and others that they helped me become the poet that I am. I have to say it helped me to be a student of Philip Roth, who accused me of writing a pornographic novella. This is Philip Roth in 1961 accusing me of writing a pornographic novella! I've got to lie when [Donald] Justice, who's a friend of mine and whom I love and who's a very decent man, told me in private, "You know, Michael, when I write this letter of recommendation I can't say how angry you are." I was considered angry because I would speak up. I would say things to Paul Engle like, "Don't you think it's important that the next time you have a black person come here, maybe from a foreign country like Nigeria, that you better check and find out whether you can get an apartment for him, because he'll be walking around here in Iowa City, maybe being run over by some farmers who are not used to seeing Nigerians walking around downtown?" He thought I was making a kind of accusation. I wasn't making any accusation. I was telling him about the world he lived in but didn't know about at the level of race relations.

So I've got to go back and be nice. Be euphemistic, forget memory. Forget loss and forget ritual.

Now here are my notes:

Notions of Prosody

Because one does not deliberately echo European conventions for prosody does not mean that one is not aware of them. One oftentimes, in a kind of counterpoint, is referencing them.

Notions of personality. How do you get the attributes of a personality into a poem at the level of phrase or the level of diction or the level of meter even, or rhyme? That's a poetic question. It's an artistic question. The analogies, the logic of vocabulary, the shaping of vocabulary—how do you make these choices so as to elicit the time, the time frame, what I call the "mode of expression"? How do you control that? The whole business of the telling of people's dreams. We in this country have nothing but nightmare to record when we talk about this "antagonistic cooperation" because we are actually at war, even now.

There are other people, this panel and people in the audience and people who've got private record collections and people who don't write in newspapers, who buy records, dance to them and tell their daughters and sons that Coltrane's the greatest musician that ever played. But let me play for you Coleman Hawkins' "Body and Soul." Let me tell you something about how he learned to play "Body and Soul" in that way. After being in Europe all those years, trying to escape racism and trying at the same time to live his imaginative life, he heard Herschel Evans' "Blue and Sentimental" on a recording, and he just said, "I just gotta go home." So he went home, and he was met by musicians, four or five hundred of them, and everybody was saying, "Man, how was Europe?" He said, "Man, where is Herschel?" Herschel had died and nobody could tell Coleman that Herschel was dead. So finally they went to a joint and he found out that Herschel was dead and he went into seclusion for a couple of days and the next thing you know, here comes "Body and Soul."

Now that little riff, that little story, was cut out of the *New York Times* review that I gave. I was furious, because I think that that kind of linkage is important for people who could never hear the musicians play in person. They ought to know that story. It's important to know that when Count Basie was a youngster and went to Cleveland, Basie was on Art Tatum's turf and didn't know it. He walked into the place and started playing and thought he was the baddest dude in the world because he'd been traveling around. He sat down and talked to the waitress and the waitress said to him, "You know, there's a local musician that'll be in here in a little while. Why don't you wait, have a drink and listen to him?" Basie was walking around and talking about "I'm going to cut and blow this cat away." And he was downstairs, he was away, and all of a sudden he hears on the piano somebody he ain't never heard before, named Art Tatum. So he goes up to the waitress and he says, "Who is that guy in there?" She says, "Oh, that's Art Tatum." Basie says to her, "Why

Coleman Hawkins. Photo courtesy of the Institute of Jazz Studies.

didn't somebody tell me I was on his territory? Why do I have to have my hands cut off by that hatchet?" And Tatum later on sat Basie down and said, "Show me a few things. What are you doing here, man?" And Tatum gave him some instruction. These kinds of things were cut out of my review.

Two other things in conclusion. The titles of my books are important. I was accused of being a sentimentalist because of *Dear John, Dear Coltrane*. But I've got that "blue and sentimental" in my background, that music going around in my head. And so the word "sentiment," is not a bad word for me. The other thing is that the titles of songs are also important, and Al Young knows some great songs. "All the Things You Are": you've got to hear Charlie Parker play that before you understand all of the residue that is in the mechanics of just assigning a title to a song. There are reservoirs and resonances.

And the last thing I have to say is that it's an honor to give testimony to people who got me through terrible times. When I was in graduate school at Iowa, the only thing that saved me was a record [album] called *Kind of Blue* [by Miles Davis]. A friend of mine, Lawson Inada, who's a Japanese-American, also had a great collection. We had apartments right next to each other, and the walls were so damn thin that if he turned his record player on first I didn't have to turn mine on. And if I turned mine on first, he'd say, "Man"—I mean, he'd do things like this: I'd meet him at the mailbox and he'd say, "Man, you played *Kind of Blue* 48 times this morning, Jack." And I'd say, "Really?" He'd say, "Yeah, let me tell you a story." He says, "You know, I bought *Kind of Blue* and I played it and wore out one side, and this morning you turned over *Kind of Blue* and it's the first time I'd ever heard the other side of *Kind of Blue*. I fell out! A two-sided record!" Nowdays you listen to a record and you find your favorite tunes, then you decide you're going to tape, and if you don't like all of the thing you take little excerpts from here and there and you put that together and then you play that over and over again. But this was before we could make cassettes. We would just play one side, or we'd play one cut! We'd play that over and over again. We didn't want to be bothered going through the entire side. And he said to me, "Kiss my ass—a two-sided jam!"

That was wonderful to me, because I understood exactly what

Louis Armstrong. Photo by Bill Smith.

he meant. He meant he'd been playing *Kind of Blue* on one side
for a year and a half, and had no idea that there was this mystery
on the other side. And to be given this at four o'clock in the
morning or whatever time it was, to actually hear a tune he'd
never heard before on a record that he'd been carrying around
with him all over the country and hadn't had the nerve to turn
over because he didn't want to be disappointed! You know, he
didn't want to be let down after listening to side one of *Kind of
Blue.*

The fact that Al Young's second memoir in his three collections of memoirs is called *Kinds of Blue* speaks volumes to me because I memorized many, many records to the point that I don't
have to play them. I know the tunes. They're running around in
my head. So when I sit down in the compositional sense these
things impact on me. In the process of making up a kind of commentary or an investigation into any one of a number of poetic
subjects, I've got those tunes in my head. They're blessings to

me and they wouldn't be there if those musicians hadn't played.

And many of them are *not* on record. Most people don't understand that musicians weren't concerned about records. Musicians that I know are not buying too many records. They've got eighty references or a hundred or a thousand. They've played "Body and Soul" eight hundred times. But I'm playing just one version on the record. It matters a great deal to me as a non-musician. Doesn't matter much to them.

Process and performance are important. Music for black musicians is almost never entertainment. Almost never entertainment. So for you to approach Armstrong through a film with Bing Crosby in it is a way of not understanding Louis Armstrong. If you want to understand Louis Armstrong, listen to "Potato Head Blues" or "What Did I Do to Be So Black and Blue?" Or look at Mr. Ralph Ellison's *Invisible Man* and ask yourself why is it that he frames his particular tale around the story of a musician [Louis Armstrong] who was perhaps the greatest innovator in music in the 20th Century. Certainly right up there with Stravinsky and all the others that you might bring to mind in talking about 20th Century culture.

AUDIENCE MEMBER: A given jazz piece can lose a lot of people real quickly because of the nature of it. People know words, but they don't know tonalities. Is jazz dying?

YOUNG: What you're talking about is life. Life doesn't die. It took the forms that we talked about up here today, but there's always a continuum. Life continues to flow. And I think that what jazz is really about, like I said before, is human spirit and life itself. I remember something that William Carlos Williams said in some of his letters. He said he thought that when society became too staid and static, the artist should throw herself or himself on the side of a little bit of chaos. When it would get too chaotic, he would seesaw a little over on the side of order. And the idea was to keep a balance. I think that people will just naturally always gravitate to whatever is life-giving and life-restoring.

KART: Regarding my saying that jazz is dying. I have some questions, which I could briefly go into, about what I think the

William Carlos Williams. Photo by John D. Schiff, courtesy of New Directions Publishing Corp.

future or the present problems of jazz are. I don't think—if I understand what postmodernism is in art—that jazz can be a postmodern art. It's an essentially humanistic art. To the degree that play with the codes, in a distant way, is what a lot of arts are up to these days, jazz can't do that. Let me quote from a piece I wrote recently about this problem:

It seems logical to assume that jazz is a music that can and should be played *con amore*, that is because jazz is this century's most humanistic art, a music whose goal, the discovery and expression of one's personal identity, can be reached only when musicians speak openly and honestly to those who are willing to respond in kind. But the belief that such transactions can take place rests on the faith that individual human beings still care to make that kind of response, a faith that is seldom found in the elaborately coded messages of this century's highbrow art and is even less prevalent in the mass-market products of our popular art. So the jazz musician, whose rebelliousness has ranged from bold cultural pioneering to romantic despair, now finds himself cast in the role of the loneliest rebel of them all, an artist who is unable to speak without evasion or artifice in an age which seems to demand little else.

That, in a nutshell, seems to be the problem that the music in general is facing today. Many of those who can and must still speak in that way, and their names are legion, don't seem to be abroad in a culture that is losing its ability to respond to that kind of speech. There are other people, many of them very well-intentioned, who are beginning to play a music that certainly derives from what I would think of as being the jazz tradition, but who are speaking behind masks, where before that was known not to be the way it could be done. And I think still is the way it cannot be done.

HARPER: I'm going to go back to what I said earlier about American speech and the American tongue. I have great belief that people as makers are never going to be mechanized in any final sense. And I think that one has to believe in the process of improvisation at every level. And I'm going to give you a couple of examples here.

I'm reading from the *Collected Prose of Robert Hayden*. "Not too long ago, he [he the persona—in this case, Hayden as he remembers himself as a youngster] decided to include as part of the design of a new series of poems, words and phrases remembered from childhood and youth. Under the title of *Gumbo Ya Ya*—Creole patois for 'Everybody talks'—he wrote down several pages, hoping of course, to make use of them in poems later on. Here are a few selections:

1. God don't like ugly and cares damn little for beauty.
2. She looks like a picture done fell out the frame.
3. Goodbye, sweet potato, plant you now and dig you later.
4. Every shut-eye ain't sleep and every goodbye ain't gone.
5. Married? The man ain't born and his mother's dead.
6. He's a bigger liar than old Tom Culpepper and you kow the devil kicked him out of hell nine times before breakfast for lying.
7. Yez, Lawd, I got me three changes a day—in rags, outa rags, and no damn rags a-tall.
8. I promised God and nine other men I wouldn't do that again.
9. Gonna hit you so hard your coattail will fly up like a window shade.
10. To be a good liar you got to have a good remembrance.

Ain't that the bad one! "To be a good liar you've got to have a good remembrance." Which is to say, you've got to be able to tell stories; you have to be able to tell stories in a true idiom, the true idiom that comes out of life. And that the kind of call-response business, which has been highlighted in black American churches, in dramaturgy, in street plays, in bars, in the kind of hopeless, soporific exchange that goes on at academic conferences—*that* can become distilled by a great poet into something which will be a commentary on our age and our culture. And I think that a phrase will sum that up. You know, musicians are terribly economic. I remember when Stevie Wonder came out with a song called "Up Tight, Out of Sight," You remember when the term was appropriated and everybody took "uptight" to mean "psychologically duressed"? You know? And I remember black folks just saying, "What is wrong with them? Don't they understand?" They'd say, "Well, I guess we'll just let them have that. You can have that. Take that and we'll come up with something else."

A native of the Gulf Coast (Ocean Springs, Mississippi), Al Young came of age in Detroit. He was born May 31, 1939 and began to read before he was of school age, by which time books had already become vital to his well-being. The author of several screenplays as well as more than a dozen books of fiction, essays and poetry, Young is also a freelance journalist whose work has appeared in *Rolling Stone,* the *New York Times,* the *Chicago Sun-Times, West (San Jose Mercury News)* and *Harper's.* The San Francisco Museum of Modern Art, Stanford, the Neighborhood Youth Corps, Rice, Foothill Community College, the University of Washington, U.C. Berkeley and U.C. Santa Cruz are institutions where he has taught writing, literature and creativity. His honors include the magazine *Ploughshares'* Cohen Award for Poetry, the Joseph Henry Jackson Award, the Pushcart Prize, the American Book Award and a Wallace Stegner Fellowship, as well as National Endowment for the Arts, Guggenheim and Fulbright Fellowships. For most of his life, Al Young has lived in San Francisco Bay Area.